W9-AGV-142

CAR
LENOIR

DATE DUE			
Feb 28 79			
Feb 20 81			

Speaking and Meaning

Studies in Phenomenology and Existential Philosophy

GENERAL EDITOR

James M. Edie

CONSULTING EDITORS

Speaking and Meaning
The Phenomenology
of Language

James M. Edie

INDIANA UNIVERSITY PRESS

BLOOMINGTON AND LONDON

Copyright © 1976 by Indiana University Press
Published in Canada by Fitzhenry & Whiteside Limited,
Don Mills, Ontario
Manufactured in the United States of America

Library of Congress Cataloging in Publication Data
Edie, James M.
Speaking and meaning.
(Studies in phenomenology and existential philosophy)
Bibliography
1. Languages—Philosophy. 2. Semantics. I. Title.
         P106.E3   1906   401   75–28909
ISBN 0–253–35425–0   1 2 3 4 5 80 79 78 77 76

For C. A. E.

Contents

Preface

THERE WAS a time some ten years ago when I believed it would be possible to work out a completed phenomenology of language. Such a study would begin with an analysis of the intentionality of consciousness and the phenomenology of the life-world, based on the fundamental primacy of perceiving consciousness over language-using consciousness; it would then move on to a consideration of the relation of *the experience of meaning* in perceptual and linguistic psychological acts of consciousness (*noeses*), and in other subjective acts, to objects of reference in the real world, to meant ideal "contents," and to the various levels of meaning in experience and in language; and then finally it would discuss the relation of the structures of language to speech-acts, the ideality of language to its historical employment and evolution, the *structures* of usage as opposed to *actual acts* of usage.

While all of these topics are interwoven and discussed in considerable detail in the following pages, it has been necessary to restrict the scope of my original proposal. The fact of the matter is that there is no completed theory of language, phenomenological or otherwise, within our grasp at the present time. And there is no present hope of such a theory. It is necessary, in the face of the complexities of language which confront us, to attack our problems one by one, to go as far as we can along one line of research while being willing to change focus and attack related problems in the optimistic expectation that, by making some progress down a different track, "the whole" of language will gradually become more clear and our "theory" of it more articulate.

These essays study *the experience of meaning in language,* that is, our human experience of being signifying, speaking, communicating beings within different contexts of our common intersubjectively constituted life-world. The *experience* of meaning and the *expression* of meaning are intrinsically bound up with language, though it is necessary to distinguish language-using consciousness from the more foundational structures of perceptual, prelinguistic consciousness (chapters one and three). Within language, once properly distinguished and specified with respect to other kinds of acts of consciousness, it is necessary to distinguish the levels of linguistic meaning (chapters three and four).

This book is clearly not an historical study of previous theories of language, nor is it limited exclusively to phenomenological authors, though the contributions of the principal phenomenologists of language up to now, namely, Edmund Husserl, Maurice Merleau-Ponty, and Paul Ricoeur, are naturally at the center of attention throughout. The central thesis which unifies these five studies and which culminates in the concluding chapter on metaphorical expression (chapter five) is that while language as a structure, as an ideal entity, is ontologically dependent on historical acts of usage, of speech-acts, which in each actual occurrence mean something new and different from anything which has ever previously been uttered, these same speech-acts logically presuppose the already ideally and objectively established formal laws *according to* which acts of linguistic meaning can take place. It is in the study of metaphor or polysemy in particular, therefore, that the true understanding of the relationship of language as a "structure" (*la langue*) to acts of speaking (*la parole*) can be set forth.

Thus, the following five essays follow both an historical and logical progression, which cannot be properly understood except in terms of its culmination in the concluding distinctions interrelating the structures of *la langue* and *la parole* made in the final chapter.

We necessarily begin with Edmund Husserl (chapters

one and two), not only the first phenomenologist of language, but the founder of phenomenology itself. Husserl's interest in language was primarily that of a logician interested in the omnitemporal and objective laws which are necessarily presupposed in any act of actual linguistic expression. Though he was also concerned with the relations between "the ideal" and "the real," between *noemata* and *noeses,* with how "the ideal" can become "immanent" in real psychological acts of speech, it is clear that his primary interest in language lay in that aspect of language which, since Saussure and the foundation of contemporary structural linguistics, we call *la langue,* that atemporal and non-psychologistic hierarchy of phonological, morphological, and syntactical structures which are presupposed by speech-acts and which logically allow them to take place. We are in these first two chapters primarily interested, therefore, in relating Husserl's objectivistic and idealistic theory of grammar to the work of linguistic structuralism and its continuation in the work of contemporary linguistics.

Merleau-Ponty, on the contrary, appears in these pages almost as an Oxfordian. This is an irony which neither he nor the Oxfordians he met during his lifetime ever adverted to: namely, like the "ordinary language philosophers" with whom he argued, disagreed, and damned, he never called into question their fundamental Wittgensteinian presupposition that the center of study in the philosophy of language was the "act of usage," the speech-act itself. It was only in his very latest reflections on language (which we develop in chapter three) that he truly came to recognize and make room for the problematic of Husserl (and the Structuralists). He was an advocate of *la parole* up until the very end, and if we occasionally make both him and Husserl say things—through our interpretation—with which they would both have been very uncomfortable, it is in order to clarify their necessary conflict and to show how it can be resolved from both sides.

The final chapters (four and five) develop the distinctions which we feel are essential to a phenomenology of language and which enable us to establish the basis for a dialectical resolution of these two *opposed,* yet on both accounts interrelated, approaches to language, i.e. as that of a logical "system of rules" (Husserl) and that of the psychological "speech-act" (Merleau-Ponty). Though we force both Husserl and Merleau-Ponty to go further than either of them wished to go, our concluding distinctions, based on their work, may place us in a position to state much more clearly and more comprehensively than they did in their published writings what an authentic contribution to a phenomenology of language—our common aim—would achieve.

A large number of the ideas which have been developed in this book have been previously presented in preliminary fashion in articles which go back to 1963. I therefore thank the following publishers and journals for permission to reproduce certain parts of previously published material: The Northwestern University Press for "Can Grammar Be Thought?" from *Patterns of the Life World, Essays in Honor of John Wild*, edited by Edie, Parker, and Schrag (Evanston, 1970), for "Husserl's Conception of *The Grammatical* and Contemporary Linguistics," from *Life World and Consciousness, Essays for Aron Gurwitsch*, edited by Embree (Evanston, 1972), and for my "Foreword" to Maurice Merleau-Ponty, *Consciousness and the Acquisition of Language*, translated by Silverman (Evanston, 1973); Quadrangle Books for "Phenomenology and Metaphysics: Ontology Without Metaphysics?" and "The Levels and Objectivity of Meaning," from *The Future of Metaphysics*, edited by Wood (Chicago, 1970); The Duquesne University Press for "The Present Status of the Phenomenology of Language," from *Language and Language Disturbances, The Fifth Lexington Conference on Pure and Applied Phenomenology*, edited by Straus (Pittsburgh, 1974); The Johns Hopkins University Press for "Vico and Existential Philosophy," from *Giambattista Vico, An International Symposium*, edited by Tagliacozzo and White (Baltimore, 1969); *The Journal of the History of Philosophy* for my review article of Etienne Gilson, *Linguistique et philosophie* (Vol. IX, 1971), and for "The Contemporary Significance of Merleau-Ponty's Philosophy of Language" (Vol. XIII, 1975); *Philosophy and Phenomenological Research* for "Expression and Metaphor" (Vol. XXIII, June 1963); *Humanitas* for "Husserl's Conception of the Ideality of Language" (Vol. XI, May 1975); *Semiotica* for "Was Merleau-Ponty a Structuralist?" (Vol. IV, 1971); *The Journal of the British Society for Phenomenology* for "Identity and Metaphor: A Phenomenological Theory of Polysemy" (Vol. VI, 1975).

Finally, in addition to Mrs. Audrey Thiel, who with indefatigable devotion and attention to detail has typed this manuscript, I would like to thank the following persons for reading parts of this work prior to publication and for making suggestions which have helped me in my reflections on the phenomenology of language: Professors Paul Ricoeur, Bruce Wilshire, Hubert Dreyfus, J. N. Mohanty, Aron Gurwitsch, John J. Compton, Wolfe Mays, Calvin O. Schrag, Klaus Hartmann, and, above all, Professor Donald Marshall, who read and criticized my work chapter by chapter as it came from my pen in Paris in the winter and spring of 1974. I also express my most sincere gratitude to the American Council of Learned Societies for granting me a fellowship for the year 1973–74, during the tenure of which I readied these chapters for final publication.

I   The Ideality of Language

IN THE CONTEXT of current linguistic discussions among philosophers the most distinctive of Edmund Husserl's contributions to the philosophy of language is his theory of *the ideality of language.* The foundation of this theory lies in the broader thesis he developed concerning the *intentionality of consciousness.*

1.   THE SENSE OF OBJECTIVITY

WE DEFINE intentionality as the ability of consciousness to entertain and hold before itself "objects," *noemata.* We thereby at once see that there are many different ways of "having objects" which are eidetically distinguishable. There is *perceiving,* with its correlatively meant perceptual world; there is *imagining* and *supposing,* with their correlatively intended worlds; there is *remembering;* and there are all the various imperfectly distinguished *affective* ways of having objects (mood, emotion, feeling, evaluating). For Husserl the realm of "the meant," i.e., the totality of interrelated objects in the world which can be distinguished correlatively to the conscious acts in which they are given, is much broader than the world of *thought* in the strict sense. The distinction between perceiving and thinking must, therefore, be particularly stressed because the very "ideal of truth" requires that we be able to determine the truth or falsity of a thought (a linguistic statement) by turning to things as they really are in our experience prior to any thinking about them. Knowledge, or true cognition, always

1

involves, over and above an analysis of the meaning of a linguistic statement, the movement of verification which turns *zu den Sachen selbst* to ask: but is it true? In simple, prereflexive perceptual experience the world is simply given, as a *plenum*, unquestioned and passively accepted. What *thinking* introduces into experience is the ability to turn away from the experienced world of real facts and events to their meanings, to entertain these meanings just as such, and to ask of some thing the properly philosophical questions: what does it mean? is it true?

Since the same consciousness which thinks the world also perceives it, the least perception includes ideal categorial features, and, conversely, the most elemental thought, as, for example, "the determination of a determinable substrate" in the assertion of a quality or property of something (*S is p*), though subject to specifically linguistic rules, must conform itself—if its *truth* is to be determined—to a relationship passively experienced in the brute, immediate perception of objects which precedes all thought. It is necessary to recall that phenomenology as the "science" of all the various kinds of "objects" which *can* be given to consciousness (and which are all subordinated to "formal ontology" or the science of "object-in-general") differentiates the various regional ontologies by eidetically distinguishing among them the correlatively given transcendental acts of consciousness which both found the distinction among these various "material" regions and reveal the transcendental conditions of any objectivity whatsoever. In short, the consciousness which *thinks* the world (in the narrow and specific sense of "thinking" we will be using here) also, correlatively and at the same time, perceives, imagines, remembers, feels, values, questions, believes, desires, chooses, hopes, and so on. Descartes was correct in stating that any complete act of consciousness is an extremely complex synthesis of elements which we can distinguish in eidetic reflection but which, in actual experience, are always given inseparably together.

What distinguishes Husserl, the "neo-Cartesian," from his contemporaries (like Meinong and Frege), with whom he otherwise bears numerous affinities both in field of interest and in method, is the extraordinarily comprehensive and systematic character of his philosophical mind. He became a philosopher through an initial disillusionment with mathematics based on the fact that mathematics, as it is studied by the mathematician (and even logic, when it is studied as a "positive science"), is unaware of and unable to account for its foundations and presuppositions. But, as we know, Husserl's interest was never limited just to the foundations of mathematics and logic but developed into an investigation of the very "idea of science" itself. Taking the various, already elaborated but always incomplete and unsatisfactory, sciences of the several regions of experience *as examples* of the exercise of theoretical reason, he attempted to elaborate a theory which could account for the laws of objectivity as these are found throughout the whole unified field of life-world experience. It was because he also laid down the foundations of a phenomenology of perception, of imagination, of memory, of temporality, that he was able to distinguish more rigorously than Descartes the realm of "thinking" from these other interrelated ways of "having objects." It is characteristic, he found, of the objectivities of preverbal experience to be "accepted passively,"[1] as "functioning associations" ruled by the laws of "immanent temporality,"[2] whereas linguistic acts always "bestow a sense"[3] and generate "objects of thought."[4]

In his later writings, from *Ideen* onward, Husserl developed his concept of "the noematic" in experience and showed that the *noema,* or "object," of consciousness as it appears in the various modes of experience is *always* an ideal correlate of an act of the mind; he found, therefore, that ideality was not something restricted to the realm of thought but extends throughout the whole of our mental life and is, indeed, constitutive of the world as experienced by men.

The return to experience (the reduction) which distinguishes Husserl's phenomenological method from the "metaphysical" conceptions of the "natural attitude" is based on the "transcendental turn" away from the transcendent world of "natural things" to our experience of the *meaning* of such realities. The transcendental attitude reveals a new and deeper sense of reality. Reality is now methodologically defined, through the reduction, as the correlate of consciousness. Phenomenology is based on the postulate that that which is real can be experienced and that everything which is experienced is, insofar forth, real. If there is an unexperienceable or strictly unknowable reality, it must be methodologically surrendered by phenomenology. No metaphysical entity, postulate, principle, or hypothesis can be admitted which cannot be reduced to experience. "What we cannot think," writes Husserl, "cannot be; what cannot be, we cannot think."[5] We must here, first of all, take Husserl's "think" in its wide Cartesian and scholastic sense (of thinking, knowing, willing, feeling, perceiving, imagining, and sensing); phenomenology replaces talk about *being* with talk about the *phenomenon of being,* because, in the last analysis, all *being* must be *phenomenon* or there could be no talk about it at all; it would fall into the unknowability and ineffability of nothingness. In this way phenomenology happily and effortlessly gets rid of a large number of the metaphysical categories and dichotomies (such as interior-exterior, substance-accidents, potency-act, appearance-reality, and phenomenon-noumenon) at the outset.

> Modern thought [Sartre writes] has realized considerable progress by reducing the existent to the series of appearances which manifest it. Its aim was to overcome a certain number of dualisms which have embarrassed philosophy and to replace them by the monism of the phenomenon. . . . There is no longer an exterior for the existent if one means by that a superficial covering which hides from sight the true nature of the object. And this true nature in turn, if it is to be the secret reality of the thing, which one can have a presentiment of or which one can suppose but can never reach because it is the "interior" of the object under consideration— this nature no longer exists. The appearances which manifest the existent are neither exterior nor interior; they are all equal, they all refer to other appearances, and none of them is privileged. . . . The obvious conclusion is that the dualism of being and appearance is no longer entitled to any legal status within philosophy. The appearance refers to the total series of appearances and not to a hidden reality which would drain to itself all the *being* of the existent.[6]

Husserl's concluson is that "Object is everything and all that is."[7] What we discover, by a phenomenological analysis of experience, beginning with perceptual experience, are objects which polarize the selective and pragmatic attention of the experiencer. Neither sense-data (the explanatory postulates of empiricism) nor forms of judgment (the explanatory "deductions" of rationalism) are primarily experienced. The whole tissue of experience consists of constituted fields of objects (perceptual objects, imagined objects, thought objects, and so on), and thus "being" as the ultimate category is replaced by the category of "object" or "thing" (understood in the sense of "something," i.e., "anything whatever").[8]

For Husserl no "object" is conceivable except as the correlate of an act of consciousness. An "object" is thus never a thing-in-the-world, but is rather something apprehended about a thing; objects are things *as* intended, *as* meant, *as* taken (*aufgefasst*) by a subject. There is neither apodictic certitude nor any apriori possible on the level of the empirical existence of things-in-the-world; apodicticity and certitude emerge only on the level of the experience of "objects" of consciousness.

A further corollary of this theory of "objectivity" is that categories of meaning (in the double sense of *Sinn*, *Meinung*—that is, unities of objective categorial "sense"— and of *meinen*—that is, acts of judgment, *apophansis*)[9] are universally and necessarily correlative to "categories of objects." Apophantic analytics, or formal logic, as the purely formal analysis of logical grammar, of the logic of consequence and implication, and of the logic of validity and truth, leads to the elaboration of the categories of formal ontology, or the science of *objectivity in general*. Formal ontology, based on the pure apriori categories of meaning, thus establishes the purely apriori science of "objectivity" as a whole. Together, apophantic analytics and formal ontology constitute what Husserl calls the *mathesis universalis*.

> We take our start from formal ontology . . . which . . . is the eidetic science of object in general. In the view of this science, object is everything and all that is and truths in endless variety and distributed among the many disciplines of the *mathesis* can in fact be set down to fix its meaning.[10]

Formal ontology, therefore, consists in the purely analytical study of the ultimate categories of objectivity, of what it is to be an object, or of "object-in-general." Formal ontology is followed by the analysis of the richer and more restricted regional ontologies, which are based more concretely on experience and which require, over and above the apriori analytics of formal logic, the instrumentality of a transcendental logic or a logic of experience in a "material" (as opposed to a merely "formal") sense. The regional ontologies involve the discovery of invariant eidetic structures of various levels of experience which are "synthetic" or "material" and which apply the laws of objectivity as such to ever more concrete "regions" of experience. Thus, for instance, the phenomenology of perception will reveal the eidetic aprioris of the perceptual object as such; it will elaborate eidetic structures of experience which cannot be *deduced* from formal ontology, and which are, therefore, "material" or "synthetic" laws applicable only within a restricted domain (that is, the domain of the physical three-dimensional objects perspectively situated in intersubjective space) and not applicable to the whole of experience as such.

> The system of synthetic truths which have their ground in the regional essence [for example, the essence of perception] constitutes the content of the regional ontology. The totality of the *fundamental* truths among these, of the *regional axioms*, limits—and defines for us—*the system of regional categories*. These concepts express not merely, as do concepts generally, specifications of purely logical categories, but are distinguished by this, that by means of regional axioms they express the features *peculiar* to the regional essence, or *express in eidetic generality what must belong* "*a priori*" *and* "*synthetically*" *to an individual object of the region*.[11]

There is very little in Husserl's formal *mathesis universalis* (formal logic plus formal ontology), with its analysis of the concept of "object-in-general" (with reference to the subordinate concepts of "thing," "property," "relation," "substantive meaning" or "fact," "group," "number," "order," "part," "whole," and so on), which could not be given a place in traditional metaphysics. It is his conception of the various regional ontologies, which require a transcendental as well as a formal logic, that makes the critical difference. Transcendental logic is the analysis of the "objectifying" and "constituting" acts of consciousness, which is necessary to account for the world of objects actually experienced. Transcendental phenomenology is based on the discovery of the law of intentionality, that is, that all experience is *experience of something*—a law which empirical psychology, for all its acuteness, was never able to thematize or "discover" because all natural experience always takes it for granted. Intentionality distinguishes conscious processes from all other kinds of processes in that they are ways of *having objects*. Since we have no access to being-in-itself except through the *phenomenon of being,* all being *quoad nos* is objectified and endowed with a meaning and value responsive to our theoretical and practical aims, needs, interests, goals, intentions, desires, and so on. Experienced being is the "world according to man" (Merleau-Ponty's phrase), a structured, objectified, intentional object, and this is why Husserl posed the problem of being in the language of "being in the world"[12] and gradually developed his thought in the direction of an "ontology of the *Lebenswelt.*"[13]

Phenomenology thereby replaces the ancient metaphysical category of "being" with the concept "world," or the "world of objects" (because to say "the world of objects" is to say the world as meaningful, as objectified, as structured by consciousness). Transcendental phenomenology discovers that "being" always already has a sense for consciousness, that it is the objective correlate of the processes of subjectivity which are the necessary and sufficient conditions of its objectivity. Perhaps the most striking contribution of phenomenology (in both its transcendental and existential forms) has been this elaboration of the notion of "world." This is not the Greek *kosmos,* an ordered and fixed totality of beings whose order and structure owe nothing to human consciousness, which is governed by "divine" laws to which the gods and men are subject. Nor is it the moral conception of "this world" of the New Testament,[14] the world of pride and concupiscence, the arena of sin under the reign of Caesar and Satan. Finally, it is not the world as the elaborate fabrication of a hidden metaphysical instinct in man, the "transcendental illusion," of which Kant spoke, which forces us to *think* a world which we can never experience.

"The world," in the phenomenological sense, is the ever-experienced horizon of all the objectifying acts of consciousness, the experienced coherence of all the objects presented in a given regional ontology, and, ultimately, the experienced concordance of the objects of all the regional ontologies within a coherent structure of experience. The *world as world* can never be given as an object in the strict sense (*as Selbst da*), but only as the field of contextual relevancy within which any given object can be distinguished, as the ultimate ground within which all experience takes place. It is never a *given* totality but rather the always presupposed "presumptive" totality, the never completed but always more closely approached synthesis of all perspectives. It is our experience of the world, as the ground of any particular experience, that founds our fundamental belief (*Urdoxa*) that all perspectives, all objectifications, will ultimately be found to coalesce in a coherent structure. In short, the "world" is the ultimate and most global objective correlate of transcendental constituting subjectivity; it is the basis on which any given "object" can be identified and distinguished from any other and can thus acquire an "objective" sense.

One of the best ways to describe "the world of objects" is to relate it to the various regional ontologies which are elaborated through the phenomenological analysis of the ways in which consciousness experiences objects and thus constitutes its *Lebenswelt*. This would also give us the key to how the various phenomenologies of perception (Husserl and Merleau-Ponty), of imagination (Sartre), of love and affectivity (Scheler), of embodiment (Heidegger and Merleau-Ponty), of will (Ricoeur), of reason (Husserl), and so on, could ultimately be fitted together.

> Every science [writes Husserl] has its own object-domain as field of research, and to all that it knows . . . there correspond as original sources of the reasoned justification that support them certain intuitions in which objects of the region appear as self-given and in part at least as *given in a primordial sense* . . . and the *primordial* dator experience is *perception*. . . .[15]

It is in the elaboration of a phenomenology of perception that we discover the primary sense of "being" or "real object." The lived-time and lived-space of our corporeally embodied existence, perspectivally situated within a world of factually given physical bodies, give us our primary experience of existence, and our primordial conception of "the world." This is the realm of fundamentally experienced and irreversible temporal synthesis (phenomenal time) on the basis of which we objectify our perceptual realities, other persons, and our own bodies as situated among others, our own past and the past of others, and on the basis of which we conceive the ideas of "objective" (standard) time and "objective" space. This is the inescapable world in which we live our lives, work, pursue our practical projects as citizens, as members of a family, or of a profession, and in which we die. Even when we are lost in the higher and "founded" regions of imagination, of categorial thought, or of scientific and philosophical theories, the perceptual world is always present in the margins of our consciousness as a perceptual imperative, as the inescapable place and time of our existence.

It is unnecessary, and in any event impossible, to recapitulate here or to discuss in detail the various structures of perceptual consciousness which have been elaborated by Husserl, Merleau-Ponty, Erwin Straus, Gurwitsch, Schutz, James, and others. It is sufficient if we can distinguish this primordial level of experience from others (the regional ontology of perceptual reality). Nor can we hope here to give a complete map of the various orders of reality; it is sufficient to point out that man does not live only on the level of perception but also has experience of "objects" (taking "objects" in the wide sense given to the term by Husserl, as the correlates of experience) of different orders of reality: the past, the unreal, the imaginary, the ideal, the cultural. To take but two examples, schematically, we can distinguish the worlds of imagination (as the correlates of imagining consciousness)[16] and the worlds of categorial thought (as the correlates of thinking consciousness) from perception.

The objects of imagination are "unreal" when compared to the objects of perception, even though the worlds of imagination are all made up of quasi-perceptual objects, possessed of their own specific temporality, their own specific thematic consistency, and so on.

Worlds of imagination as exemplified by any epic poem, play or novel, may exhibit considerable complexity of events and happenings as inter-meshing with one another. The most diversified relationships may exist between personages involved; persons human, divine, and even animals. . . . For a world of imagination to appear as *one* world, it must contain no contradictions, nor inconsistencies. . . . Contriving a world of imagination or, as in reading, following the imagination of an author, we proceed from phase to phase. At every moment of our imagining, whether productive or merely receptive, a certain phase of the imagined world appears as present and refers both backward to earlier phases and forward to later ones.[17]

The time of imagination does not correspond isomorphically to perceptual time; we can relive the whole of the lives of *The Brothers Karamazov* in a few hours of our own lifetime; their world exists as a separate realm for the imagination which we can discover, leave, and return to—"as identically the same as imagined on a previous occasion"[18] —at will. In short, the worlds of imagination are not and cannot be perceived, and are possessed of a noematic consistency and coefficient of reality utterly distinct from the perceptual world, all the while being "founded" on perceptual structures which cannot ever be completely escaped but which can be manipulated by imagining consciousness so as to effect a veritable *metabasis eis allo genos*.

When we turn to the worlds of ideality, of categorial thought, and of the theoretical attitudes of consciousness, we discover "objects" (Husserl likes to use the more abstract term "objectivities" here) of a still different nature. Such "objects" are the purely ideal orders of logical systems, geometrical systems, number systems, and of scientific and philosophical theories, which constitute specific eidetic domains. Needless to say, we need invoke no Platonic *chorismos* to discuss such "objects," and there is no question of treating mathematical and conceptual entities as if they were perceptually real. Since every eidetic domain is considered as an autonomous order of existence, the sense of being and reality attributed to "ideal" entities must be defined in function of that particular contextual realm of experience.[19]

It is in this sense of "being" that we can most easily distinguish phenomenology as a science of experience from traditional metaphysics. The status given to ideal entities is *just that* which accrues to them in experience. Since we can live in the realms of ideality as effortlessly as we live in the world of perception, the realms of ideal relationships can be shown to have their own distinctive thematic consistencies, in this case essentially atemporal and unaffected in their objectivity by phenomenal time, and to be, as the correlatives of acts of thinking, genuine "objects" of consciousness. As such, ideal entities are subject to laws of logical validity, propositional truth, wholly independent of the laws which pertain to mundane perceptual reality. Thus the "reality" which we ascribe to them is of a different order, but for that reason no less "real" and "discoverable" *mutatis mutandis* than the objects of perception. In fact, it is here, in the treatment of ideal objects, that the true value of substituting the metaphysically neutral concept of "object" for the more naively realistic term "being" comes to the fore. The reality-status of objects of consciousness is totally in function of the acts of consciousness (perceiving, imagining, and thinking) in which they are experienced.

> To experience an object then means to apprehend that object within a wider context, the order of existence [regional ontology], having a certain systematic form of unity and continuity, in virtue of a specific constitutive relevancy-principle. Accordingly, when an object appears as existing, it presents itself as existing within a certain specific order.[20]

We are now, then, in a better position to define the phenomenological sense of "world." It is constituted of all the objects correlative to a consciousness which at the same time perceives, imagines, remembers, and *thinks* it. In order to elaborate this phenomenological notion completely it would be necessary now to pose the stronger form of the thesis of the "primacy of perception" which Merleau-Ponty has advanced concerning the interrelations of these various regional ontologies and the correlative phenomenologies of perception, imagination, and thought. To argue this thesis we would have to show how all the "higher" levels of experience are "founded" on the perceptual level (though irreducible to it), and how it is ultimately impossible to account for perception without taking into account the structures of operating-imagination, operating-memory, categorial thought, affectivity, and emotion. (We will be dealing with this question in more detail in chapter three below.) These structures of experience, which can and must be distinguished for the purposes of phenomenological analysis, are not, *in actual experience*, ever separated *in actu exercito*, and the "world according to man," that is, the *Lebenswelt*, is the complex and interconnected structure which polarizes all of man's various powers at once. The least perception contains categorial structures, and there is no perception isolated from the derealizing powers of imagination and thought which accompany and surround it. Conversely, the most purified realms of irreality and ideality are never completely freed from their dependence on certain perceptual structures.

2. THE INTENTIONALITY THESIS IN ITS GENERALITY

THUS WE SEE that much more is involved in Husserl's theory of intentionality than the ancient Platonic (*Sophist*, 262e) and Scholastic dictum that "all consciousness is consciousness of something," or that all consciousness is self-transcending and objectifying. According to Husserl, intentional *Erlebnisse*, or "acts" of consciousness, issue in "intentional objects" (*noemata*) which are "ideal" in character and which serve as the means through which it is possible (1) to identify a given "object" as being the *same one meant* through a period of time, and (2) to synthesize or bring together in structural relationships all the various acts which can be directed toward a given "sense-content" (or "intentional object"). We must always, according to Husserl, take care to distinguish between the psychologically and historically real (*reel*) acts of consciousness (such as believing, positing, naming, thinking, expecting, remembering, knowing, etc.) and their intentional objects. We must also always distinguish the *real thing* intended from the *intended object*. The "intentional object" may *refer* to a real thing or state of affairs, but the intentional act itself does not in any way entail that the intended object really exist (in whatever modality posited) but only that it be so intended.

This distinction between the *intentional object* and the *real* thing(s) in the world to which an intentional presentation refers is Husserl's way of formulating the Fregean distinction between meaning and reference (the things referred to through meanings), and it is essential to the concept of intentionality that the intended object, that is, the object merely presented to thought and held before the mind as such, *not logically entail the real existence* of the (real) object intended. Otherwise, the distinction between meaning and reference would collapse and we would be left with some kind of (early Wittgensteinian or logical positivistic) "picture theory of meaning" or something of the sort.

The criteria which recent analytical philosophy has set up for "intentional" (or "psychological") verbs, namely, "existence independence," "truth-value indifference," and "referential opacity," all equally well qualify the act of intending an "intentional object" *as it is intended.* Whether the act be one of belief, of doubt, of imagination, of thought, or whatever, its correlative "intentional object" must be entertained according to the mode in which it is intended; but this logically entails only that such objects be *believed, doubted, imagined,* or *thought,* and not that they really exist. A number, a unicorn, or Hercules can as easily be "intentional objects," therefore, as a tree, a university, or the Declaration of Independence. It is, in fact, this very distinction between "intentional objects" and the kinds of realities to which they refer, and which might or might not verify them in intuition, which separates phenomenology from metaphysics: the "intentional object" as intended must always be distinguished from that to which it refers in the realm of being, that referent which would enable us to verify it, to give it truth-value, and thus bring an "empty" meaning-intention to knowledge.[21]

Two further characteristics of the "intentional object" must also be emphasized. First of all, not only does the mere entertaining of the intended object (the intended "meaning" or the "meant object" as such) *not* logically entail the real existence of that to which it refers in the real world, but this *intended object* alone is that which can be thought again and again, which alone is affected with *sameness* or *identity*. *Identity* (sameness, synonymy) is never anything *real*. It is not ever anything which actually occurs in the real world of chairs and tables and spatially situated "things" that we experience in the world of primary perceptual consciousness.

Secondly, sameness does not affect actual *acts* of thinking. Acts of thinking (*noeses*) are psychological events taking place in this or that organism which intend various objects through various periods of psychological time and, thus, being real events in the *real* world, can never be identically the same as previous or other similar psychological events. The *same noetic act* can never occur again as identically the same act as it was on an earlier occasion, but *what can* occur again is *the same meant object*, or the same meant content.

Finally, therefore, the intentionality thesis involves the ability of the mind to hold before itself the same intended object through successive pulses of time. In other words, it involves the ability of the mind to transcend time as a physical and psychological temporal process of becoming.

Now, to refer this to language, we would have to say that language is the essential instrument we have for making the phenomenological reduction, of turning toward meanings. It establishes our ability to turn away from, to take a distance from, and thus to suspend (or forget) perceptual consciousness—the world in which we are immersed immediately and directly through our senses—and to turn just to the realm of *the meant as such*, namely, words and sentences.

To examine our words and sentences as our way of holding before ourselves our thoughts or meanings is not to deny that these meanings *may* refer back to perceptually given things. In fact, whether the meanings we may simply entertain, *even in their referential capacity*, can ever be fully justified or completely "verified" by a turn to the perceptual situation(s) in which they first arose or which they permit us *to think in isolation* involves us in the gradual and asymtotic "pairing" of meanings with things in the world which, by definition, must remain always incomplete and beyond our grasp.

The investigation of meanings independent of their referentiality ushers us into the linguistic realm of the apriori; it is for this reason, among others, that we must keep the structures of thinking and the structures of perceiving *eidetically distinct,* even though in the complex acts of "having objects" in actual life-world experience they are always intermingled and inseparable. But if we are not to erase the eidetic value and importance of the distinction between meaning and reference, which is the final implication of the intentionality thesis in Husserl's phenomenology, we cannot *reduce* thinking to perceiving.

3. THINKING, LANGUAGE, AND THOUGHT

BY NOW it is evident that the realm of ideal "objectivities" is much more encompassing than the idealities of language, though it is through language alone that we are able, after the fact, to discover the apriori and ideal characteristics of such realms of experience as perception and spatiality. Geometry is built not upon our sensuous perception of shapes but on the idealization of those shapes —namely, exact figures, surfaces, volumes, and so on— which remain "spatial" even after they become fully "ideal" for thought.

Furthermore, we must take account of the extensions of Husserl's theory of intentionality in the work of his successors, particularly that of Merleau-Ponty and Ricoeur, to whom we will return in the following chapters. The whole thrust of Merleau-Ponty's philosophy of the lived-body is to show that in its very motility, in its most basic sensory-motor behaviors, bodily acts distinguish and objectify the realities around us and bestow a sense on the objects of our surrounding world. He has shown that the "content" of a perception is a noematic entity which is neither an individual psychological event (since it is "objective" for any experiencer) nor a real material thing (since it does not exist in the world of things-in-themselves independent of the organization which experience imposes on things). Then, as Ricoeur in particular has shown, there is also the intentionality of the "unconscious." Mental states of volition, of need, of affectivity are clearly intentionally structured in terms of objects even though these states may be partially or wholly "unconscious" and the activities which they unleash opaque to unaided reflexion. An unconscious desire or an unconscious hatred is not for that reason an objectless desire or an objectless hatred. Just what the "object" in any given case may be may have to be deciphered by analyzing the behavior, but when it is finally brought to the level of consciousness it is recognized as having been the polarizing object of that behavior all along.

Intentionality, therefore, is not simply a matter of consciousness, but is also present in subconscious bodily behaviors and in the unconscious structures of volition and action as well.

Thus, for the philosopher of language, it is necessary to make the kinds of distinctions which Husserl made at the beginning of *Formal and Transcendental Logic* in order to distinguish the linguistic realm of "thinking" from all the other modes of intentionality.

At first sight the first chapter of *Formal and Transcendental Logic* looks very traditional, very Greek. The study of language, Husserl says, is the study of *logos* in all its principal interrelated senses: as the act of meaning, and its correlative meant *sense;* as the process of reasoning, and its correlative *rational norm;* as stating and judging, and the correlative faculty of reason itself. But when we look more closely we find that the strictly traditional (i.e., Greek) component in Husserl's approach to language lies exclusively in his refusal to separate the analysis of speaking from thinking, of language from thought. The question "what is speaking?" is but one specific way of posing the question "what is thinking?" And to ask "what is the structure of language?" is but another way of asking "what is the structure of thought?" In Husserl's sense the analysis of speaking and thinking is an analysis of what some of our contemporaries call speech-acts, or *use* (*la parole*), whereas the analysis of "thought" is a grammatical and logical analysis of the structures of language, *la langue*—and the two are as strictly correlative and mutually implicating as the application of a rule in a given, factual situation is to the ideal rule which is here momentarily applied. But since *acts* of thinking can only be specified in terms of their objects, Husserl's primary focus is the "meanings" or "objects of thought" which are given by means of acts of thinking.

Husserl defines "thinking" very strictly. Though he calls himself a "neo-Cartesian," he has left Descartes' definition of thinking far behind. When Descartes asks what it means for us to experience ourselves as *cogito*, as an ego which thinks, a thinking thing, he answers that a *res cogitans* is a thing "that doubts, affirms, denies, that knows a few things, that is ignorant of many (that loves, that hates), that wills, that desires, that also imagines and perceives."[22] This definition of *pensée* or *cogitatio* was useful when we were discussing intentional consciousness in its generality. But if we wish to distinguish "thinking" from the other dimensions of intentional experience we must be more specific and restrictive. Thinking (as distinguished from perceiving or imagining) is always "done in language" and is "entirely bound up with speech."[23] Thinking, as distinct from the other modalities of consciousness, is thus always linguistic, always some use of language. Any definition of thought broader than this would lead us into confusing thinking with other phenomenologically distinguishable conscious and intentional processes.

Henceforth, we will be interested primarily *in language* and the manner in which language, as a notational system, introduces ideality into experience and enables us to "live" in the ideal realms of numbers, concepts, theories, myths, cultural institutions, and so forth, just as effortlessly as we "live" in the real perceptual world of spatial location and irreversible temporal sequence. For Husserl, an "object of thought" in the strict sense is distinguished from other kinds of "objects" in that it is always, even if it consists of but one word, "syntactically formed," that is, it possesses an articulated structure which can ultimately be accounted for by the various interrelated and purely formal laws of phonology, morphology, and syntax. Husserl focused his own phenomenology of language on the study of the "pure apriori grammar," which gives the laws by which we are able to detach ourselves from immediate, intuitive experience of the world in order to generate objects of thought and thus bring our experience to full reflexive clarity by laying it out in syntactically well-formed sentences which express and reflect its own *gegenständlich* articulations.[24]

But before we continue this analysis of the specific ideality of linguistic objects (that is, "thought" objects), a short digression is in order. It is a commonplace even for empiricistically inclined logicians to admit the distinction between, let us say, sentences and words on the one hand and "propositions" and "terms" on the other. Sentences and words are actual occurrences (spoken or written) in the real world which have all the empirical properties of any other actual existing things and events, even though, *as understood,* they have, over and above their various acoustic or graphic qualities, the property of being signs which carry meanings. Sentences and words as uttered or written in the course of daily living have all the characteristics of other unique, unrepeatable, temporally and spatially determined physical, perceptual things.

No two occurrences of a given sentence or word are ever, strictly speaking, physically identical with any other, and their physical properties do not, in themselves, guarantee that this particular employment of these particular sounds will or will not carry meaning either for the one who actually here and now utters the linguistic string or for the hearer to whom it is addressed. It is essential to linguistic sounds and marks that they carry meaning; it is not essential to them that this meaning be actually and in fact understood either by the speaker or the hearer in any particular historical utterance. There is, therefore, a sound motive for distinguishing the meaning of sentences and words from the physical occurrences themselves and thus designating the meaning of a sentence by the locution "proposition" and the meaning of a word by the locution "term." Terms and propositions, unlike words and sentences, are indifferent to temporal and spatial locations, to tones of voice, to idiosyncracies of accent, to whether they are spoken in one natural language or another. They are, in short, ideal types or "meaning contents" which remain ideally the same each time they are "cashed in" by producing their tokens in actual speech. They have, moreover, intensional and extensional properties which are wholly "ideal" and "logical" as opposed to the "real" properties of their tokens.[25]

To this generally accepted (and, indeed, inescapable) distinction Husserl added nothing spectacularly new; what he did was to provide the phenomenological evidence for this kind of ideality and examine its meaning; in this way he was able to justify the place of ideal laws, such as the laws of logic, within the concrete texture of life-world experience and not just "add them on" as an inescapable but theoretically incomprehensible feature of our experience in the manner of Hume and the logical positivists who place "experience" on the one side and the "laws of logic" on the other, accepting both but finding no organic interrelationships between the purely empirical and the purely conceptual.

Husserl is concerned not only with the independence of these two realms but with their interrelationships; like James he is concerned with *why* "the world plays into the hands of logic"[26] and of how logic, on its side, enables us not just to think emptily in the abstract, but "to think the world," and ultimately to produce its "science."

In fact one might say that the "foundation of phenomenology" in the work of Husserl lay precisely in the development of the strictly phenomenological, that is, experiential, evidence for the ideality of meanings. Empiricists and nominalists have always based their refutations of conceptualism on the fact that the only *real* entities are the particular, singular, individually time-bound and space-bound physical things available to sense intuition. To speak independently of ideas or thoughts or concepts seems equivalent to postulating the existence of "queer entities," "quasi-beings," "meinongian ghosts," and whatnot, and empiricists have generally felt it sufficient to refute both Meinong and Husserl by accusing them of "Platonism." But the fact of the matter is that Husserl, at least, never denied the principal empiricist contention: ideal entities are not *real*, either as acts of the mind or as things in the world; they are wholly correlative to experience, a phenomenological and not a physical kind of reality. They do not exist anywhere in the "real" world as a plenum of temporally evolving things and processes, of realities "in themselves" independent of and indifferent to consciousness.[27] The ideal (and all that concerns the realm of *the meant* as such, the apriori, etc.) is not "of the world" at all but only "of our experience of the world." The ideal therefore emerges only on the level of experience and its only evidence must be phenomenological. But once this has been understood, evidence abounds, and Husserl gives a surfeit of arguments in each of the *Logical Investigations*, but most particularly in the *First*.

It is unnecessary and would be uninstructive to repeat here Husserl's arguments or examples in detail. He begins with the *Faktum* of the existence of some natural language, taken as a specimen or example of what it means for there to be a natural language at all (whether one were to take German, or French, or Latin, or Hebrew, or Bantu would be a matter of complete indifference). And he sees that languages, as opposed to other categories of "signs" (*Anzeige*), which serve only to motivate us and to give us grounds for thinking of something else, enable us to express *meanings* or *thoughts* (taking "thought" in its objective sense and not as the *reel* psychological *act* of thinking).

Such linguistic meanings (whether incomplete words or complete sentences) are what is essential to *any* language or notational system and are precisely *that which* language enables us to entertain. The concept of meaning in general (to which Husserl reserves the more vague term *Sinn* and, later on, *noema*) extends far beyond language, and its investigation takes us into the phenomenology of perception and other modes of experience; but this latter is a generalized concept and in some sense a limit-concept of meaning. Here we are concerned only with linguistic as distinguishable from nonlinguistic meanings. Language, then, as a system of linguistic signs, gives us our first and surest route of access to the experience of meanings, and it is doubtful whether a creature which could not use language could experience even the perceptual world as fully meaningful.

The important thing here is that what we *mean* by a language, that is, a system of linguistic signs proper (*Ausdrucke*), is that it enables us to entertain and express meanings which are experienced as ideally independent of the physical sounds or marks which are nevertheless their necessary embodiment. What is expressed by a word (term) or a sentence (proposition) is not just our present mental experience or our personal dispositions (these are only "indicated" or "conveyed," not *meant* by the expression). What is *expressed* is a meaning which, ideally, can be repeated in any other possible natural language, which can be understood *in the same sense* by different persons at different temporal and spatial locations, and so on. When I (and my students) go through the demonstration of the Pythagorean theorem, let us say, here, now, in this classroom, we are thinking *the same objective concatenation of thoughts* which Pythagoras and the early Greek geometricians also thought and which has been available to anyone who is capable of understanding what the signs mean to think at any time since the sixth century B.C. We are thinking (at least in *ideal intention*) something which remains invariant in its meaning, no matter where, no matter when it is thought, and in fact would be identical in its sense even if no mind had ever *de facto* thought it through or not. The first characteristic of the ideality which language enables us to achieve is thus *the sense of sameness*, which is the phenomenological foundation for the concept of identity. This keel of the mind which makes it ideally possible that any "thought" can be thought again, repeated, translated into another idiom, this experience of the *objective identity* of meanings through the various mental acts in which they can be presented, is what Husserl primarily refers to when he attributes the institution of idealities to language.

But if this were Husserl's only major contribution to the phenomenology of language, even though it is still something which linguistic philosophers of today are very loathe to confront, much less to accept, we would have to say that he had not brought us very far or, at least, not as far as we wish to go. Contemporary philosophy of language is centered on the analysis of speech-acts, of usage, of the phenomenon of speaking (*la parole*). Scientific linguistics, on the contrary, is centered on formal linguistic structures as an ideal system of phonological, morphological, and syntactical laws which are logically presupposed by speech-acts and which underlie them (*la langue*). Does Husserl have anything to say that would help us bring together these two sides of linguistic investigation and help us on the way toward a unified philosophy of language?

First of all, it is not enough to recognize the importance of the discovery of "the ideal" within language; we must also distinguish the several kinds and levels of ideality, how they function, and what they mean. Primarily we must distinguish the ideality of the "intended sense" from the ideality of the linguistic structures which enable us to intend such an ideal sense. Secondly, we must relate "the ideal" to "the real," and, in Husserl's words, attempt to "clearly grasp what the ideal is, both intrinsically and in its relation to the real, how this ideal stands to the real, how it can be immanent in it (*wie es ihm einwohnen kann*) and so come to knowledge."[28]

Here we are confronted with the essential paradox of any phenomenological investigation, namely, the discovery of ideal objectivities which owe their status in some sense to psychic processes (since they are not real empirical things but exist only for some experiencer) and yet which nevertheless impose themselves as inescapable objectivities for any mind which would think the world. This is the paradox of logicism and psychologism, of the ultimate relations between the noematic and the noetic, which Husserl ultimately solves by means of his theory of transcendental consciousness.

Ideality is a correlate of experience; it has no empirical status in the real world independent of experience and would thus seem to be something which psychic subjects "add" to the real-in-itself or to "nature"; yet this coating of ideality which consciousness seems to introduce into being and to spread over its phenomenal surface is not something subjectively created by individual acts of thought or by the subjective dispositions of individual experiencers. On the contrary, its laws are more strict, more coercive, more general, and *in their sense* more unalterably "objective" than any of the generalizations of empirical science or everyday commonsense. The phenomenology of language, as a special field of investigation within phenomenology, derives its primary importance from its strategic location as the focal point and illustration of this mysterious relation of the ideal to the real, of logic to psychology, of conceptualism to empiricism, of *noema* to *noesis*.

We have been speaking of the logician's distinction between words and terms vis-à-vis sentences and propositions, and the manner in which this distinction reveals the ideality of the meanings ("intended senses"), and we have discovered that the two characteristics of ideal entities (such as terms and propositions) are (1) identity of meaning in different empirical expressions and (2) repeatability. Nothing in the real world is, strictly speaking, repeatable; only when one is dealing with an ideality of some kind does the possibility of its being repeatable make sense. No *event* in the real world can ever recur as exactly the same event, because real time is irreversible; no *thing* is ever the same as itself through the successive instants of time. Only the mind can identify *sameness*, using criteria of a conceptual and intentional nature; in itself, every empirically real thing or event is ineffably unique and therefore unrepeatable.

It is important at this juncture to make a distinction which has only been hinted at in the foregoing. When we are speaking of general ideas or abstract concepts and the particular instances in which they are realized or which fall under them, it is useful to use locutions such as the type-token distinction or the essence-instantiation distinction. But in the particular linguistic invariants expressed by phonemes, morphemes, or words (and perhaps even by "texts"), this distinction is not useful. The reason for this is that phonemes, morphemes, and words are not universals at all but "individuals."

Language presents us with a whole hierarchy of ideal laws and their corresponding ideal individuals. Husserl had a clearer awareness of this characteristic of languages than most contemporary linguistic philosophers, even though he had, of course, no knowledge of what discoveries contemporary linguistic science would bring. Words, he says, carry meanings and must necessarily do so, for this is what we *mean* by words. But a "word," just of itself, independently of *its* meaning, is already an ideal and highly abstract entity. Whether understood, misunderstood, mispronounced, used in a proper or an improper sense, the word keeps its ideal unity—just as a possible vehicle of meaning in this natural language.

Contemporary linguistics has, of course, gone beyond Husserl in developing this aspect not only of "words" but also of "morphemes" and "phonemes." There was an initial attempt to define "phonemes," the minimal elements out of which phonological systems of natural languages are built up, as "sound segments." But it soon became apparent that phonemes—as described by structural linguistics—are not *sounds* at all. The search for an absolutely complete and reliable International Phonetic Alphabet led to the essential distinction between the study of phonetics (the actual sounds produced in speaking any natural language) and the study of phonemes (which are purely ideal, distinctively "opposable" elements in an ideal, abstract system of phonological laws). Within the limits of pitch, intensity, emphasis, and intonation which the human vocal apparatus is capable of producing, there are no fixed limits. For instance, in a system of tones which stand for phonemes which are contrasted as "high" and "low," the *high* must always be higher than the *low* with which it can be contrasted, but this contrast is utterly independent of the absolute sounds produced. A child's low tone may be absolutely higher in pitch than the high tone of an adult speaking the same language.[29] Thus, though the study of the phonetics of a language gives us our first clue to its phonological structure, this structure itself is ideally independent of phonetics. Phonemes are not "sounds" but opposable ideal elements which stand in contrast with each other in the phonological system of the language. They can be defined only negatively, in terms of their opposability to other elements of the same order.

A narrowly accurate determination of the physical sounds accepted in any given natural language is impossible. No two "intended repetitions" of the *same sound* even by any one individual speaker can be shown to be precisely and in every respect the same on different occasions, and between different speakers of the same language (following rigorously the same phonological laws) they are often demonstrably not the same.[30]

Linguists like Charles Hockett illustrate in detail that when spectographic analyses of actual speech are done there may occur very great differences between the sounds which are actually produced on given occasions and what the speakers and hearers engaged in conversation actually recognize, such as the interpretation of sounds as different as /píj/ and /ká/ as being *the same*.[31] Clearly, the spectograph, which is only a machine, records the sounds which were actually produced; but human beings interpret the sounds they actually hear in terms of the abstract phonological system of their natural language as well as in the total context of a given conversation. Thus it is absolutely essential to distinguish the raw phonetic material involved in speaking from the idealities involved in *taking such raw sounds* as such and such a phoneme.

To quote Hockett at some length:

Since the element *p* in English is something different from the various other elements, we are trained to pronounce it, by and large, in such a way that it cannot easily be mistaken for any of the other elements; and, as hearers, we are trained to catch even the subtlest clue of pronunciation which identifies what we hear as *p* rather than as any of the others. But this does not mean that we must necessarily pronounce *p* in exactly the same way every time, and we do not. So long as what we say sounds sufficiently unlike any of the other elements which might occur in the same context, yielding a different utterance, our hearers will interpret what they hear as *p*. This affords us more leeway than we realize. ... It is difficult to demonstrate to a speaker of English that his pronunciation of an element like *p* does vary quite widely. But it is easy enough to demonstrate comparable irrelevant ranges of variation in other languages. For example, if we listen to a Menomini Indian saying several times his word with the meaning "he looks at him," we hear in the middle of the word now a sound something like our *p* and now a sound more like our *b*. We hear the difference because English trains us to hear it. But the Menomini does not hear it, because in his language this particular difference of sound never functions to keep utterances apart—and therefore he has no reason to *need* to hear it. Conversely, a speaker of Hindi, hearing us say *pin* a number of times, will report that we fluctuate between two initial consonants, the difference between which is functional in his language, but not in English.[32]

In other words, unless there is a "reason"—in the form of an abstract and ideal system of phonological laws—to distinguish various allophones (or groups of *similar* sounds) from one another, these distinctions will not be made. What is essential is not what is physically pronounced but what these sounds are *taken as* representing in terms of the phonological structure of our language.

Our point here is, by way of example, that there is only one phoneme /p/ in the English language and, though this one phoneme has the characteristics of "sameness" and "repeatability" and is therefore an "ideal" entity rather than an empirically real sound, it is not a general concept in the way a common name for objects exhibiting certain defined characteristics is. The same is true, *mutatis mutandis*, of morphemes and words. We must, therefore, following Husserl, admit *ideal individuals* (of the kind the elements of language uniquely give us) as well as *ideal universals* (in which alone the essential laws of typification and the defining of instances in terms of essences properly come into play). There are, of course, in this latter case—corresponding to ideal universals—*real individuals* as well, namely, the examples, instances, occurrences of such universal ideas. (Husserl remains innocent of Platonism for the simple reason that there is no room in his analysis for "real" universals.) As for *ideal individuals*, like phonemes and words, what is characteristic of them is that, though ideal, they are subject to historical contingency, temporal change, and development in a way that concepts (as for example, the concepts of number in mathematics or the concepts of proof-forms in logic) are not. This does not at all mean that they are not fully "ideal," but only that there are forms and functions of ideality other than purely formal concepts.[33]

This characteristic form of ideality pervades the whole range of linguistic phenomena, from the most basic elements (phonemes and the laws of phonology), through words and the laws of the syntactical "formation" of words into sentences, to the ultimate end-products of language, namely, the literary text, the scientific demonstration, and the philosophical (or theological) argument.

> In a treatise . . . every word, every sentence, is a one-time affair, which does not become multiplied by a reiterated vocal on silent reading. Nor does it matter who does the reading, though each reader has his own voice, his own timbre, and so forth. The treatise itself (taken now only in its lingual aspect, as composed of words or language) is something that we distinguish, not only from the multiplicities of vocal reproduction, but also . . . from the multiplicities of its permanent documentations by paper and print, parchment and handwriting. . . . The unique language-composition is reproduced a thousand times . . . we speak simply of the *same* book with the same story, the same treatise. And this self-sameness obtains even *with respect to the purely lingual composition*. . . .[34]

Thus "a system of signs by means of which, in contrast to signs of other sorts, an expressing of thoughts comes to pass," namely language, presents us with specific forms of the ideality, sameness, and repeatability of meanings which are specifically distinct from the other operations of intentionality. As an objective product of thinking by means of some notational system, language has the same properties as other mental products, like the *Kreutzer Sonata,* the *Constitution of the United States,* or Shakespeare's *Hamlet,* namely, a specific form or ideal individuality susceptible of indefinite repetition and re-actualization in the very same real world from which it first historically originated. The word-sounds or musical notation which constitute such scores or texts are "obviously not the sounds dealt with in physics," nor are they "the sounds . . . pertaining to sensuous acoustic perception." The *Kreutzer Sonata* and Shakespeare's *Hamlet* are ideal unities, not only *of sense* but also of the "constituent sounds" of which they are composed—"sounds" which are every bit as "ideal" as the significational contents of these meaningful cultural objects, though exhibiting an ideality of a distinctive "lingual" kind.

> Just as the one sonata is reproduced many times in the real reproductions, each single sound belonging to the sonata is reproduced many times in the corresponding sounds belonging to the reproductions. Like the whole, its part is something

ideal, which becomes real, *hic et nunc*, only after the fashion of real singularization.[35]

4. CONSEQUENCES AND COMPARISONS

HUME WAS ONE of the philosophers to whom Husserl felt closest, particularly for his descriptions of the structure of mental life. Hume and James were the two philosophers Husserl most insistently recommended to his students as the best preparations for reading his own writings. However, there was one fundamental point in Hume's phenomenological descriptions which greatly distressed Husserl and this was Hume's inability to account for sameness, i.e., the concept of identity. Given a large number of "perceptions" or "impressions" closely resembling one another, and after any number of interruptions during which we perceive other things, we have, says Hume, a *propension* to consider these interrupted but perfectly similar perceptions as the same, and a *propension* to grant their objects a continued existence. This is evidently a purely psychologistic and mentalistic explanation of sameness or identity, and it *will not do*. Hume shares with the whole tradition of British empiricism since Ockham, and with a large number of those philosophers who adopt the "methodological nominalism"[36] characteristic of much contemporary philosophy, two theses which Husserl undertakes to refute in the *Second Investigation* with much more painstaking detail than we can repeat here.[37] These theses are (1) that the only realities are singular, individualized, concrete real things and events (and ultimately states of affairs), which Husserl concedes as the "objects of reference" (*Gegenstände*) of mental acts, and (2) that ideas (whether as perceptions, impressions, or images) are acts and processes which take place in the mind and nothing more.

Husserl requires that over and above these two givens, namely real things and events in the real world and, secondly, acts of the mind which are also unique, datable occurrences which never occur twice in the history of any given individual, there are—*purely on the descriptive level*—"meanings" (*Sinne*) or "objective contents" of thought, *noemata*, which are wholly ideal in character, which can be *meant again* (and again) by the same person or others, and which are thus affected with the properties of (1) being identifiable through time as being *the same* "objective contents" meant—such as judgments like "two plus two equals four"—and (2) being "repeatable" in the sense that they do not change *in their sense* when they are meant by various individuals separated in time and space or by the same individual at different moments of his psychological life.

> Each attempt to transform the being of what is ideal into the possible being of what is real, must obviously suffer shipwreck on the fact that possibilities themselves are ideal objects. Possibilities can as little be found in the real world, as can numbers in general, or triangles in general.[38]

The history of philosophy has seen two principal errors regarding "meanings" as they are taken here. There was the Platonic attempt at the "metaphysical hypostatization" of the universal, based on the belief that species, kinds, and types really *do exist externally* to thought. And there was the nominalistic attempt at the "psychological hypostatization" of meanings based on the assumption that ideal objects somehow exist *in* the mind, that forms and species somehow *get into* the container-consciousness and are, in fact, nothing other than psychological acts.[39]

> Expressions such as "universal object," "universal presentation" certainly arouse memories of old, burdensome errors. But, however much they may have been historically misinterpreted, they must still have a normal interpretation which justifies them. Empirical psychology cannot teach us this normal meaning: we can learn it only by going back to the self-evident sense of propositions which are built upon general presentations and which relate to general objects as subjects of their predications.[40]

It is thus that Husserl's phenomenological analysis of meaning escapes the Scylla of idealism on the one side and the Charybdis of empiricism on the other. *Meaning* clearly involves the mind and arises as the structure of the world only for psychological subjects, as it clearly refers to real (or possible) objects of experience, but in analyzing "the meant" as such, not only what "I mean" but what "is meant" by such an experience or such an expression, we are led from our subjective, private, inner psychological states toward the "objective sense," or *Sinn,* which has an *eidetic structure.* There are no eidetic structures *in rebus;* they exist only for the mind; they are, in a sense, what the mind adds to nature; but neither are they the individual acts of individual consciousnesses, since any description of the content of experience must recognize the *objectivity of the ideal,* of the typical, of the structural, in our experience of the world. Nowhere is this more evident than in our analysis of the meanings of verbal expressions.

By way of conclusion I would like to refer briefly to three arguments which have been advanced by contemporary philosophers who would seem to fall among the "methodological nominalists" we have referred to above but which seem, nevertheless, to provide a basis, given some interpretation, not only for a rapprochement with Husserl's position but even for its support.

(I) In his recent work, *Languages of Art,* Nelson Goodman has suggested making a distinction, in the realm of aesthetic theory, between *autographic* works of art (such as paintings or pieces of sculpture) and *allographic* works of art (like plays and symphonies), which depend on a "notational system" and which can, and even must be, enacted or performed according to an ideal linguistic model in the *hic et nunc* of our presently real perceptual time and space.[41]

With an *autographic* work of art you either have it or you don't. It may be in fragments like the *Venus de Milo* or the *Victory of Samothrace,* or it may be whole and entire like the *Mona Lisa.* But *copies* are not *it.*[42] Autographic works of art have the historical continuity and uniqueness of any *real* thing in the world; if they are lost or destroyed they are gone forever. The *allographic* work of art, which depends on the introduction of a "notational system," is not *a particular thing* in the same way. There is, of course, the "autograph" of the *Summa Contra Gentiles* in the Vatican Library; there are some authentic folios of Elizabethan plays; the original scores of Beethoven can be examined. But clearly that particular manuscript or folio or score is not the literary work, the play, the symphony *itself.* Clearly the allographic work of art, in Goodman's sense, is not exhausted in any *particular* (perceptually real) presentation or performance of it.

It is not contained in any particular published version of the original text or in any actual performance. Though Goodman does not use such language, it seems clear that an allographic work of art (of literature or of music) possesses an ideality specific to its linguistic or notational structure such that its existence, though perfectly individuated, is always "ideal"; that is, it possesses a system of ideas or norms which in some sense is represented in *every* enactment or performance and which yet transcends *any particular* enactment as the ideal *"telos"* in terms of which we can and must judge the present, real reproductions as to their authenticity.[43]

I suspect that Goodman's allegiance to nominalism is so strong that he would be uncomfortable with the manner in which I am putting his distinction. Would he not want to say that the "texts," "sentences," "words," and "phonemes" we have are *classes* of particulars, of tokens? Certainly it makes sense to say, within a given natural language, that the "phoneme" can be considered to be a *particular range* of sounds, and that *this particular* copy of *The Brothers Karamazov* consists, whether on the level of words, sentences, or of the text as a whole, only of tokens of (ideal) types. This is, indeed, the strategy of one of Goodman's first critics, Paul Ziff. Without going into the details either of Goodman's argument or of Ziff's interesting criticisms, what seems to stand out is that if Goodman's theory is to withstand nominalistic criticism, it requires a theory of intentionality. Suppose, Ziff argues, following a weak point in Goodman's presentation of his thesis, that if a "wrong note," for instance, is to disqualify a particular performance of a Bach fugue from being a genuine instance of that allographic work of musical art, then we must be able to determine when we have a "wrong note." Ziff avers that Goodman believes that the pitch á can be specified in terms of physical frequencies of sounds as 440 cycles per second. But, in musical history, we know that the pitch á has ranged from frequencies of 370 to 567.3 cycles per second. For example, writes Ziff, "the great organ in Strasbourg Cathedral, dating from 1713, has A_4 [*sic*] at 393.2; Handel's tuning fork is 422.5; the organ at St. Jacobi Kirche, Hamburg, approved by Bach, is 484.2."[44]

What this kind of argument lacks, or perhaps consciously eschews, is any intentional analysis of experience. The subliminal frequencies which *we recognize,* for some given purpose, as the pitch á, or the range of allophones or other gradations of sound which *we recognize,* for a given natural language, as being *the same* phoneme, are essentially irrelevant on the phenomenological level. How does one distinguish a given *particular range* of sounds as being *one and the same phoneme*? Certainly not by studying the physical frequencies emitted by this or that speaker, since some languages make finer distinctions here, grosser distinctions there, or no distinctions at all over the large ranges of actual physical, phonetic sounds. What is essential is *the noetic act* which takes certain real occurrences in the world *as instances* of an ideal *intended content.*

This may not really say more than that what interests us most in this distinction may be something which the author himself was unaware of or uninterested in: namely, the manner in which any "notational system" founds ideality in experience. The fundamental place Goodman gives to music is basic and has great importance for the study of language, since language consists, like music, of strings of modulated sounds (or strings of marks on paper) which have distinctive structures or "grammars." There is a sense in which words are fitted together meaningfully in a sentence like sounds are in a melody. Simple juxtapositions of sounds bring about noise, not sense, not even musical sense. Music is not just any ordering of sounds but one which imposes an intelligible structure which conveys direct and immediate meaning to the hearer. Unlike language, this musical meaning is nonconceptual, but this level of the meaning of patterned sounds also exists in language.

When we move to natural languages and then to the artificial languages of logic and mathematics the distinction between the mere "sound" and its "meaning" becomes more and more emphatic—to such an extent that in the artificial languages of logic and mathematics "sounds" and "marks" play almost no role independent of their meanings. In natural languages, however, the sounds themselves are important as the *necessary vehicles* of meaning; it is the sounds themselves which are "taken to be the same" in order for us to experience the same word again and again. And, in music, of course, meaning and sound are so fused together that it is impossible to speak of the "meaning" of a musical piece other than by simply playing it again; the sounds *mean just themselves* in their particular melodic "grammar" and cannot be translated into another idiom.[45]

Music and natural languages are, clearly, "notational systems" which enable the creation of "cultural objects," such as novels, symphonies, plays, poems, and so on, which have an ideality and a repeatability which is characteristic of language taken as a system of structures, which Saussure called *la langue.* Husserl developed his ideas on this most explicitly in his little work on *The Origin of Geometry,* a work which has occasioned the great efflorescence of "grammatology" in French Structuralists like Jacques Derrida.[46]

> The important function of written, documenting linguistic expression, writes Husserl, is that it makes communication possible without immediate or mediate personal address; it is, so to speak, communication become virtual. Through this, the communalization of man is lifted to a new level. Written signs are, when considered from a purely corporeal point of view, straightforwardly, sensibly experienceable; and it is always possible that they be intersubjectively experienceable in common. . . . as linguistic signs they awaken, as do linguistic sounds, their familiar significations.[47]

It is not sufficient to speak in Aristotelian fashion of the "notational system" of writing as a system of "signs of signs" with primacy being given to the spoken (*la parole*) over the written word. Though we may be inclined to give the chronological priority to spoken sounds over their written transpositions, it is not at all clear that we should give "logical" priority to the spoken words. The analysis of speech sounds, which *writing* accomplishes, was, no doubt, always implicit in the spoken word, but the laws of phonology, morphology, and syntax, which the structural analysis of speech discovers, would have remained unanalyzed, subunderstood, and perhaps even unconscious operations of the human spirit except for the invention of writing. Linguistic scientists have been telling us since the turn of the century that the only valid object for scientific research in their domain is the spoken word *as such,* but the only possible way they can have of studying this object is to put it down in writing and to transpose it into a form which on their own terms cannot be the authentic object of their science. This puts scientific linguistics in a false position. As *linguistics,* its primary object is spoken language prior to and independent of any written transposition of it; but as *scientific,* such a study must transform the spoken into the written, and thus, by "scientifically" observing its primary object, it necessarily alters and deforms it. The only possible conclusion to this dilemma has to be that written language cannot be taken as something secondary and derived with respect to spoken language but that spoken and written language must be *exactly the same language* in two different states of explicitation, with "logical" priority to be given not to verbal but to written language.[48]

Thus the discovery of the place of "notational systems" within linguistic expression is extremely important and permits us to pose the fundamental problem of the relations between *la langue* (the purely atemporal, ideal, structuralist, and "allographic" aspect of language) and *la parole* (those actual, "autographic" speech-acts and acts of patterned linguistic usage whose historical and temporal structure needs to be uncovered).

The "concept" we have of our maternal tongue as native speakers, that is, the ability we possess to speak and understand this language, is a "concept" which is in our possession through usage, which we have grasped on a level beneath the level of fully reflexive thought. No linguist has ever yet completely described *all* the rules of any natural language, and neither the words nor the grammatical usages of any natural language have ever been completely codified, nor will they ever be. The description of a particular grammar is, in effect, an attempt to bring to full reflexive clarity all the rules operative in a given language, in their various hierarchically ordered levels, and to make them fully explicit. And yet the knowledge of these rules *must* be in our possession, in some sense, prior to any attempt to clarify and describe them. Even though the native speakers of a given language cannot (without instruction) state to themselves or to others in any clear way what these rules are, they can always recognize instances of grammaticalness and ungrammaticalness in their own language—independently of and prior to the work of the grammarians who explain to them what the rules of good usage in their language really are.

What, then, is *writing* other than the means which we use to bring to articulation these very (preunderstood, subliminal, and dumbly known) rules? The linguist who insists that he is studying only *spoken* language must always write it down, must invent a dictionary, and, in order to invent a dictionary, must create an international phonetic alphabet. Without an international phonetic alphabet (one of the perennial goals of scientific linguists—which eludes them like the pot o'gold at the end of the rainbow) it is said to be impossible to establish definitively what the phonemes of any given language are and how they are interrelated so as to be able to produce the words of that language. But there is no need to look for or demand perfection; a phonetic alphabet sufficient to distinguish most natural languages from one another has been achieved and, by this very token, it has become pellucidly obvious that the linguist has transposed the spoken sounds he primarily studies into a written text.

But what is even more significant, and more to the point here, is that when we use writing to transpose our thoughts, to get them down on paper, whether in an ordinary book or in a great work of literature such as *Faust*, once these thoughts are objectified, written down as printed symbols in the real world, they all exist in the same simultaneity of objective time. The last concluding words of Dostoevsky's *Brothers Karamazov* exist in the same standard time as the first sentence, once they have been written down and published. But, if we are now going to read this work of literature and to understand it, to reactivate its meaning for ourselves, we have to reintroduce the temporality of lived existence into it by beginning, at one point in time, at the beginning, and, reading from left to right, through a temporal sequence of moments, gradually arrive, after a period of time, at the conclusion. The living-through this period of time rules our access to the *meaning* of the book from beginning to end, no matter *when* the book may have been completed or printed or when we may have stumbled upon it and actually begun to read it. This characteristic of *la parole,* the temporality of the actualization of meaning in which each use of words is an event and in which no use of words and no comprehension of words have exactly the same meaning twice, has to be related to the syntactical and formal structures which writing alone enables us to comprehend, and to transcend time for the purposes of *fixing* meaning as a cultural object, an institution of our intersubjective life. There is something intrinsically atemporal about the written word, something intrinsically temporal about speaking and understanding.

How, ultimately, the interrelationships between *la parole,* the speech-act, and *la langue,* the codified language, are to be accounted for in a unified theory of language is something we will be dealing with in the later chapters of this book. The point of these remarks in this first chapter is to show how the problematics of philosophers as diverse as Husserl and Goodman lead to the posing of the same questions.

(II) The second argument from contemporary philosophy, which I would like to touch on briefly, comes from William P. Alston. Alston qualifies the theoretical observations he develops in chapter two of his *Philosophy of Language* (on "Meaning and the Use of Language") as "pioneer work."[49] This qualification is justified and remains valid even if we are able to impose a phenomenological interpretation upon it—of which I fear neither he nor Husserl would approve.

But we are, after all, now becoming aware of the possibility that what Wittgenstein did when he took contemporary philosophy around the "linguistic bend" was to turn it back in the direction of Kant, and that the "linguistic turn" involves, in its method, at least a limited "transcendental turn" as well. I am using the term "transcendental" here in a restricted, but authentically Kantian and Husserlian, sense: namely, the search for *the necessary conditions of the possibility* of something being the case, whether on the level of the formal analysis of meaning-structures or on the level of the analysis of the material conditions applicable to a given region of objectivity. If, in addition, the necessary conditions of the possibility of acts of consciousness should turn out to be necessary conditions for the possibility of objects (and of their correlative meanings),[50] then we would have operated a *complete* transcendental *revolution*. I am not suggesting, of course, that anything like this is in the offing. Even the restricted claim that linguistic philosophy has taken a "transcendental turn" in this minimal sense may be asserting too much, but I believe there are Wittgenstein scholars who would not object.[51]

Wittgenstein's "battle against the bewitchment of our intelligence by means of language" issued in a program of defining the meanings of words by their *use*. But, at its inception, this program was beset by an instructive and almost insurmountable ambiguity. When we say that the meaning of a word *is* its use, we may mean that it is a specific kind of human behavior which operates according to "rules" (if we are logically and rationalistically inclined) or "regularities" (if we are more stringently empiricist) which delimit the field of the possible occurrences of such a word, both by giving us rules for all possible instances in which it could actually occur in speech and by excluding all the rest. Such rules (or regularities), for any given language, are quite complex, and it is unclear in the Wittgensteinian literature whether primary emphasis is to be placed on the structuralist (or syntactic) sense of *use* or on the semantic sense of *use* in speech-acts, acts of intentional usage. The question must be: how is a word "used" to make sense, how is it effectively brought under a rule at all? And how does our knowledge of the rule (that superordinate category which defines all the possibilities of the actual "use" of a given word and which can only laboriously be discovered by philosophical analysis) give us the *meaning* of the word?

After all, we already know how to *apply* these rules even though we have no *explicit knowledge* of them. Stated in this way, the problem is not essentially different from that posed by Kant in the *Critique of Pure Reason* when he found that, since experience and concepts are heterogeneous, a *schematism* and a theory of use (*Gebrauch*) were necessary to show how it is possible to put a thing (an experience) under a rule (concept) at all. This is something that occurs in ordinary experience effortlessly prior to any reflection about it. We know, therefore, that it is possible. What we do not know is exactly *what* we are doing when we perform such elaborate acts as speaking a language, and thus making sense. This is why we need theories: to bring to the level of fully reflexive and discursive awareness what we already know (*in actu exercito*) but cannot say (*in actu signato*).

On this subject the Wittgensteinians seem to present all the possible shades of doctrine from the extreme linguistic behaviorism of a Paul Ziff to openly intentional and psychological interpretations of usage (Hampshire, Strawson). Wittgenstein himself seems to vacillate between the two extremes.[52] Therefore, his cryptic dictum *the meaning is the use* is in need of interpretation which puts Wittgenstein in touch with a tradition he was not thinking of. The Wittgensteinian revolt against traditional philosophy must be tempered by the realization that in some instances the tradition stood on solid ground, which is not to say that the disciples of Wittgenstein will not eventually bring about the renaissance of German Idealism.

Throughout the *First Investigation* Husserl always operated with the primary structure of linguistic expressions: *someone saying something about something to someone.* Alston seems to be amenable to such a starting point.

Let there be a *speaker*, what he says, a *thing* about which he is speaking, and a *hearer*. What is essential to *meaning* in this situation? Not the *thing about which* the speaker is speaking, because we have already separated meaning from reference. Not the *hearer*, because the speaker could be speaking to himself or to a "putative" listener (a dummy, or a distracted or deaf person).[53] What is *essential* is that there be a speaker and that he *say something* (express a meaning). Or, since we are concerned only with the *essence*, that there be a *speech-act* (meaning-act) and *something said* (meaning-content). To be sure, such an act always takes place within a wider context of behavior, in terms of which it is understood, but just *what* it is that is to be understood, the *meaning* of the behavioral act itself, must be distinguished from everything else. This is what Husserl called the *meaning-content* of an act of expression, and what Alston, following J. L. Austin, calls the "illocutionary" force of the speech-act. And since, as Alston says, "the concept of an illocutionary act is the most fundamental concept in semantics and, hence, in the philosophy of language,"[54] it is appropriate to attempt to distinguish the illocutionary act from what it is not. It is above all what "constitutes sameness of meaning"[55] in terms of the "illocutionary act-potential" of sentences which are otherwise distinct.

If the illocutionary value of a given word or a given sentence did not change when another word or another sentence was put in its place, it would have the same meaning. It is to be distinguished from the "perlocutionary," that is, from all the effects (and intentions to produce effects) which the speech-act may carry with it incident to its meaning but intrinsically unrelated to the meaning as such. The illocutionary-perlocutionary distinction is similar to the distinction Husserl made between the ("objective") presentational character of an act of meaning and all its nonpresentational aspects.[56] For instance, while I am speaking I may either deliberately or inadvertently cause my interlocutor to realize that I am tired, or happy, or exuberant, or depressed, that I want something, that I am interested in something, that I value something, and I may, by addressing my wishes, commands, pleas, whims, or requests to him, get him to do something and I may thus bring about an external change in him and in my environment. These *effects* of language, and their source in my own lived, psychological dispositions, as they are experienced in acts of consciousness, lie outside the meaning of *what* I am saying when I am saying something. It is indeed true that every nonpresentational act (wish, command, commendation, evaluation, and so on) must have as its basis a presentational act ("an illocutionary act can be a means to a perlocutionary act, but not vice versa"),[57] but it remains that the felt desires or moods it may convey to my hearer and the external effects it may produce are distinct from such presentational meanings as such.

How, then, are we to establish just what a sentence *means* (its illocutionary force) over and above these aspects of its "environment"? Alston proposes that we accept a vaguely "behavioristic" approach by specifying "the situation of utterance as a determinant of meaning" in terms of "what speakers are doing when they use language."[58] This *turn to the* "*speaker*" (which has been strangely absent from most behavioral theories and is Alston's important innovation) must distinguish between the bare "situation in which the speaker operates" (the conditions we have been enumerating) and "what the speaker is doing in that situation." This *Wendung zum Subjekt*, to be sure, falls far short of Husserl's turn to meaning-intending acts and the discovery of transcendental constituting acts of consciousness. For Husserl it makes no sense to speak either of "meaning" or "object" except in terms of the structures of subjectivity to which and for which objects are objectified and thus receive meaning.

But Alston, in effect, takes a limited "transcendental turn" when he attempts to explain the meanings of sentences, in that which is strictly "illocutionary," by showing that we must list the semantic conditions which make the sentence produced by the speaker meaningful *just as such*, without reference to any other behavior than that of just saying something. Husserl, also, did not turn to the experiencing subject in order to *reduce* meaning to the *psychological acts* of the subject, but to show that objective *meaning-contents* ("the meant as such") can occur only for a subject. Language does not speak all by itself; it speaks only when it is used by a subject. The meaning of language is thus always a function of some *use*. The essential thing, for our purposes here, is to distinguish the properly linguistic sense of use from an infrahuman behaviorism on the one hand and psychologism on the other. The *meaning* of an expression is itself "objective," according to Husserl, and must be delineated by an eidetic analysis which will result in thematizing the apriori conditions necessary for the possibility of such an expression to have such a meaning.

Granted that the analysis of the meaning of sentences is not something which can be accomplished in one fell swoop, that sentences can frequently have more than one meaning (all of which *can*, nevertheless, be clearly distinguished from one another given sufficient time), that there are levels of meaning, and that there are various levels of generality on which meaning can be specified, Alston gives a sample of what he means by specifying the conditions of an act being an illocutionary act by listing, for instance, the conditions necessary in order to understand the meaning of a simple request to open a door.[59] If we ask someone to "Please open the door," such a request implies, among other conditions of intelligibility, (1) that there be a particular door to which attention is directed, (2) that the door is not already open, (3) that it is possible for the hearer to open that door, (4) that the speaker wants the hearer to open the door, and so on.

Now, we can say that if any one of these conditions is not satisfied, there is something wrong with making such a request on the part of the speaker. That these meaning-conditions primarily concern the sentence as uttered and meant *by the speaker* is clear from the fact that they are necessary conditions only of what he *means* and are not necessary conditions of the performance of the act requested. Whether or not the hearer obliges the speaker is irrelevant to the *meaning* of the request. What is not so obvious, but which is nevertheless true, is that these meaning-conditions are also semantically "objective" with respect to the speaker.[60] They do not require that the speaker effectively mean what he asks, but only that he *mean to say* what he asks.

It is true that the speaker is the one who expresses the sentence and, therefore, it is to his situation that we turn to understand what he means. But there are cases in which a speaker can discover what he really means only by speaking (which is the reason why the psychological intentions of the author of a sentence are not the *only* criterion of its meaning).[61] For instance, suppose the speaker did not really want the door to be opened and was just testing his hearer to see if he would obey (as in boot camp). This does not at all mean that the fourth condition listed above ceases to hold for this expression; the *meaning* of the expression requires that this condition hold. It is the sentence which *means* in this case, and the speaker can always be brought to recognize this, even though what the sentence he utters *means* may be irrelevant to his peculiar intentions in uttering it. In an extreme limit-case, such as would occur, for instance, if the speaker, after requesting me to open the door, were then to evince shock and surprise that I did so by saying something like "But, I did not mean that!", we would rightly say either that he did not yet understand the

the meaning of the sentence, even though he himself had produced it, or that we were confronted with a pathological case.

Since rules of semantics are rules, they can be broken like any others, but this does not alter their "ideal," "objective," and necessary character. The speaker who does not understand the meaning of his sentences can be led to see just why what he said in this language means just this and can mean nothing else (by listing apriori semantic conditions). In short, the speaker *must* (is obligated to) know what his sentences mean under pain of expressing only nonsense. This is not a psychological but a semantically objective obligation that affects him not as a moral person but as a user of this language. He is, willy-nilly, governed by apriori laws of contextual consistency and coherence of which he is not the master, although he is the only user.[62]

In short, it seems that the kind of "behavioral" analysis of meaning being pioneered by Alston, though it speaks a different language and is still subject to the accusation of psychologism, can be interpreted in an eidetic sense.

If one takes seriously the distinction between sense and reference, it becomes clear that meaning is not some entity like a perceptual object, or an image, and that the phenomenology of thought has a specificity which distinguishes it from the phenomenology of perception or the phenomenology of the imagination. Thought deals with "idealities" by which one need not mean "another realm of things" similar to perceptual objects or imaginary objects, but rather, in the case we have been discussing, *necessary conditions of possibility*—conditions of meaning which are, for thought, as inescapable and "objective" as the physical objects over which we stumble in the real world are for perception.[63]

We thus see that there are approaches to the Husserlian sense of "objectivity" developing within contemporary behavioristic philosophy of language which owe nothing to phenomenology but which are nevertheless convergent with it.

(III) My final example will be very briefly given. It is the interesting argument John R. Searle develops in the first chapter of his book on *Speech Acts.* Searle shows that the very failure of nominalists and behaviorists to find any criterion for analyticity (or synonymy) itself presupposes that "we *do* understand analyticity" and therefore are in possession of a conceptual basis on which to distinguish analytic and synthetic judgments.[64] There simply are neither extensional, formal, nor behavioral criteria for such concepts as "meaning," "analyticity," "synonymy"—but this does not at all entail that such concepts are spurious or meaningless or unnecessary for philosophy. Whether the argument against analyticity be extensional, formal, or behavioristic, we must proceed by way of examples, in which we find many "borderline" cases. Searle's argument hinges on the "phenomenological" fact that though we can find no such independent criteria, *we can and do* recognize borderline cases, and our very recognition of our failure to find independent criteria, as well as our ability to recognize borderline cases as "borderline," presuppose that we are in possession of the concept of analyticity itself.

Searle writes:

> . . . I have no operational criteria for synonymy, ambiguity, nounhood, meaningfulness, or sentencehood. Furthermore, any criterion for any one of these concepts has to be consistent with my (our) knowledge or must be abandoned as inadequate. The starting point, then . . . is that one knows such facts about language independently of any ability to provide criteria of the preferred kinds for such knowledge. . . . My only point . . . is that where certain preferred models of explication fail to account for certain concepts it is the models which must go, not the concepts.[65]

Though we must content ourselves with this very brief reference to Searle's argument, our reason for mentioning it at all is that it strongly recalls to those bred in a different tradition the arguments of Husserl, and others, as to the centrality of the concept of identity (which analyticity and synonymy clearly presuppose) to our mental life. Plato had already argued in the *Parmenides* and elsewhere that the concept of "The One" (or Identity) was a more fundamental concept even than that of "being," because in order to recognize a "being" it is necessary to be able to identify it and thus to distinguish it from everything else while being able at the same time to recognize it again should it reappear. The concept of identity thus cannot be derived from the similarities of empirical being or empirical experience. Aristotle, the empiricist, reportedly defined "identity" as the "highest degree of similarity." But this will not do, as Husserl and countless others have shown:

> We cannot predicate exact likeness of two things, without stating the respect in which they are thus alike. Each exact likeness relates to a Species, under which the objects compared, are subsumed. . . . this Species is not, and cannot be, merely "alike" in the two cases, if the worst of infinite regresses is not to become inevitable.[66]

In other words, *similarity* can be recognized only because we are already in possession of the more fundamental concept of *Identity*, and that is Husserl's explanation of why all behavioristic and operational quests for a criterion for such a concept must fail. This is the basis of Husserl's theory of objectivity, intentionality, and the ideality of experience and language. Identity is a concept so fundamental to our mental life and so pervasive of experience that it is involved *in the least experience* and is always presupposed by everything else.

II   Husserl's Conception of *The Grammatical* and Contemporary Linguistics

Since the middle ages philosophers have periodically made proposals for a universal apriori grammar, frequently suggesting that such a grammar be considered as a branch or an application of formal logic. These researches have never progressed very far, not even during the period when grammarians were themselves primarily logicians. In the modern period, since scientific linguistics has vindicated its own independence of logic and philosophy, philosophical proposals of this kind have fallen into "scientific" disrepute. Thus, Edmund Husserl's project for a "pure logical grammar"—which is probably the most recent full-scale proposal in this area from the side of philosophy—has fallen upon deaf ears. But now, within the past decade, Noam Chomsky has begun to propose, from the side of linguistics itself, a program for the study of grammar which, if it were to succeed, might seem to justify the earlier intuitions of rationalistic philosophy and to give a new grounding to its ancient quest. Might it not be, after all, that what was needed was a more sophisticated development of grammatical studies themselves before such a proposal could be sufficiently clarified to be prosecuted with any confidence?

Husserl's studies on logical theory could be interpreted as an explicit renewal of the hoary rationalistic attempt to establish the bases of a universal logical grammar. This

Wiederholung of a program of research, which goes back to Roger Bacon and the Franciscan theologians of the thirteenth and fourteenth centuries, to Descartes, Leibniz, and the Port-Royal logicians, was endorsed by Husserl in the *Fourth Investigation* and clearly motivated the work of his student, Heidegger, on the *Grammatica Speculativa* of Thomas of Erfurt (which Heidegger mistakenly attributed to John Duns Scotus). But on the whole Husserl neglects not only scientific linguistics but even the philosophical tradition. It is true that he mentions Von Humboldt[1] and Scotus (Thomas of Erfurt)[2] and refers in a general way to the seventeenth-century French grammarians, but he attempts to restate the problem completely independently of tradition, starting once again from the beginning, *de novo*. He is interested in establishing the basis for an eidetics of language within his general phenomenology of reason and thus is concerned with the purely apriori structures of grammar which can be uncovered by the techniques of phenomenological reflection on our experience of speaking a language.[3] Such an approach will not provide a complete or totalitarian account of language; in fact, it will be limited to an examination of certain apriori characteristics of languages, which might, at first glance, seem to be no more than the enumeration of a series of trivialities[4] which—in their abstract generality—may seem to emasculate the phenomenon of language by reducing its enormous and known complexities and rich resources for expression to some unreal and emaciated "essence."[5]

But if it should be the case that natural languages obey certain apriori laws and manifest an "ideal framework" which is "absolutely stable," in spite of the empirical and accidental differences proper to each particular language, then the neglect of this aspect of linguistic reality would render the linguist ultimately unable to account rationally for his science. And Husserl firmly believes this to be the case:

> Language has not only physiological, psychological and cultural-historical, but also apriori foundations. These last concern the essential meaning-forms and the apriori laws of their combinations and modifications, and no language is thinkable which would not be essentially determined by

this apriori. Every linguist, whether or not he is clearly aware of the fact, operates with concepts coming from this domain.[6]

The very fact that one can meaningfully ask such questions as: How does German, Latin, Chinese, and the like, express "the" categorical proposition, "the" hypothetical premise, "the" plural, "the" modes of possibility and probability, "the" negative, and so on, shows the conceptual validity of such an inquiry into the aprioris of grammar.[7] Against his contemporaries, among whom the sense of the apriori had "threatened, almost, to atrophy," Husserl asks philosophers to "learn by heart" that, wherever philosophical interests are involved, "it is of the greatest importance sharply to separate the apriori."[8] We must not ignore "the great intuition of Kant." It does not become philosophers, who are almost the sole guardians of "pure theory" among us, to let themselves be guided merely by questions of practical and empirical utility and, in the case of grammar, to allow this study to be simply parceled out among a number of ill-defined empirical sciences, since it is also governed by a framework of unified apriori laws which define its true "scientific" boundaries.

Husserl's study of grammar locates this discipline as the first or lowest level of formal logic and states that a phenomenological approach to logic must "be guided" by language. He means by this, not that the empirical, psychological, physiological, historical, and cultural bases of language be incorporated into philosophy, nor that logic is dependent on any given natural language, but rather that the study of "the grammatical" (not a given, empirical "grammar") is the *first level* of logical reflection. The two primordial types of intentional experience, according to Husserl, are (1) the experience of the world and (2) the experience of language. The theoretical elaboration of the first is logically posterior to the theoretical investigation of the second, namely, *language*.[9]

To consider language in itself is to operate an implicit phenomenological reduction, to turn from the *Lebenswelt* of factual experience in which meanings are instantiated in factual situations to the separated meanings themselves, as they are experienced in their ideality, independently of any possible factual reference.[10] The experience of language is the experience of meaning par excellence; it is our route of access to the realm of "the meant," of "sense" and "signification." If one distinguishes the realm of significations (what Husserl calls "categories of signification" as opposed to the "categories of the object") from the realm of objects signified *through* language, one isolates within formal logic the territory of "apophantic analytics," or the purely formal study of the structures of judgment.[11]

Now, the *first level* of the implicit phenomenological reduction (if we can call it that) which is operated by the "linguistic turn" away from the world toward language itself is that of the discovery and analysis of *the grammatical.* Husserl calls this the study of the "pure morphology of significations" (*reine Formenlehre der Bedeutungen*) or "pure apriori (logical) grammar." Such a study is strictly apriori and purely logical, a study of "the grammatical," as opposed to the empirical and historical investigation of comparative grammars; it constitutes the first level of "apophantic analytics," to be followed by the second (the logic of noncontradiction) and the third (the logic of truth) levels of the formal analysis of signification.

No philosopher can escape the apriori rules which prescribe the conditions under which a linguistic utterance can have unified, intelligible sense. The study of grammar, in this sense, is necessarily philosophical. Pure logical grammar (or apophantic morphology) is, according to Husserl, that first branch of formal logic which establishes the formal grammatical rules necessary for any statement to be meaningful at all; it is prior to and independent of all questions of the formal validity and the truth value of statements. Every judgment must, for instance, respect the apriori grammatical rule that in a well-formed sentence a substantive must take the place of S (in the "primitive form" S *is* p) and a predicate must be substituted for p. If this rule is violated, nonsense (*Unsinn*) results. We get strings of words like "King but where seems and," "This frivolous is green," "Red is world," "A man is and," etc., which are devoid of any unified meaning; the words individually may have meaning, but when they are arranged ungrammatically, they have none. It is the purpose of pure logical grammar to derive from the originary form of judgment (*S is p*) the laws which govern the formation of potentially meaningful affirmative, negative, universal, particular, hypothetical, causal, conjunctive, disjunctive, etc., forms. It is in this sense that *das Grammatische selbst* founds the second and third levels of formal logic and establishes rules which are always already taken for granted in the logic of non-contradiction and truth. These purely formal grammatical laws are wholly independent of the truth or falsity of the statements which they rule and guarantee only that the statements formed in accord with them will be free of *Unsinn* (nonsense). They have no relevance to the material contradiction (*Wiedersinn*) involved in such well-formed sentences as "Squares are round" or "This algebraic number is green." The laws of logical grammar save us from *formal nonsense* only; it is the other levels of logic which save us from contradiction and countersense.

However, thus to vindicate the value of pure grammatical aprioris is not to assert that logic is based on ordinary language or empirical linguistics. Husserl insists on this: logic is founded not on grammar but on "the grammatical":

> It is . . . not without reason that people often say that formal logic has let itself be guided by grammar. In the case of the theory of forms, however, this is not a reproach but a necessity—provided that, for guided by grammar (a word intended to bring to mind *de facto* historical languages and their grammatical description), guidance by the grammatical itself be substituted.[12]

This is grammar raised to the level of the analysis of the formal conditions of thought. It is here that Husserl joins the seventeenth-century proponents of a *grammaire générale et raisonnée* in conscious opposition to the accepted views of his historicist and psychologistic contemporaries. The task of logical grammar is to study and furnish the apriori rules which govern the structural coherence of "parts of speech" with one another in sentences. Such grammatical rules are not just historical accidents or conventions but are *necessary* conditions of meaningfulness and for the avoidance of nonsense; they are not, without the higher levels of formal logic built upon them, *sufficient* conditions for the avoidance of contradiction and error:

Nothing else has so greatly confused discussion of the question of the correct relationship between logic and grammar as the continual confounding of the two logical spheres that we have distinguished sharply as the lower and the upper and have characterized by means of their negative counterparts: the sphere of nonsense and the sphere of countersense.[13]

Thus, Husserl vindicates the place of grammar (*reinlogische Grammatik*), as a theory in its own right, within his phenomenological hierarchy of "sciences." But grammar is, so to speak, the emptiest and the most formal science of all. Its rules provide the barest minimal conditions necessary to avoid nonsense in forming linguistic statements. They exclude only the purest nonsense, which it would never occur to anyone to utter. Pure grammar establishes rules which are always subunderstood and already taken for granted in all the formal systems which study and establish the sufficient conditions for meaningful expressions. But the fact that the uncovering of these conditions has no "practical" value and even seems to make a science of what is trivially obvious is no reason to despise it. Its theoretical value for philosophy, Husserl tells us, is "all the greater." Husserl takes pride in this discovery; he even glories in the fact that only philosophers are concerned with the apriori, with the discovery of truths so fundamental that all the other sciences take them for granted. It is, he believes, precisely such "obvious" trivialities as those expressed by the rules of pure grammar that mask the deepest philosophical problems, and he sees that, in a profound, if paradoxical, sense, philosophy is the science of trivialities.[14] The clear distinction which he was able to establish between pure grammar and the "higher" level(s) of formal analytics seemed to him to be a theoretical discovery of the first magnitude and a necessary point of departure for the elaboration of a phenomenological theory of consciousness.

1. Pure Logical Grammar

WE CAN BEST give a general outline of what Husserl means by pure logical grammar by taking his earliest discussion of this problem in the *Fourth* of the *Logical Investi-*

gations together with his more developed discussions of *Formal and Transcendental Logic.* These discussions, in turn, are but one application of "the logic of wholes and parts" of the *Third Investigation.* A grammatical unit is, indeed, one of the best illustrations of Husserl's doctrine of wholes and parts.

> If we enquire into the reasons why certain combinations are permitted and certain others prohibited in our language, we shall be, in a very great measure, referred to accidental linguistic habits and, in general, to facts of linguistic development that are different with different linguistic communities. But, in another part, we meet with the essential distinction between independent and dependent meanings, as also with the apriori laws—essentially connected with that distinction—of combinations of meanings and of meaning modifications: laws that must more or less clearly exhibit themselves in the theory of grammatical forms and in a corresponding class of grammatical incompatibilities in every developed language.[15]

A linguistic expression, whether dependent (like a word which functions as a syntactical category within a sentence) or independent (a sentence or proposition), is a string of sounds whose unity is founded in its "meaning." Any string of sounds devoid of a unified sense (or meaning) is just that: a string of noises. What makes a string of sounds a linguistic expression is its unified meaning. A "nominal" (substantival) or an "adjectival" (predicate) expression are examples of dependent meanings; only a fully propositional meaning, which joins such dependent parts into a unified whole, is independent. The first task of logical grammar is to establish the "pure categories of meaning" as they can be related in this dependent-independent relationship.[16] (It is not necessary here to follow Husserl into his detailed discussions of simple and compound meanings in relationship to simple and compound expressions and the relations of these to simple and compound objects or "referents," though this would be necessary in any complete account of his thought.)

What is important is that any linguistic expression is a "whole" composed of "parts" which are *members* (or "moments") of the constituted whole rather than merely *pieces* (discrete elements) only incidentally and *de facto* attached to one another; a *member* of a whole obeys laws which are distinctive of the role it plays within this unified system and which are not the same as it would exercise were it, *per impossible*, detached from the whole of which it is an integral part. The members of a whole interpenetrate and codetermine one another and, as such, are inseparable from one another and from the whole of which they are parts. Mere "pieces," on the contrary, would be just what they are even if separated from the whole of which they are, by analysis, found to be parts. An example of parts which codetermine one another as members of a whole would be the "extension," "surface," "color," and "brightness" of a physical, perceptual object. One is not present without the other; there cannot be brightness without color, or color without surface, or surface without extension. As did Plato before him,[17] Husserl considers color and surface to be related according to an apriori law (which is "synthetic" or "material" rather than "analytical," since the idea of color is not analytically contained in the idea of surface or extension) given in perception.[18] Such an apriori law is not the result of any personal or cultural conditioning; it is not an empirical psychological fact about my experience, nor is it based on some statistical probability. It is a law founded in the very *meaning* of color and extension; what I mean by color and what I mean by extension require that every instance of one be an instance of the other; and once I understand this, every experience which illustrates the one will illustrate the other, and I can know this without any appeal to future experience. That brightness entails color, color entails surface, surface entails extension is an apriori law of the constitution of perceptual objects, and no act of perception will or can contradict such a law, because it is part of what is *meant* by a physical, perceptual object. Another way of stating this is to say that a physical, perceptual object is a "whole" which consists of parts which are integrated into the whole as constituent members of this unified object.[19]

We can apply this notion to grammar immediately by noting that an independent meaning, namely, a proposition, is a formal structural whole which consists of at least a minimal number of constituent parts which are related to one another by apriori laws which govern their meaning-functions within the one unified whole which *is* a complete, meaningful sentence. In other words, what one *means* by a complete, unified, independent linguistic expression (*S is p*) is that its parts be related to one another by apriori laws of composition which we call "syntax."[20] A dependent term also has a unified kernel of meaning, but this meaning requires that it be completed according to certain rules if it is to function within the meaningful complex which is a whole sentence. In short, a sentence will be grammatically well-formed, and hence potentially meaningful, if and only if certain apriori rules for the correct integration of partial meanings into a whole meaning are observed. These rules are the laws of pure logical grammar; they are laws which govern the potential meaningfulness of sentences and are independent of and prior to the laws which govern internal consistency and possible truth. Meaningfulness is a prior condition for noncontradiction. The string "King but or blue" is meaningless (*unsinnig*), whereas the string "There are some squares which are round" is inconsistent or contradictory (*wiedersinnig*); the former, but not the latter, violates apriori and purely formal "grammatical" rules. The rules of grammar are sufficient only to guarantee grammatical coherence; they are not sufficient, though they are necessary, to guarantee logical consistency in the full sense. Pure logical grammar classifies meaning-forms and is concerned with "the *mere possibility of judgments as judgments*, without inquiry whether they are true or false, or even whether, merely as judgments, they are compatible or contradictory."[21] Truth and falsity, according to Husserl, pertain not to propositions as such but to the laws of the *assertion* of propositions and thus belong to a higher level of logic.

The second step in the elaboration of a pure logical grammar (after establishing the "pure" or formal categories of meaning, such as S, p, S is p, etc.) concerns the laws of the *composition* of partial meanings into well-formed wholes or sentences.[22] At the limit, no word can be taken and defined without relation to its possible grammatical functions within a complete, unified meaning-whole; the grammatical distinctions ("parts of speech," etc.) given in dictionaries bear testimony to this fact. Wherever there is found some grammatical distinction (or "marker") attached to a word, this is the mark of a certain incompleteness of meaning; and thus grammatical distinctions are guides to essential meaning-distinctions within sentences.[23] Sentences, unlike words, have no such "markers."

We begin with the analysis of the pure syntactical categories. When words are combined to form sentences, they are necessarily given a syntactical "form" which permits their integration as partial or dependent meanings into a complete or independent expression. This requires. that there be a restricted number of primitive connecting forms, such as the predicative, attributive, conjunctive, disjunctive, hypothetical, and so on, and that there be pure syntactical forms, such as the substantive, the predicative, the propositional, and so on. This is the basis for the fundamental distinction between *syntactical forms* and *syntactical stuffs* and for the recognition that the propositional form presupposes the subject form and the predicate form. Whether I take a given word as the "subject" of a sentence ("This paper is white") or as the "object" ("I am writing on this paper"), the word—as a "term"—bears a core of meaning (and reference) which remains identical though its syntactical form varies in each case. The specific meaning and referentiality of the proposition (to a "state of affairs") is mediated through the meaning and referentiality of its constituent terms. That is to say that the proposition is a higher categorial unity "founded" on the meaning of its constituents through its giving them the syntactical form necessary to produce a unified and complete sense. Now, it can be readily seen that the number of syntactical stuffs can be infinite while the number of syntactical forms is limited and capable of complete formal definition.

Husserl calls a given unity of syntactical stuff and form the *syntagma*. All the members (that is, the constituent parts) of a proposition are *syntagmas* [and we can here neglect the analysis of the infrasyntagmatic elements or "pieces" of words and sentences which belong to phonology], and the proposition as a whole is also a *syntagma* of a higher order ("a self-sufficient predicational whole . . . , a unity of syntactical stuff in a syntactical form").[24] Different members of a proposition can have the same form and different stuffs and, conversely, can have different forms but the same stuff; and these forms can be fitted into hierarchies in which what is syntactically formed on one level becomes the "stuff" of a higher form; for example, when the proposition itself (*S is p*) is formed, and when it is modified modally (*Is S p?, S may be p, If S is p, Then S is p, S must be p*, etc.), these more complex modal forms are constructed on the basis of the *Urfrom* (*S is p*), which is itself composed of the infrapropositional *syntagmas S* (substantive), *is* (copular unity-form), and *p* (predicate).[25]

We must note, of course, that, when a word actually occurs in a sentence, it has already been modified according to its proper syntactical form (and this form retrospectively dictates the manner in which it is defined in dictionaries under its proper "parts of speech"), since a "pure nonsyntactical stuff" is only a limit concept which can nowhere be found in actual, meaningful language (all of which is already always syntactically formed):

> The forming, of course, is not an activity that was, or could have been, executed on stuffs given in advance. That would presuppose the countersense, that one could have stuffs beforehand—as though they were concrete objects, instead of being abstract moments in significations.[26]

All the members of a proposition are "non-self-sufficient" under all circumstances; they are only what they are in the whole. I can reach the "pure stuff" of an expression only by an ideal analysis. For instance, if I examine the "syntactical stuffs" given in the sentence "This tree is green," I am left with such words as "tree" and "green." These *can* be considered as "unformed stuffs," but they are not completely unformed and thus should be called "nonsyntactical forms." For instance, if I freely vary in imagination words like "green," "greenness," or "similar," "similarity," as they can appear in different syntactical forms, I reach a kernel of nonsyntactical meaning (*Kernform*) which remains essentially the same in its various syntactical formations; such a meaning-form "animates" a pure *Kernstoff*, which is essentially prelinguistic—the very stuff of prepredicative experience itself. Nonsyntactical stuff (*Kernstoff*) and nonsyntactical form (*Kernform*) constitute the *syntactical stuff* which is "formed" by the pure laws of syntax (*Kerngebilde*). Nonsyntactical matter and form are only abstractions from experience; they are nonindependent constituent parts of the lowest meaningful unit, namely, the "syntactical matter" of a sentence, or what we might call the "word."[27]

Now it is clear that "syntactical form" is something much more general and "formal" than syntactical stuff. If we vary different material terms like "paper," "man," "humanity," "sincerity," and so on, we find that, in spite of their differences in meaning and referentiality, they possess in common an identical "form," namely, that of "the substantive." The same is true of "the adjectival" (which Husserl divides into "attributes" and "properties")[28] and the other basic syntactical forms.

The third and final task of pure logical grammar is, then, the construction of a closed system of basic syntactical forms and a "minimum number of independent elementary laws" for their combinations. Husserl here introduces the notion of grammatical "operation" according to which sentences can be generated. There are two interrelated tasks here which can be distinguished.

1. The fundamental forms of judgments establish laws according to which subordinate forms can be generated *by derivation* from the most fundamental (and, in this case, most general and abstract) forms. This is possible because the most general forms dominate the whole of pure logical grammar: the formation of a given sentence is an "operation" according to an abstract and formal rule which carries with it the law of its possible reiteration:

> This, moreover, should be emphasized expressly: *Every operative fashioning of one form out of others has its law;* and this law, in the case of operations proper, is of such a nature that the generated form can itself be submitted to a repetition of the same operation. *Every law of operation thus bears within itself a law of reiteration.* Conformity to this law of *reiterable operation* extends throughout the whole province of judgments, and makes it possible to construct reiteratively (by means of fundamental forms and fundamental operations, which can be laid down) the infinity of possible forms of judgments.[29]

Thus the form *S is p* is more original than the form *Sp is q*, which is an operational transformation of it by the "operation" of converting a predicate into an attribute. These are operations, which Husserl calls "nominalization,"[30] by which predicates can be transformed into substantives and also by which whole sentences can become substantives in later, *derived* judgments; these manifest *a hierarchy of possible derivations.* "This paper is white" (*S is p*) ⟶ "This white paper is before me" (*Sp is q*) ⟶ "This white paper before me is wrinkled" ((*Sp*)*q is r*), and so on.[31]

2. The second manner in which the "primitive" form of judgment (*S is p*) can be transformed is through modal operations upon it. The form *S is p* is originary with respect to its further "doxic" modifications of the type *If S is p, So S is p, Because S is p, S may be p, Let S be p,* and so forth. Through the process of *modalization* the fundamental structure of the judgment [*doxische Ursetzung*][32] is not essentially changed; it is merely modified by special "doxic" qualities (the hypothetical, the optative, the causal, etc.), and this holds also of the more complex forms derived from the *Urform* (thus, *If Sp is q* is a modalization of *Sp is q*, etc.).[33] It is the task of pure logical grammar to discover the basic, minimal number of laws of the *derivations* and *modalizations* of the primitive *apophansis* (*S is p*) which will account for all the possible forms of judgment which *can* make sense. Grammar thus is lifted up to the level of the philosophical study of language in general and becomes a part of the logical study of the formal conditions of thought:

> It gives us the primary and ideal structure of the expression of human thought in general, the ideal type of human language. This ideal structure [*ideales Gerüst*] is an *exemplar* or an *apriori* norm which defines the proper sphere of "the grammatical" [*das Grammatische selbst*], that is the formal law of expressions having meaning.[34]

2. TRANSFORMATIONAL GENERATIVE GRAMMAR

Husserl thus limits himself to giving an outline of what a pure logical grammar would be if it were to be worked out within his general phenomenological architectonic of interrelated and properly subordinated "sciences." But this is sufficient to relate his project to the contemporary aprioristic approach to grammar adopted by Chomsky and some members of his school. We cannot recapitulate the whole theory of transformational generative grammar here, but we can perhaps outline its most fundamental presuppositions.

For Husserl, apophantic morphology (pure logical grammar) is the science (or "theory") which delimits (that is, describes and defines) the whole infinite set of possible well-formed sentences thanks to a finite system of apriori laws which state the necessary (but not always sufficient) conditions of meaningfulness. Stated in this general way, there is an obvious similarity between what Husserl claimed could be done in the analysis of grammar and what Chomsky is in fact trying to do. They both believe that the study of grammar will illustrate certain basic laws of thought and that the "universals of grammar" are not merely the result of empirical coincidence or statistical regularities based on cross-cultural borrowing, linguistic analogies, and the like, but are ideal necessities of all human thought as such. For his part, Husserl explicitly recognizes that there may very well be strictly empirical universals, in grammar as elsewhere, which are due to universal traits of human nature, to the contingent, historical life of the race, and that there is much in particular grammars which depends on the history of a people and even on an individual's life-experience; but the apriori aspect of grammar (the "ideal form" of language) is independent of such empirical facts about men and culture.[35] There is a slight, and perhaps important, difference from Chomsky here, inasmuch as Chomsky wants to account not only for "formal" but also for what he calls "substantive" universals, whereas Husserl does not expect to build up a universal grammar in all its breadth but only a pure grammar which can serve as the basis for logic. Thus he admits that his apophantic morphology does not contain the totality of *all* the aprioris which would be relevant to universal grammar.[36] In short, Husserl does not discuss the possible "material" aprioris which might be found in a phenomenological study of language; he leaves this door open.

There are more important and fundamental differences. Like Plato and Descartes, Chomsky seems to feel that from the very fact that it is possible to locate and describe certain apriori (and therefore universal) features of language, these aprioris must be treated as "innate" ideas or even as "biological" constituents of the human organism. Husserl would certainly never draw such a conclusion, because it would involve him in the kind of "psychologism" which he spent the first half of his philosophical life learning to avoid. Chomsky, on the other hand, is unafraid of psychologism and mentalism and freely illustrates his work (as does, for instance, Merleau-Ponty from a different perspective) with what is known about the psychological processes involved in the acquisition of language; he concludes that these facts point toward the existence in the human mind of a categorial structure ("linguistic competence," *innere Sprachform*) which would be unlearned, innate, and temporally as well as logically prior to experience. But if his notion of "linguistic competence" can be divorced from the Cartesian theory of "innate ideas," as I think it can be, we need not tarry over this difference from Husserl.[37] If, in short, it is possible to interpret the "formal universals" of language which constitute the *base rules* of deep grammar as aprioris in Husserl's sense, then we can easily separate the essence of Chomsky's work from the Cartesian folklore in which it is imbedded in his own writings.

In fact, the notion of "linguistic competence" which Chomsky is attempting to elaborate is based on the very straightforward linguistic fact that native speakers and hearers of a language can produce and recognize on the proper occasions an infinitely varied number of appropriate and new sentences for which their empirical linguistic habits and experience up to any given point can have prepared them only in the most abstract and schematic manner. Moreover, most speakers of a language, i.e., those who know how to speak grammatically and how to distinguish grammatical from ungrammatical sentences in their language, are not aware on the level of conscious reflection just which grammatical rules enable them to give definite interpretations to ambiguous sentences, nor can they in general explicitly state the rules which enable them to for-

mulate and distinguish well-formed from deviant utterances. Most speakers thus operate according to a complex
system of hierarchically ordered linguistic rules (which
must be applied in series) without explicit awareness of just
what these rules are; these rules must therefore be a subconscious possession of the speaker of a language (and in
fact we know that the grammar of no natural language has
been completely and explicitly codified up to now).

In order to avoid all misunderstanding, when quoting
Chomsky's psychologistic vocabulary we must emphasize
the essential difference here between him and Husserl. We
are attempting to give a "transcendental" interpretation of
his concept of "linguistic competence." There is no need
to suppose that the structures by which a child comes to
understand the grammar of his language, or to learn a new
one, are *temporally* prior to this learning or somehow *innate in the organism prior to the acquisition of language;* a
logical priority of the universal structures which are found
in the experience of speaking itself and which enable the
child to grasp its grammatical style (without explicit conceptualization, to be sure) in the very act of speaking is
sufficient.

One can therefore interpret what Chomsky attributes
to the subconscious possession of the human race in a
nonpsychologistic way. It is clear that language learners
do not know, on the level of explicit awareness, what the
laws *according to which* they recognize and reject grammatically meaningful sentences are. As Chomsky has
shown, the cyclic application of phonological rules and the
fact that certain properties of nominalization correspond
only to deep and not surface structures—aspects of language which have been only recently discovered[38]—are used
by all language-users without conscious awareness of what
these laws are or how they can be made formally explicit.
But this only establishes once more the old Husserlian distinction between *the explicit knowledge* of some formal law
and our *acting in accord* with it. All the sciences devised by
man must proceed *according to* the laws of formal logic, and
we can know apriori that if any physicist, or physiologist,
or psychologist violates any law of formal logic, his theory
is subject to error; but very few physicists or physiologists

or psychologists have ever studied, or have any need to study, formal logic *ex professo*. Neither the laws of logic nor the laws of language can be discovered by simple introspection, but only by an analysis of the data produced by language users.

But the simple fact is that Chomsky, in his theory of "innate ideas," has fallen into a relativistic psychologism of an almost Spencerian crudity.[39] It is dangerous to speak of linguistic ability as "species specific" unless one immediately ties this to the ability (of any "intelligent" being) to comprehend grammar and thus formulate propositions which are theoretically translatable into *any* other language. We do not grant to the subhuman animals of this planet the ability to speak, in the full and *true* sense of the word, precisely because they cannot formulate propositions or assert beliefs. They can give signals which enable a degree of communication to take place and they may have something like words (even bees can *denote* it seems), but they cannot express fully complete units of meaning which the possession of a grammar alone would assure. To approach the same fact from the other side, it seems safe to state that *all* students of linguistics today (not only the apriorist grammarians like Husserl or the transformationalists like Chomsky, but also the empiricists like Hockett) would agree that of the some four thousand languages presently known to man none deforms thought, none has any claim to primacy over any other, that each is adequate for all purposes of human communication—in short, that *every* natural language is *capable* of expressing everything.

The ultimate basis for the equivalency or "translatability" of languages, Husserl would argue, is precisely their basis in an apriori logical structure of thought which he calls "the grammatical," or the first level of formal logic. This is not to deny that there may very well be "untranslatable" aspects of given natural languages, tied either to their phonetic sound-structure or to the semantic circumstances and contexts of given historical usages. But insofar as languages issue in statements and propositions, this propositional element (that is, the "meant content" of a sentence), which is founded on grammaticality, can always be made understood from one linguistic field, from one tongue, to another.

This must be true not only of the presently existing languages but also of all past and "lost" languages and of any which will be invented in the future.

Every intelligent creature can, in principle, learn any language. Thus it is "relativistic," "psychologistic," and philosophically unacceptable to tie the underlying universals of grammar to the emergence of our own species on the planet Earth or to the DNA code in the genes of the homo sapiens species. Since apriori grammatical constraints on the meaningfulness of sentences belong to the first level of formal logic, Husserl would argue that they are *constraints on understanding as such* and that, if there be intelligent life on some planet other than Earth, or in the "spiritual creatures" of medieval theology, then, in principle, it would be possible for us to learn their languages and communicate with them. What divides Husserl and Chomsky, then, is whether the universals of grammar are to be understood in a genetically biological (and thus necessarily psychologistic) sense or whether they are to be understood in terms of the logical transcendentalism of Kantian and Husserlian phenomenology.

But the great originality of Chomsky is to have given us a coherent, consistent, highly developed and brilliantly creative theory about the *deep structure* (competence) common to all languages and of the transformational rules by which this deep structure is converted into the phonological *surface structure* (performance) of given, natural languages. He has thus enabled us to transpose the essentials of his discoveries into the "logical" and "transcendental" mode of eidetic analysis.

"The central idea of transformational grammar," Chomsky writes, is not only that the surface structure of a language is *distinct* from deep structure but that "surface structure is determined by repeated application of certain formal operations called 'grammatical transformations' to objects of a more elementary sort."[40] In short, a given sentence can be studied either from the point of view of its physical shape as a string of sounds or morphemes or from the point of view of how it expresses a unit of thought, and the latter is not adequately accounted for by the surface arrangement and phrasing of its component parts. Sentences with very similar surface structures can be seen to require very different grammatical interpretations (as, for instance, "I persuaded John to leave" and "I expected John to leave").[41] We are not interested just here in the intricacies of Chomsky's analyses, and philosophers will probably grant him more readily than structural linguists will that the deeper "logical form" of sentences is frequently belied by their surface grammatical forms. This kind of distinction between surface and deep grammar is exactly what Husserl was aiming at when he distinguished "the grammatical" from empirical grammars,[42] though he nowhere anticipated the spectacular developments in linguistic theory which Chomsky has initiated without him.

We must limit ourselves here to a brief account of the nature and structure of deep grammar as Chomsky postulates it. In order to account for the full range of infinitely variable "new" sentences which we are capable of producing and recognizing on the surface level, there must be a highly restricted and hierarchically ordered system of recursive rules (what Husserl called "reiterable operations") which constitute, in fact, the deep structure of language, and, then, a set of transformational rules which can account for the productions of the surface level. The transformational rules differ for each natural language; but what Chomsky calls *base rules* (which establish the basic grammatical categories and subcategories and the rules of their combinations) are "formal universals" common to all languages. They are "the universal conditions that prescribe the form of human language . . . ; they provide the organizing principles that make language learning possible."[43] But to say in this way "that all languages are cut to the same pattern"[44] is not necessarily "to imply that there is any point-by-point correspondence between particular languages":

> To say that formal properties of the base will provide the framework for the characterization of universal categories is to assume that much of the base is common to all languages. . . . Insofar as aspects of the base structure are not specific to a particular language, they need not be stated in the grammar of this language. Instead, they are to be stated only in general linguistic theory, as part of the definition of the notion "human language" itself.[45]

Thus there can be no language which violates such basic universal rules, but not all of these rules need be explicitly incorporated into every natural language; we are dealing with formal, apriori conditions only.[46] Of course, one must ask *how* these rules are discovered and elaborated, and the answer can only be by reflection and the analysis of some one or several known languages. Though Chomsky does not say so explicitly, the method he employs would seem to be a variant of the method which Husserl called "eidetic intuition," namely, argument on the basis of examples chosen from empirical experience: a free variation and comparison of a number of examples sufficient to give one an eidetic insight into the essential structure of what is being examined—in this case, linguistic behavior. We cannot directly inspect "linguistic competence," Chomsky admits; and the very existence of the deep structures by which "competence" is described and defined must be "theoretical." But it is not necessary to know whether the details of Chomsky's theory are true in order to understand what that theory means and how it is to be elaborated as a "working hypothesis" which, at the limit, would account for the phenomenon of language in all its generality.

Here there are striking parallels with Husserl's approach. Whether we attempt to explain the "linguistic competence" of a native speaker-hearer or attempt to thematize the deep structure which *is* this competence, there are apparently no "inductive procedures of any known sort" which we can follow. Certainly a speaker's "internalized grammar . . . goes far beyond the presented primary linguistic data and is in no sense an 'inductive generalization' from these data":[47]

> It seems plain that language acquisition is based on the child's discovery of what from a formal point of view is a deep and abstract theory—a generative grammar of his language—many of the concepts and principles of which are only remotely related to experience by long and intricate chains of unconscious quasi-inferential steps. . . . In short, the structure of particular languages may very well be largely determined by factors over which the individual has no conscious control and concerning which society may have

little choice or freedom. On the basis of the best information now available, it seems reasonable to suppose that a child cannot help constructing a particular sort of transformational grammar to account for the data presented to him any more than he can control his perception of solid objects or his attention to line and angle. Thus it may well be that the general features of language structure reflect, not so much the course of one's experience, but rather the general character of one's capacity to acquire knowledge.[48]

Even if one refuses to jump to Chomsky's conclusion that such considerations as these necessitate the postulating of "innate ideas," one can still give them the more sensible kind of aprioristic interpretation which would be natural in a Husserlian framework. According to Husserl, fact and "essence" are inseparable in experience. Every fact, in order to be understood, must be brought under an eidetic law which defines its essential meaning-structure,[49] and thus linguistic facts must exemplify essential and necessary apriori structures no less than perceptual facts. It would seem that nothing essential is lost to Chomsky's theory if its "universals" are understood as eidetic aprioris of the kind discussed by Husserl.

There is a further point. If there *are* eidetic or apriori structures of language *as such,* it ought to be possible, at least theoretically, to establish such structures on the basis of even one well-selected example, a single instance of the apriori law in question, since no instance of the phenomenon in question could fail to illustrate its essential and necessary structure.[50] And we find that Chomsky makes a claim for his theory similar to this well-known Husserlian axiom. He writes:

> Study of a wide range of languages is only one of the ways to evaluate the hypothesis that some formal condition is a linguistic universal. Paradoxical as this may seem at first glance, considerations internal to a single language may provide significant support for the conclusion that some formal property should be attributed not to the theory of the particular language in question (its grammar) but rather to the general linguistic theory on which the particular grammar is based.[51]

And also, like Husserl, Chomsky believes that the aprioris of grammar ("the grammatical") reveal the structures of thought itself:

> The central doctrine of Cartesian linguistics is that the general features of grammatical structure are common to all language and reflect certain fundamental properties of the mind. . . . There are, then, certain language universals that set limits to the variety of human language. Such universal conditions are not learned; rather they provide the organizing principles that make language learning possible, that must exist if data is to lead to knowledge.[52]

If we were able to examine the claims of transformational generative grammar in greater detail than we can permit ourselves here, we would be able to bring out a number of theoretical claims which appear to be just as Husserlian as we should expect on the basis of these general methodological statements. Let us limit ourselves here to the parallel discussions of "nominalization" which we find in Husserl and Chomsky. Various kinds of nominalizations are Husserl's most frequent kinds of *operations* which can be applied to judgments and judgment forms. There is a whole hierarchy of such possible operations. There is, first of all, the "operational transformation . . . of converting a predicate into an attribute,"[53] through which what had been a predicate in a proper judgment becomes absorbed into the substantive as a determining characteristic which is no longer affirmed but simply presupposed as the basis for further predication. Furthermore, any predicate (any "adjectival") form can be nominalized and become the subject of further judgments of itself (for example, "The quality p is appropriate to S," "The green of this tree is beautiful," and so on).[54] Finally, and more importantly, the proposition itself (and through it the state of affairs to which it refers) can be nominalized and thus become the substrate for a new judgment ("The fact that S is p" becomes the subject of a further predication). This is possible because, in the most fundamental sense, the primitive form of all judging (S *is* p) is itself "an operation: the operation of determining a determinable substrate"[55] and, as such, can always be *reiterated* and thus generate higher and more complex forms having the same (though now hidden) formal structure. In this way the primal form can generate the infinite set of possible sentences. If we attend only to the *form* of propositions, we leave aside whatever complexities might be discovered by a material analysis of the terms of an actual judgment and grasp the subject (*S*) of the judgmental operation as a "simple object," ultimately just as "something" or "one" (*Etwas überhaupt*), as subject to determination in general (without specifying the particular kind or appropriateness or validity of any particular determination other than to say that any given determination, whatever it may be, must be compatible with the *sense* of the subject).[56]

It is on the basis of these considerations that Husserl affirms within pure logical grammar the "pre-eminence of the substantival category."[57] Adjectives (predicates, whether relations or attributes) can always be substantivized, Husserl shows, whereas the converse is not the case. The proposition, as the operation of determining a determinable substrate, is necessarily ordered in terms of its substantival member, and an analysis of the manner in which a predicate *can* be chosen as a determination of a given subject form must be established on each level of apophantic analytics, that is, on the level of the minimal formal rules of meaningfulness, on the level of analytical noncontradiction, and on the level of possible referential truth. The "pre-eminence of the substantive" thus expresses an absolutely fundamental structure of the logic of discourse.[58]

Now, if we turn to the claims of transformational grammar, what do we find? Chomsky believes that the Port-Royal grammarians were the first to discover the distinction between deep structure and surface structures as well as some transformational rules for converting semantically significant structures of the base (deep structure) into the more derived surface structures in which their true, underlying form is obscured. In their analysis of the derivations of relative clauses and noun phrases which contain attributive adjectives, the Port-Royal grammarians postulate a recursive ("operational") rule in the base such that each relative clause and each modified noun phrase is derived from a propositional structure which is essentially the same as Husserl's most abstract form (*S is p*). "The invisible God created the visible world" is, on the surface level, an implicit way of saying that "God, who is invisible, created the world, which is visible"; and this structure in turn implies a series of propositions such as: "God is invisible," "The world is visible," "God created the world," and so on. The most abstract underlying structure (S *is* p) is what determines the semantic interpretation of the surface structure, and each relative clause and each modified noun phrase (which is but a further derivation in the same line) has a proposition at its base:

> The principal form of thought . . . is the judgment, in which something is affirmed of something else. Its linguistic expression is the proposition, the two terms of which are the *"sujet . . ."* and the *"attribut. . . . "* In the case of . . . the sentences just discussed, the deep structure consists of a system of propositions. . . . To form an actual sentence from such an underlying system of elementary propositions, we apply certain rules (in modern terms, grammatical transformations). . . . It is the deep structure underlying the actual utterance, a structure that is purely mental, that conveys the semantic content of the sentence. This deep structure is, nevertheless, related to actual sentences in that each of its component abstract propositions . . . could be directly realized as a simple propositional judgment.[59]

Thus we see that what Husserl discussed in terms of "nominalizations" receives an interpretation in terms of the transformational rules which derive surface structures from the more universal structures of the base. But, there is at least one more claim on the part of transformational theory which goes quite a bit beyond this one. Chomsky argues that, in deep structure, noun phrases which are subjects logically precede verb phrases and that verb phrases are subject to selectional rules determined by the nouns. Though verbs can be "nominalized," nominalization is a transformational process of mapping deep structure onto surface structure and does not affect the essential and necessary distinction between the class of nouns and the class of verbs. Like Husserl, Chomsky requires that every sentence have a subject and a predicate and that the former logically determine the selection of the latter. Nouns thus enjoy logical priority over verbs; and no language, it is asserted, is thinkable which would not contain nouns and which would not give nouns logical priority over verbs in such wise that one cannot select verbs prior to the selection of the nouns which they must modify. There is thus some kind of ontological structure to language, in its possible relation to its own referential use, which parallels in some way the necessary perception of the world in terms of "objects." Moreover, there are strict context-free subcategorization rules operative on the selection of nouns themselves. These are rules of the base and therefore have some universal validity and coerciveness, according to transformational theory. A noun can be either a count or a noncount noun; only if it is a count noun can it be animate or inanimate; only if it is an animate noun can it be human or nonhuman; only if it is not a count noun can it be abstract, and so on:

> There is a binary choice at each stage, and the derivation is hierarchical because the rules impose an ordered set of restrictions on the syntactic features which can be associated with nouns and limit the classification of nouns to the possibilities enumerable by the rules. As a decision in linguistic research this implies that the optimum representation of the grammar of any language contains these rules. They identify an aspect of the mechanism of language use which is fundamental.[60]

Thus we see that transformational grammar has discovered a way of making explicit the *kind* of universal conditions on grammar which a philosophy of language affirming the "preeminence of the substantival" might expect.[61] At the present state of linguistic research it would be most hazardous to draw the parallel any further.

3. CONCLUSION

IN CONCLUSION we cannot consider all the arguments which have been or might be brought against this unified conception of apriori grammar; but, granting ourselves that the unity of purpose we have discerned behind the grammatical projects of Husserl and Chomsky is acceptable, we can, perhaps, touch on *one* typical argument which we find in the writings of Merleau-Ponty vis-à-vis Husserl[62] and in the writings of "structural linguists" like Hockett vis-à-vis Chomsky.[63] This argument is based on the diachronic development of languages through time, an evolutionary development which subjects languages to all the vicissitudes of cultural history. The vast proliferation of historical human languages and their known diachronic changes, it is argued, renders highly dubious the claim that there is some fixed universal, nonhistorical structure of language independent of the surface structures of the natural historical languages which I speak and which I learn. It is not only that there are gradual but never ceasing changes in sound structure and phonology, but the very forms and senses of words also change; and, if we compare languages over a long period of time, we can see fundamental changes in (surface) syntax as well. (English syntax is no longer what it was in the days of King Alfred or Chaucer; French and Italian do not have the syntax of Latin, etc.) Are not such fundamental and apparently all-pervasive historical changes—to which all natural languages are subject—sufficient to cause us to reject the rationalistic hypothesis of a universal logical grammar? The fact that many languages, like Chinese and Bantu, seem to lack the subject-predicate structure of the Indo-European languages studied by Husserl and Chomsky has led some linguists to argue that these languages have a "grammar and logic" different from that of the Indo-European languages and even that they escape the logical categories of Aristotle and Leibniz altogether.[64]

To this challenge we can give here no more than a schematic answer, but one which, if true, is sufficient to meet it. If we restrict ourselves to the fundamental Husserlian distinction between empirical grammars and "the grammatical itself," I believe Husserl would (and Chomsky could) point to at least one structure of language which would resist the thrust of this "empiricist" observation. There are certain linguistic facts—such as the translatability of all natural languages into one another, the recognition that every natural language is sufficient for all purposes of human expression and that none is privileged, that anything which can be said in any language can, in principle, be said equally well in any other—which point in the rationalistic direction. It is not necessary that there be *no* loss of meaning in the movement of translation from one language to another (clearly the levels of meaning tied directly to phonological systems and even to morphophonemics are only incompletely translatable), but only that some categorial level of identifiable *sameness of meaning* be reproducible in any natural language. This, Husserl would say, is primarily the unit of meaning carried by the syntactically well-formed sentence. A sentence which is formed in accord with the fundamental apriori laws of signification *must necessarily have a sense,* and this sense must necessarily be *one.* This is the *apriorisches Bedeutungsgesetz* which normatively determines and guarantees the possibility and the unity of a given independent meaning in his sense.[65] There can be no language, Husserl would argue, which is not formed on the basis of units of meaning (that is, sentences as "wholes" composed of syntactically formed "members"), because this is what *is meant* by language. It is these units of meaning which are—in the primary sense—translatable from one language to another and, in principle, expressible in any. Certainly the manners in which the Bantu, the Chinese, the Semitic, and the Indo-European languages, for instance, express the various kinds of propositions differ as to their morphology, and there will be some languages whose morphology will explicitly incorporate forms for the expression of meaning that other languages must express in some other (perhaps nonmorphological) manner. But would we call a language a human language if it had no means of expressing the units of independent and unified meaning which can be thematized in logical propositions? If we answer this question negatively, we will have recognized the *fundamental form* of linguistic meaning from which all other possible forms *can* be derived; and this recognition will not be based on statistical probabilities or on an appeal to future experience but will be a conceptual or "eidetic" claim about the nature of language and thought *as such.*

III Merleau-Ponty's Structuralism

It is now becoming fairly common among both phenomenologists and Wittgensteinians to look on linguistics as the newest, the best, and perhaps the *only* authentic model of what a "human" science can and should be—a "human" science being defined as one that gives a systematically complete explanation of some delimited area of human behavior methodologically distinguishable from the sciences (and the scientific methods) concerned with explaining "physical" or infrahuman (i.e., not *specifically* human) nature. This structuralist model may very well serve in the near future to free all the social sciences from their awkward and increasingly indefensible reliance on the "Galilean" model of scientific explanation used in the physical sciences. Though most social scientists still pretend to be using a model of explanation received from physics and chemistry, the day of Structuralism is dawning and hardly anyone who has reached his intellectual maturity since around 1960 doubts that the discoveries of structural linguistics (and the various less well developed structuralisms it has spawned) will revolutionize scientific work as it applies to specifically human social behavior.

Thus *linguistic structuralism*, which in the work of Saussure and his now myriad followers served as the foundation of modern scientific linguistics, is more and more being found to have epistemological and even ontological implications for the philosophy of man and the philosophy of science that are of greater importance than would normally be the case for just *any* new developed scientific hypothesis or method. Among the philosophers who were the first to recognize and attempt to assess the importance of these implications was Merleau-Ponty, the first of the phenomenologists of language to take account of linguistic structuralism. Husserl himself was almost totally innocent of scientific linguistics, though it can certainly be argued that his contributions to the philosophy of language are and remain of greater contemporary interest than Merleau-Ponty's hasty attempt to reinterpret them would lead his readers to believe.[1] It is evident that other major phenomenologists, like Heidegger and Sartre for instance, are equally innocent of scientific linguistics, and it is safe to say that phenomenologists on the whole (and particularly the Heideggerian existentialists) have remained uninterested in these developments except and to the extent that, primarily in this country, they have found themselves arguing points of the philosophy of language with Wittgensteinians.[2] But this dialogue, in American philosophy, is only about to begin; one cannot say that it has already begun.

In France, however, where Structuralism has now become a generalized theory, even a "philosophy," which has gone far beyond its origins in the structural linguistics of Saussure, and is being applied in almost all the human sciences, phenomenologists have not been permitted to ignore its claims and, indeed, have found themselves in danger of being displaced in the affections of the young and the avant-garde by the Structuralists, who now have them on the defensive.[3]

Thus, from the point of view of the philosophy of language, Merleau-Ponty holds a unique place in contemporary phenomenology; he is about the only phenomenologist whom the Structuralists are wont to treat with respect and whose authority and support they readily invoke.[4]

Was Merleau-Ponty, then, a structuralist? In order to answer this question we must first make some preliminary observations and then examine Merleau-Ponty's philosophy of language as a whole. As all his readers know, Merleau-Ponty is one of the most "dialectical" thinkers in the whole history of philosophy; he introduced into phenomenology a style that Husserl, for one, would have found incredible: he is, *consciously*, never simply on one side or the other of any given question but always, from his chosen point of view, on both sides at once. Readers with "linear" minds constantly get confused; they read along in *Phenomenology of Perception*, nodding their heads in agreement with the soundness of the argument, only to discover to their dismay, a few pages later, that this was the position Merleau-Ponty meant to destroy. He always puts *himself* into an argument and presents it in its most appealing and forceful form. There is nothing relaxed about his style; it is tense and taut. Reading his major works is much like reading Wittgenstein's *Philosophical Investigations;* it takes time and effort to distinguish the interlocutor from the philosopher, and it takes considerable agility of mind to hold onto all the threads at once so as to avoid being misled into confusing the position he means to defeat with the theses he is attempting to propound. This dialectical style, more than anything else, has led Merleau-Ponty's expositors and detractors into confusion; very few philosophers are cited so frequently as holding theses they would have disowned.

No oppositions were too extreme for his attempts at dialectical reconciliation: Descartes, the philosopher of the *cogito* and of subjectivity, can be seen in his eyes to be making the same points as Marx, the materialist, or Freud, the philosopher of the unconscious. The structure of *Phenomenology of Perception* is indicative of Merleau-Ponty's style at its best, though this style is maintained in full force through his posthumous work, *The Visible and the Invisible.* In chapter after chapter we begin with well-argued statements on attention, on sense-data, on memory, on the structures of perception, and so on, from two or more of the most opposed points of view, from intellectualism and empiricism, from idealism and realism, from naturalism and subjectivism, only to find that both of the opposed possibilities are in error, and, what is more important, *are in error for the same reason.* When we have discovered the central point at which explanations of the same phenomenon diverge while at the same time *admitting the same phenomenal facts,* at that central point that must be incorporated into each of the opposing systems but that can always be ambiguously expressed, i.e., can seemingly be equally well accounted for in the language of intellectualism or the language of empiricism, or whatever, we have reached the point from which we will be able to start again and to finally account not only for the way things really are in our experience but also for the errors of the opposing explanations. The truth is never wholly to be found on either side, particularly when both involve long traditions in philosophy whose arguments have been reworked and refined sometimes for generations and centuries, but somewhere else, namely, at a point from which all these opposed accounts can be seen to be *ambiguous* with respect to the primary explicandum and capable of being absorbed, dialectically, into a new perspective that will do justice to both. Merleau-Ponty worked hard to earn his title as *the philosopher of ambiguity,* and this should not be overlooked in any exposition of his thought. We need not claim that he was always successful in his dialectical resolutions, or even that he fully justified his own method or his own style, to be fully aware of the nature of our task when we attempt to state his arguments and conclusions in a faithful and properly nuanced manner.

Thus to the question, *is Merleau-Ponty a structuralist?* the answer we should expect is that he is neither a pure structuralist nor a pure phenomenologist (if these are properly opposable categories, as the Structuralists themselves do not for a minute doubt) but something else, a Merleau-Pontean.

1. MERLEAU-PONTY'S EARLY PHILOSOPHY OF LANGUAGE

HAVING ISSUED this first, general caveat, whose importance will become clear as we proceed, let us turn to Merleau-Ponty's philosophy of language. His writings on language can be divided into three periods. The *first period* reaches its culmination in the chapter on "The Body as Expression and Speech" in *Phenomenology of Perception.*

Shortly after finishing the *Phenomenology of Perception,* which was published in 1945, Merleau-Ponty began reading scientific linguistics, particularly Saussure. This was also the period when he was writing *Humanism and*

Terror and thinking of the problem of the philosophy of history. Saussure does not occur in the bibliography of either the *Phenomenology of Perception* or *The Structure of Behavior* and is not mentioned in the text of the celebrated chapter on "The Body as Expression and Speech" in the former. Saussure's work was first used in the course on language which Merleau-Ponty gave at Lyon in 1947–48 and then in the lectures he gave on Saussure in Paris in 1948–49. We will take up Merleau-Ponty's interpretation of Saussure shortly; here let us focus our attention on the reason Merleau-Ponty would find Saussure's theory of the linguistic "sign" so congenial.

In Merleau-Ponty's early works, the study of language is only an adjunct to his development of "the primacy of perception," that is, the thesis that among the various phenomenologically distinguishable modalities of experince, the structures of perception are the most fundamental and paradigmatic whose analogues or derived equivalents reappear at all the other levels. From this point of view, language is important only as an example or an illustration of a more general thesis concerning the origin of meaning and value within the texture of experience. Language, as a system of words that make up our vocabulary and our syntax, is one of the "stores," one of the "sedimentations," of the multitudinous sources of meaning through which men, through time and conjointly with one another, give to nature a human signification; language gives us not nature as it is *in itself,* but the "world according to man."[5] Acts of speaking must therefore be inserted into the framework of the more fundamental prelinguistic and nonlinguistic behaviors that constitute—emanating from the experiencer —the articulations of the experienced world. Perception, gesticulation, the dance, the chant, which precede and accompany speaking, produce an actively preconstituted world whose contents and articulations can then be named and "thought" in language. Words, Merleau-Ponty says, are continuous with the primordial acts of giving meaning to things, which the human body accomplishes in its active, motile, affective perceivings of objects. Words, in short, are gestures.

The spoken word is a genuine gesture, and it contains its meaning in the same way as the gesture contains its. . . . The linguistic gesture, like all the rest, delineates its own meaning. . . . The phonetic 'gesture' brings about, both for the speaking subject and for his hearers, a certain modulation of existence, exactly as a pattern of my bodily behavior endows the objects around me with a certain significance both for me and for others. The meaning of a gesture is not contained in it like some physical or physiological phenomenon. The meaning of a word is not contained in the word as a sound. But the human body is defined in terms of its property of appropriating, in an indefinite series of discontinuous acts, meaningful configurations which transcend and transfigure its natural powers. . . . Here and there a system of definite powers is suddenly thrown out of kilter, broken up and reorganized under a new law unknown to the subject or to the external witness, and one which reveals itself to them at the very moment at which the process occurs. For example, the knitting of the brows intended, according to Darwin, to protect the eye from the sun, or the narrowing of the eyes to enable one to see sharply, become component parts of the human act of meditation, and convey this to an observer. Language, in its turn, presents no different a problem: a contraction of the throat, a sibilant emission of air between the tongue and teeth, a certain way of bringing the body into play suddenly allows itself to be invested with a *figurative sense* which is conveyed outside us. This is neither more nor less miraculous than the emergence of love from desire, or that of gesture from the uncoordinated movements of infancy. For the miracle to come about, phonetic 'gesticulation' must use an alphabet of already acquired meanings, the word-gesture must be performed in a certain setting common to the speakers, just as the comprehension of other gestures presupposes a perceived world common to all. . . .[6]

In his chapter on "The Body as Expression and Speech" in the *Phenomenology of Perception* it is therefore clear that Merleau-Ponty's interest in language is limited to an investigation of the role that speech-acts play in the bodily and perceptual constitution of our lived-world, of how the structures of speaking are related to, embedded in, and affect perception. He develops a "gestural" theory of expression.

The body is expressive of meaning in many ways more fundamental than speaking; speaking is but the refinement, specification, and extension of preverbal behaviors which already bestow a human sense on the world. Our very motility and acts of bodily attention polarize our sensory faculties, select objects, and objectify reality; the selection of perceptual objects and the recognition of their affective tonalities are accomplished through sensory-motor behaviors which do not require the use of words. Moreover, the expression of our mental states in gestures, such as expressions of desire, frustration, concern, anger, pleasure, joy, and so on, gives us the paradigm notion of what a "sign" is, namely, the physical embodiment and expression of a meaning in which the meaning expressed is strictly inseparable from its bodily expression. An expression of anger does not transmit a pure thought from one mind to another; like a mother's smile which communicates an affective state which is immediately understood and responded to by the child—without concepts and without analogizing—the bodily expression signifies itself. It *is* the physical appearance of meaning.

It was natural for Merleau-Ponty to extend this gestural notion of "sign" to the linguistic "word." He did this without reference to Saussure but later interprets himself as having anticipated what he would find in Saussure. Saussure defined a linguistic sign as the indissoluble unit of a meaning (*signifié*) with a physical sound or mark (*significant,* acoustic image). He wrote in one place:

> People have often compared the bilateral unity [of the physical aspect and the meaning aspect of linguistic signs] to the unity of the human person, composed of body and soul. This analogy is unsatisfactory. It would be more exact to think of a chemical compound, like water, which is a combination of hydrogen and oxygen. Taken separately, each of these elements has none of the properties of water.[7]

Whatever we may think of this wild chemical analogy (which, by the way, is clearly false since anyone can verify, simply by listening to a foreigner speak a language he does not understand, that the meaning-aspect and the physical-aspect remain completely distinct in all the uses and transformations of speech), it does serve to stress Saussure's notion that the physical expression of a meaning and the meaning expressed are somehow *inseparable*, if not indistinguishable, and that linguistic meaning cannot be found or investigated otherwise than through a study of the words in which it is fully incarnate (though the fusion of meaning and word-sounds is hardly comparable to the chemical combination of two gasses to get *tertium quid* which possesses none of the properties of its component elements). But this stress on *the unity of the meaning and the sound* in speech is of the essence of Merleau-Ponty's position in the *Phenomenology of Perception* and it leads him into a rather paradoxical position.

He writes:

> . . . it must be recognized that the listener receives thought from speech itself. . . . People can speak to us only a language which we already understand, each word of a difficult text awakens in us thoughts which were ours beforehand, but these meanings sometimes combine to form new thought which recasts them all, and we are transported to the heart of the matter, we find the source. Here there is nothing comparable to the solution of a problem, where we discover an unknown quantity through its relationship with known ones. For the problem can be solved only if it is determinate, that is, if the cross-checking of the data provides the unknown quantity with one or more definite values. In understanding others the problem is always indeterminate because only the solution will bring the data retrospectively to light as convergent. . . . There is, then, a taking up of others' thought through speech . . . an ability to think *according to others*. . . . Here the meaning of words must be finally induced by the words themselves, or more exactly, their conceptual meaning must be formed by a kind of subtraction from a *gestural meaning*, which is immanent in speech.[8]

Merleau-Ponty then proceeds to endorse the ultimate consequences of this notion: the relation of the word-sound to *its* meaning cannot be purely "conventional."

> If we consider only the conceptual and delimiting meaning of words, it is true that the verbal form . . . appears arbitrary. But it would no longer appear so if we took into account the emotional content of the word, which we have called above

its "gestural" sense, which is all-important for poetry, for example. It would then be found that the words, vowels and phonemes are so many ways of "singing" the world, and that their function is to represent things not, as the naive onomatopoeic theory had it, by reason of an objective resemblance, but because they extract, and literally express, their emotional essence. If it were possible in any vocabulary, to disregard what is attributable to the mechanical laws of phonetics, to the influence of other languages, the rationalization of grammarians, the assimilatory processes, we should probably discover in the original form of each language a somewhat restricted system of expression, but such as would make it not entirely arbitrary to call night by the word *nuit* if we use *lumière* for light. The predominance of vowels in one language, or of consonants in another, and constructional and syntactical systems, do not represent so many arbitrary conventions for the expression of one and the same idea, but several ways for the human body to sing the world's praises and in the last resort to live it. Hence the *full* meaning of a language is never translatable into another. We may speak several languages, but one of them always remains the one in which we live. In order completely to assimilate a language, it would be necessary to make the world which it expresses one's own, and one never does belong to two worlds at once. . . . Strictly speaking, therefore, there are no conventional signs. . . .[9]

That the meaning of a word and *its* sound cannot be purely "conventional" sounds paradoxical. On the one hand the very existence of a plurality of different languages in which we can all speak of the same things differently seems to point to some kind of "natural convention" thanks to which, in a given language, certain phonemic patterns are paired with certain meanings. But, on the other hand, we recognize that "conventions are a late form of relationship between men" and that the different groups of languages cannot have arisen through any explicit grasp of the rules according to which sounds and meanings are to be paired.

If we are properly attuned to the dialectical cast of Merleau-Ponty's thought and style, it is not to the point to attempt an empirical validation or refutation of this unverified, and probably unverifiable, hypothesis, as did Alphonse de Waelhens—who strongly challenged Merleau-

Ponty on this point on the seemingly sound basis of his own perfect bilingualism.[10]

As always, Merleau-Ponty is bringing into the clearest opposition possible two theoretically possible viewpoints on the phenomenon of language, neither of which is *exclusively* true, namely, that different languages can speak of the *same things* in different phonemic patterns following different phonological rules, while at the same time there remains, beneath the level of what these patterned sounds enable one to think conceptually, an untranslatable, primitive level of meaning distinctive of that language and expressive of its primordial melody intonation and poetic "chant." And it is the latter fact that is at least chronologically and existentially prior to the former. For the speakers of a given language, for the child learning the language, and for the mature speaker or writer using it to express what has not before been said, the pairing of meanings with word-sounds is accomplished by "an unknown law" that enables us to make use of our bodies and their natural powers of vocal gesticulation for purposes that transcend them, namely, to mean, to express, and to understand the world as humanly comprehensible, as the intended correlate of behaviors that themselves "make sense" and confer a sense on the objects that polarize them. In this, every language is equally "natural" and equally conventional; it is natural to man to speak, but no particular use of his speech apparatus, no particular "natural" language is inscribed in human nature. It is as "natural" for man to "sing the world" in Japanese as in English.

> The psycho-physiological equipment leaves a great variety of possibilities open, and there is no more here than in the realm of instinct a human nature finally and immutably given. The use a man is to make of his body is transcendent in relation to that body as a mere biological entity. It is no more natural, and no less conventional, to shout in anger or to kiss in love than to call a table a "table."[11]

And the most fundamental discriminations that distinguish one language from another occur on a deeper level than that of vocabulary and syntax. One cannot learn a language by looking up the meanings of words in a lexicon, for the simple reason that one must already know the meanings of words in order to begin to use a dictionary. A child does not learn words one by one, and the adult speaker does not use words to "translate" his clear and distinct interior thought into an external representation of it.

> Here the meaning of words must be finally induced by the words themselves or more exactly, their conceptual meaning must be formed by a kind of substraction from a *gestural meaning*, which is immanent in speech . . . in a foreign country, I begin to understand the meaning of words through their place in a context of action, and by taking part in a communal life. . . . In fact, every language conveys its own teaching and carries its meaning into the listener's mind. A school of music or painting which is at first not understood eventually by its own action, creates its own public, if it really *says* something; that is, it does so by secreting its own meaning.[12]

If Merleau-Ponty's assertions occasionally seem to go beyond the bounds of acceptable (or at least verifiable) theory, they nevertheless serve to bring out one central phenomenon of language neglected in earlier theories, namely, that there is a level of phonological meaning in language "whose very existence intellectualism does not suspect."[13] He credits Saussure and phonological analysis, not himself, for this discovery.[14]

Thus we find in Merleau-Ponty's earliest writings on language two doctrines which he later finds in Saussure. The first is the definition of a "sign" as the indissoluble unity which binds meaning to *its* word(s)—a thesis which leads Merleau-Ponty to deny the possibility of an eidetic, universal, apriori grammar.

The second is the closely related discovery of a level of meaning in speech which is more fundamental and more primitive than that of translatable conceptual thought with which philosophers are usually uniquely concerned. Merleau-Ponty is a philosopher of language who is concerned primarily with the primitive phonemic processes which terminate in the production of *words*. He hardly ever goes beyond the consideration of words to the questions of syntax, which, for Husserl no less than for the logical grammarians, are primary. Merleau-Ponty's attitude toward language is quite idiosyncratic for a philosopher and, in this, is extremely original. He discovers and pays special attention to what no philosopher from Plato on down ever had any interest in, namely, the level of meaning which exists just on the level of the phonemic patterns that are capable of being accepted (given the natural phonology of that given language) by that language's native speakers. He calls attention to, and orchestrates, the primordial melody, intonation, and musical contour which characterize the babbling of children as they are learning their first words, the kind of babbling that in children of around two years of age results in their first true speech.

At the period Merleau-Ponty began reading Saussure he was given the post of professor of child psychology at the Sorbonne, and it was in the course he gave there in 1949–50 on *Consciousness and the Acquisition of Language*[15] that he first formulated the conclusions of his early reflections on language. A short digression is in order to relate his own conclusions to contemporary work.

Linguistic expression is specific to the human species; all normal human subjects learn to speak a maternal tongue as a process of ordinary social maturation. A child learns to speak as he learns to use his body, i.e., without ever reflexively learning the rules which govern such complex behaviors in the form of explicit judgments. When a child learns to smile he does not bring his bodily muscular control under a general concept through an act of judgment. Moreover, the ability of normal children to learn language (in the form of gesture and speech) bears no correlation to the degree of their native intelligence or to the efforts of their parents or those around them to "teach" them words and sentences.[16] Language is not, strictly speaking, *learned,* and it is certainly not *taught* (like swimming, reading, writing, or arithmetic). Even the intellectually backward human subject develops (what the most intelligent apes do not)[17] the ability to utter and recognize grammatical (i.e., well-formed) sentences in his maternal language just from being exposed over a period of time to the linguistic environment into which he was born. This ability extends systematically far beyond the empirical samples of correct speech to which he has been in fact actually exposed in the course of his chronological maturation.

Here we come upon an obvious empirical fact about the acquisition of language: it is an ability to utter a restricted system of sounds according to a certain well-defined style (i.e., grammatically) without explicit knowledge of the rules of grammar. The illiterate, medieval Russian peasant spoke a highly inflected, highly complex, and difficult language without the least knowledge of the rules of Russian grammar—rules which were scientifically codified only centuries after the language to which they apply was in existence. To learn a language is in some sense to be "imprinted" by the whole, given, historical language at once on the basis of very imperfect and incomplete factual examples of it. Each child, as we know, "reinvents" for himself the whole structure of his maternal tongue on the basis of his own perspectival, restricted experience of it, and, miraculously, this is just the language which his whole world understands and speaks.

A second, equally important, linguistic fact is that though all human subjects learn to speak (and in this sense, language is "species specific"), not all humans speak the *same* language. We find here, empirically, one of the motives for distinguishing between surface-grammar and deep-grammar. The particular phonological, morphological, syntactical style of any given natural language is not pre-established in the organism as such.

We can go further. *Speaking* is not a "biological" but a "cultural" use of the human body. If the ability to speak is somehow "innate" in the human organism, its empirical forms are strictly indeterminate so far as the bodily organism itself is concerned. The physiological structures of the human organism do not prescribe any particular way of speaking, any *one* natural language, nor do they, apparently, prescribe the development of language at all. The organism, taken just as a natural entity and as a part of nature, has no need to speak. There is no organ which is used in speech— the lips, tongue, palate, throat, lungs, diaphragm, and so on—which does not have a specific physiological function utterly independent of its superordinate and special employment for the purposes of speaking. Moreover, many scientists believe that, from the point of view of purely physiological development, there are certain other higher primates who lack nothing of the physiological apparatus which the human species employs for linguistic purposes.[18] Language is, therefore, a phenomenon of a higher order than biological life; it involves the use of biologically determinate organs for "another purpose," with another intention—in the words of Merleau-Ponty, "to sing the world."

This much is true of the development of language in general, but we also know that it is not enough for two members of the human species to have the same organs or the same nervous system for them to make the same "natural" signs, to utter the same speech sounds, to use the same phonemes according to the same rules, that is, to develop the same language. Our psychophysiological equipment leaves open many possibilities and is, in itself, indifferent to the use we make of it—whether to "sing the world" in English or in Japanese or in any other "natural language." Speaking is the using of a given physiological system, which has its own proper biological teleology independent of speech, for "cultural" purposes transcendent to the biological itself, namely, for the purposes of expressing, making sense of, and articulating experience in language. Thus there is an equivocation in the term "natural language." Though it is *natural* for men to speak, no *given language* is inscribed in human nature as such.

In his psychological study of the way in which children learn to speak their mother tongue, Merleau-Ponty gives special attention to the phenomenon of "babbling."[19] During its first months, the child begins to make expressive movements, to utter sounds, to babble. This babbling is of an extreme richness and diversity and comprises phonemes of every conceivable variety, many of which do not exist in the language being spoken in the child's environment. The child's babbling is a polymorphous and spontaneous language in which all the natural possibilities of the human organism are used to make sounds. When (around the age of two) the child moves from the stage of babbling to that of gradually learning to say his first *words* in imitation of those speaking around him, he first of all begins to imitate the peculiar intonations, the conversational tone, "the melody of the phrases" of those in whose company he is speaking. Thus the German child begins to place the tonic accent on his babbled sounds which corresponds to the German accent, the French child babbles in French, the English child in English, and so on.

Then with the acquisition of closer and closer approximations to the kinds of speech sounds which follow the rules of the "natural" language of his environment, the child *greatly restricts* the number and quality of the phonemes he is capable of uttering and the rhythm and frequency with which they are used. If he is German, he begins to restrict the phonemes he recognizes and can reproduce to just those which are recognized and employed in the German language; and if, some years later, he is required to learn a language like English or French, which employ different phonemes according to different phonological rules, he will be able to lose his native accent only with great difficulty and effort, if at all. Learning to speak a given language, then, requires that the child grasp its distinctive phonetic style, and this requires a selection and *impoverishment* of the natural sounds his bodily organism could naturally produce. We see that this *selective activity,* even in a child of four months, involves the (of course unexpressed) *intention to speak,* and, in repeating sounds made to him in a conversational tone, and in producing quasi-linguistic effects, the child, without doubt, has the experience of doing just what those around him are doing and of fully participating in the world of discourse. Little by little, during the first years of his life, the child moves from his first words, which are really word-sentences of very global meaning-character, to sentences grammatically construed according to the morphological and syntactical regularities of his native language, until, around the age of five or six, he begins to grasp the symbolic and analogical character of language as such.

We cannot here trace or analyze this linguistic development in complete detail. One of the things Merleau-Ponty is most concerned to show is that the child learns a language as an adult learns the style of a hitherto unknown work of art or of music. One first grasps it globally, as a whole, but very vaguely, and then, through further experience, is enabled to discover the articulated parts which constitute the whole and distinguish it from any other. Speaking originates in a personal affective and emotive gesticulation, which only

little by little, through a play of diacritical oppositions sufficient to distinguish one phoneme, one sound, one word,
from another, begins to take on an increasingly explicit and
determinate sense. In short, men begin to think through the
most global and generic categories and, through these,
descend gradually to the clear and distinct ideas of fully
reflexive language.

What primarily impressed Merleau-Ponty, then, in his
studies of language-learning, was the fact that a language
is grasped—through a period of "incubation" which begins
to peak around the second year—"as a whole" (whose
"parts" or elements are then capable of indefinite articulation in their interrelations with one another), as a *style* of
expression which imposes itself and which contains an
"inner logic" that is grasped dumbly and inarticulately (by
an *"esprit aveugle"*)[20] prior to any ability to conceptualize
the meanings for which it stands or which it enables us to
express. Beneath the level of *words,* and beneath the level of
sentences, spoken language is a coherent system of phonemic variations which render the existence of words and
phrases themselves possible. Words and phrases are composed of phonemic "signs," which in themselves do not
mean anything at all (in the sense that they do not designate
or denote anything independent of this semeiological system itself) but are, rather, only the diacritical marks necessary to distinguish one word-sound from another according
to certain patterns. The language, as a phonemic (semeiological) system, carries its meaning within it, as a global
reference to the whole world of experience, capable of expressing an unlimited number of things, which only gradually take on a specific sense. Long after the child begins
to learn specific words, he continues to babble ("to sing the
world") in a generalized way. What the child *means* to say
by such phonemic gesticulation is never *fully* expressed.
There always remains an immense mass of subunderstood
meaning even in the most articulate, adult language, and
adult speech, according to Merleau-Ponty, is only a continuation and gradual explicitation of the original phonemic
babbling.[21]

The study of the acquisition of language leads us back,
according to Merleau-Ponty, to an activity that is *prior to*

cognition, properly so called. The acquisition of language is the acquisition of an "open system" of expression, which becomes a semeiological system capable of being used as the instrument to designate, denote, refer, and speak about meanings transcendent to itself but which has an immanent sense to the speaker prior to and independent of its categorial semeiological functions. Language is acquired not by means of any genuine intellectual operation (which would require an awareness of language as a "sign" of something else), but by means of a kind of "habituation" to others through one's body and its phonetic possibilities.

> The speaking power the child assimilates in learning his language is not the sum of morphological, syntactical, and lexical meanings. These attainments are neither necessary nor sufficient to acquire a language, and once the act of speaking is acquired it presupposes no comparison between what I want to express and the conceptual arrangement of the means of expression I make use of. The words and turns of phrase needed to bring my significative intention to expression recommend themselves to me, when I am speaking, only by what Humboldt called *innere Sprachform* (and our contemporaries call *Wortbegriff*), that is, only by a certain style of speaking from which they arise and according to which they are organized without my having to represent them to myself. There is a "languagely" (*langagière*) meaning of language which effects the mediation between my as yet unspeaking intention and words, and in such a way that my spoken words surprise me myself and teach me my thought. Organized signs have their immanent meaning, which does not arise from the "I think" but from the "I am able to."[22]

That words carry, beneath their conceptual meanings and forms, an "immanent" "existential meaning,"[23] a "value of use," an "affective value" which is not merely *rendered* by them but which *"inhabits them,"* leads Merleau-Ponty to question the possibility or validity of a universal grammar which could ultimately dispense with the vicissitudes of empirical speech.

In learning a language, the child first grasps some sound or sequence of sounds as "opposed" to all the others; he makes the most general, abstract opposition *first*, and then, little by little, the more specific contrasts opposable according to the phonological rules observed in his environment. That such a general structure is observed in the learning of all the various languages of the human race is sufficient to show us why language is such a difficult and "ambiguous" instrument for the expression of meaning. Hegel liked to say that *Die Sprache ist das Dasein des Geistes,* and this is certainly correct. The relations between consciousness and language are such that consciousness cannot become fully conscious of itself and its world except through language. The spirit requires language to *exist.* But the spirit which exists in a natural language is not a sovereign spirit, is not a god who could view the whole of creation all at once, from every point of view, without perspective, without emphasis. The spirit which speaks is embodied, and the problems of the relation of language to meaning are our only route of access to the problems of the relation of body to mind.

2.   THE TURNING POINT: STRUCTURALISM

BY THE TIME Merleau-Ponty finished his course on *Consciousness and the Acquisition of Language,* his conversion to Saussure's version of structuralism was complete. For a few years his expression of discipleship to Saussure was total. From 1949 onward his writings on language multiply rapidly.[24] Language begins to become his central preoccupation; it is no longer treated as just one example among many of the specifically human institution of meaning, but now becomes the privileged model of the whole of our experience of meaning. From being a peripheral, though always essential, consideration in his phenomenological program, the analysis of language now begins to take central place. In 1951, in a paper which he read at the first *Colloque international de phénoménologie,* he attributes his own preoccupation to Husserl as well:

> Precisely because the problem of language does not, in the philosophical tradition, belong to first philosophy Husserl treats it much more freely than the problems of perception or of knowledge. *He puts it in the central position,* and the little he says of it is original and enigmatic. This problem, therefore, permits us better than any other to question

phenomenology and not only to repeat Husserl but to continue his work, to take up again the movement of this thought rather than to repeat his doctrines.[25]

This attempt to present phenomenology as a generalized theory of language grows stronger in Merleau-Ponty's later writings and, in this, he can clearly be seen as a precursor of present-day Structuralism. Moreover, in his Inaugural Address to the Collège de France in 1953 he went so far as to credit Saussurian linguistics with developing a "theory of signs" that could serve as a sounder basis for the philosophy of history than the thought of either Marx or Hegel.[26] He did not, perhaps, believe, like Wittgenstein, that the study of language would solve all philosophical problems, but he did believe that linguistics would give us the paradigm model on the basis of which we would be able to elaborate a theory of the human sciences and thus establish a universal, philosophical anthropology.

Most of his specifically linguistic essays fall in the years 1949 to 1959. By 1953 he had already half completed his work on what was to be his major, comprehensive treatise on the philosophy of language, *The Prose of the World*. That year, when he moved to the Collège de France, marks the high-water mark of his Saussurian enthusiasm and his new interest in structural linguistics. There were other philosophical commitments, which he had made and to which he held tenaciously, which required a very *special* interpretation of what structuralism could do for a phenomenological philosophy.

When Merleau-Ponty presented himself as a candidate for a chair of philosophy to the body of professors of the Collège de France in February 1952, he furnished them with a comprehensive plan for future research which would, by building on the works he had already published in the fields of the phenomenology of perception, art, and history, proceed to the investigation of the realms of speaking and writing (in a projected work to be called *La prose du monde*), of thinking and knowing (in a book to be called *L'Origine de la vérité*), and which would, after having thus established a theory of truth, culminate in a metaphysical treatise, *L'Homme transcendental*. He had formulated for himself as early as 1946[27] the major philosophical goal of his life's work. This goal was certainly *not unambitious;* it was to take its point of departure in a phenomenology of perception, thence to go on to an investigation of the higher-order levels of conscious experience founded on perception, finally to culminate in the formulation of a transcendental metaphysics "which would at the same time give us the principle of an ethics."[28]

As we know, none of these works were completed during his lifetime. He abandoned *La prose du monde* (less than half completed) that same year, 1952, and seems to have definitively lost interest in it after 1959.[29] The manuscripts which had been variously entitled "L'Origine de la vérité," "Généalogie du vrai," and "Etre et monde" were all put together after 1959 under the new title, *The Visible and the Invisible,* the book Merleau-Ponty was working on at the time of his death and which we possess in the posthumous form of a half-completed treatise followed by an intriguing but unfinished mass of "working notes." As for *L'Homme transcendental,* the ultimate metaphysical conclusion towards which he was working, there is hardly a trace except for what we can now work out for ourselves along the lines he had projected, by discovering in the texts he has left us the true intentional thread of his unfinished thought.

From 1946 onward, once the *Phenomenology of Perception* had been completed, Merleau-Ponty began to speak of the "immense task"[30] which lay before him of investigating the relationships which obtain "between intellectual consciousness and perceptual consciousness"[31] and thereby of establishing the differences, similarities, and interrelations which obtain between "ideal truth and perceived truth."[32] In the *Phenomenology of Perception* he had already tried to show how the least perception possesses an "ideal of truth" which it cannot at each moment fully account for but which is nevertheless "the horizon of its operations."[33]

When I stand before a landscape in the company of a friend and attempt to point out to him the bird sitting on the limb of the tree some fifty yards ahead of us, or the face of the owl in one of the clouds passing overhead, I make a demand on him within this perceptual situation which is a claim for the objectively necessary and universally valid truth of my own perceptions. There is not in this experience *my private world* juxtaposed to *his private world* which we can communicate to one another only by using linguistic signs which enable us to analogize each other's experiences; rather, there is given but one "objective" world—in the phenomenological sense of "objective"—correlative to our, and any other possible, acts of perception into which we are both "geared." If my friend does not yet see what I see, I insistently point it out even to the point of becoming impatient; I *demand* that what I see be seen by him also. This is because in the least perception there is given—as the very meaning of that perception—the claim that what I see here before me now must be seen by any other perceiver who would stand where I am standing. That my present perception may require later revision and reinterpretation is totally irrelevant to *this* experience of the ideally objective truth of *this* perception. Whatever corrections later experience may bring to what is now an immediate, present experience, my present perceptual experience here and now of just these objects just now before me requires that I recognize them as being objectively "true," as being really there just as I perceive them.[34] And this is an eidetic, not merely an empirical, claim about perception.

The same, according to Merleau-Ponty, is the case for the experience of freedom, choice, and value. Like all other experiences, evaluative experiences take place in temporal sequences which are undergirded by the perceptual awareness of my being in a "place" (my body) through time. *Since* every perceptual experience, in turn, is a "pro-ject" (a leap toward the not-yet-experienced future) within a field of possibilities, and *since* whatever aspect of a thing I may be presently given is surrounded and escorted by an infinite field of other possible presentations and other possible explorations of this same thing, *to say* that this thing is now presented to me from this given angle is to imply that there is no intrinsic necessity of its being so presented, that it *could* be presented otherwise, and that in fact I experience *whatever* perceptual objects may be given to me as being experienced and as being experienceable from an indefinite number of other perspectives—perspectives which I do not now occupy *de facto*, but which I *could*, at least in principle, occupy *de jure*. Thus there is a subjunctivity to perceptual experience which is the experienced perceptual foundation of freedom. Since no particular approach to reality is fatally inscribed either in nature or in history, there is a margin of indeterminacy for human free choice which is the foundation of "objective" value.[35]

According to Merleau-Ponty, therefore, perception as the most basic stratum of experience "is our presence at the moment when things, truths, values are constituted for us. . . ."

> [Perception] is a nascent *logos* . . . it teaches us, outside all dogmatism, the true conditions of objectivity . . . it summons us to the tasks of knowledge and action.[36]

There is here no question "of reducing human knowledge to sensation," but rather of recovering "the consciousness of rationality" which lives in perceptual consciousness and which founds the unity which we experience among all the diverse levels of intentionality. Merleau-Ponty does not attempt to reduce the higher-order structures of thought and value to perception, but rather attempts to show how the most fundamental structures of perception reappear in a transformed and more complex, but still recognizable, manner in such higher-order activities as speaking, thinking, reasoning, imagining, choosing, evaluating, knowing, and so on. Thus we see that the phenomenology of perception leads to the posing of the question of the relationships which obtain between perceiving consciousness and all the other levels of consciousness which are "founded" in it.

For traditional philosophers Merleau-Ponty's *Phenomenology of Perception* appeared, on first reading, to be a rather strange document. In what other historical account of perception was it ever found necessary to include discussions of sexuality, affectivity, thought (*cogito*), freedom, temporality, and even of mathematical and formal reasoning? Are *these*, also, *perception*? Clearly, the phenomenology of perception, in Merleau-Ponty's eyes, involves the whole of philosophy and leads us into a new way of posing the most fundamental questions.

We are concerned here only with the central thread, namely the investigation of the relationship between thought (language-using consciousness) and perception (the prelinguistic objectification of the world). This is the study of the nexus of these various structures of experience which Husserl termed *Fundierung*. For Merleau-Ponty this problem took the form of a special investigation of the relation of apriori truth to factual or empirical truth, and led him to attempt to show that they were somehow mutually implicating, only two facets of the same experience, apparently situated within a continuum of experience rather than being absolutely and apodictically opposed as two different ways of knowing.

> Thus [he wrote] *every factual truth is a rational truth, and vice versa.* The relation of reason to fact, of eternity to time, like that of reflection to the unreflective, of thought to language, or of thought to perception, is this two-way relationship that phenomenology has called *Fundierung:* the founding term, or originator—time, the unreflective, the fact, language, perception—is primary in the sense that *the originated* is presented as a determinate or explicit form of *the originator,* which prevents the latter from reabsorbing the former, and yet *the originator* is not primary in the empiricist sense and *the originated* is not *simply derived,* since it is *through the originated that the originator is made manifest.*[37]

This seems to me to be one of the most pregnant and important statements of his fundamental problem which Merleau-Ponty has left us. It is a thesis which stands at the center of his work; it is not something that either he or Husserl claimed to have demonstrated; it is rather the framework of their phenomenological investigations, a working hypothesis which would have to be worked out by a generation of phenomenologists. And it seems—let us admit it at once—to present us with almost insuperable problems. On the one hand there is the "objectivity" characteristic of perceived objects in the real world; on the other hand there is the "objectivity" characteristic of such ideal (linguistic) entities as analytical and synthetic apriori truths and their *logical* implications. In his *mémoire* to the Collège de France of 1952, Merleau-Ponty wrote:

> I found in the experience of the perceived world a new type of relation between the mind and truth. The evidence of the perceived thing lies in its concrete aspect, in the very texture

of its qualities, and in the equivalence among all its sensible properties—which caused Cézanne to say that one should be able to paint even odors. Before our undivided existence the world is true; it exists. The unity, the articulation of both are intermingled. We experience a truth which shows through and envelops us rather than being held and circumscribed by our mind.[38]

Hence the proper philosophical approach to the problems of perception is not to ask, from the standpoint of a dogmatically rationalistic theory of truth, whether we *really* perceive the world, but rather to begin with the phenomenological decision to call *what we in fact perceive* "the world." As he says in another place: "The [perceived] thing imposes itself not as true for every intellect, but as real for every subject who is standing where I am."[39]

But it is characteristic of perceptual truth and of perceptual reality to be always incomplete, subject to revision, never adequately given, intrinsically in need of reinterpretation in the future, and thus subject to a process of unending and never completeable verification. Any empirical fact in or about the world can never have more than a "presumptive" validity.

This does not seem to be the case, however, for "the field of knowledge properly so called—i.e., the field in which the mind seeks to possess the truth, to define its objects itself, and thus to attain to a universal wisdom, not tied to the particularities of our situation."[40]

Merleau-Ponty thus recognizes the sharp distinction between "factual truth" and "rational truth." It is characteristic of apriori truths to be truly independent of any appeal to experience. Since they are based on language rather than on *that to which* language enables us to refer (the real world), they are matters of *meaning* only and are thus ideally independent of the world of real facts and events.

We are, therefore, confronted with an *aporia* and we are perplexed. Merleau-Ponty delighted in such perplexities. We are, at the same time, in no doubt from the beginning about what Merleau-Ponty's conclusion is going to be. But we are sometimes uncertain about how he is going to reach it, as he, no doubt, was also—since he was unable to finish his book on *The Origin of Truth*. He adopts, he tells us, a "methodological rationalism" (as opposed to the "dogmatic rationalism" of a Hegel),[41] by which he means a conceptual, and therefore eidetic, investigation of the *meaning* of various kinds of experience. But how does the *eidos* emerge in experience?

In his phenomenology of perception he showed that we are given a single, objectively unified "world," conditionally "true" for any possible experiencer (this "lived-world" being the only field within which human choice and action can take place). Later, in his historical writings, he developed the notion of "the idea of a single history or of a logic of history" which is "implied in the least human exchange, in the least social perception."

> For example [he writes], anthropology supposes that civilizations very different from ours are comprehensible to us, that they can be situated in relation to ours and vice-versa, that all civilizations belong to the same universe of thought, *since the least use of language implies an idea of truth*. Also we can never pretend to dismiss the adventures of history as something foreign to our present action, since even the most independent search for the most abstract truth has been and is a factor of history. . . . All human acts and all human creations constitute a single drama, and in this sense we are all saved or lost together. *Our life is essentially universal*.[42]

Finally, in his writings on the philosophy of language, and particularly in his unfinished and unpublished *La prose du monde*—though he feared and denigrated Husserl's attempt to establish the basis for a universal, apriori, formal grammar—he nevertheless developed his own explanation of the universality of meaning and intention which is postulated in *the very attempt* of one man to address another. He concludes, in *La prose du monde*, that there are not *many* languages, but "to be precise, there is only *one language* in a state of becoming."[43] We will return to this below.

But our problem is not to discover from his texts what Merleau-Ponty saw either as the point of departure or as the ultimate goal of his own thought; this is perfectly clear. *Our problem is with what stands in between*. For his part, he proceeds dialectically, using an existentialist version of what analytical philosophers call "Ramsey's Maxim." Ramsey's Maxim states that in those cases in which apparently antithetical or contradictory positions, neither one of which is satisfactory, are in conflict, "it is a heuristic maxim that the truth lies not in one of the two disputed views but in some third possibility which has not yet been thought of, which we can only discover by rejecting something assumed as obvious by both of the disputants."[44]

Merleau-Ponty's method is to reconcile two opposed positions in a higher synthesis which will explain why each of the alternatives is indisputably right from its own perspective but yet makes an error (in the form of some fatal assumption)—which is, for the sake of the elegance of the presentation, found to be the *same* on both sides—and that, once this error is eliminated, both of the supposedly competing explanations can be incorporated in a new and more comprehensive explanation which now accounts for both without conceding the right completely to either.

Thus in discussing the relations between necessary, universally valid, and therefore apriori ("conceptual") truths on the one hand and perceptual truth on the other, Merleau-Ponty denies the rights of neither side; he accepts all the evidence which the rationalists and empiricists have accumulated, and yet attempts to show that these are not necessarily two opposed, absolutely different, completely isolable ways of knowing, but that one is "founded" on the other. Perceptual consciousness, which operates according to the dumb rules of objectivity which govern the constitution of perceptual objects (and which are revealed in a phenomenology of perception), gives us the *real world* of things and events, and *this* world of perception is the "founding term" or, he says, the "originator" of thought. The structures of thought are therefore of a different order from the structures of perception—which are "absolutely" prior to thought—but at the same time *it is only through thinking* that the structures of perception are "made manifest."

We need not dwell over a few already well-understood points. Clearly the sense of "origin" or "priority" here is not temporal or historical, but *logical;* the same consciousness which *perceives* the world also *thinks* it, and language (or thought) is contemporaneous with the silent objectifications which surround it and which it enables us to articulate.

Secondly, we need not dwell on Merleau-Ponty's obvious delight in showing that categorial, conceptual thinking takes time, that every new theory and every new idea originates in determinate cultural surroundings as the answer to some determinate question, that each idea carries its "date" and has its "birthplace,"[45] since this would be admitted by empiricists and intellectualists alike and in no way affects the logical independence of *what is thought* from its psychological and historical conditions.

What is more important is to see the way in which apriori truth can be fitted into new historical contexts and thus have its significance altered, not only with reference to the really perceived world but also with reference to other categorial schemes which it itself "founds" or makes possible.

> Once launched, and committed to a certain set of thoughts, Euclidean space, for example, or the conditions covering the existence of a certain society, I discover evident truths; but these are not unchallengeable, since perhaps this space or this society are not the only ones possible. It is therefore of the essence of certainty to be established only with reservations. . . .[46]

Merleau-Ponty orchestrates his mediating viewpoint with examples taken from geometry. This is particularly pertinent inasmuch as geometrical truths figure most prominently among those which such archrationalists as Husserl unequivocally situated in "the kingdom of truth," as not being in any way dependent on empirical experience or science, as being strictly apriori, known deductively from self-evident axioms, independent of time and any and all "psychologism."

Merleau-Ponty takes as his primary example our perceptual intuition of the idea (*eidos*) of a "triangle." His argument here is based on an analysis of our actual, intuitive "perception" of the idea (*eidos*) of a "triangle," which precedes and "founds" all the later and derived deductions and proofs which we may formulate linguistically about this *eidos*. If I want, for instance, to *prove* that the angles of a triangle are equal to two right angles, such a truth is not evident from the inspection of the figure of the triangle and is not known simply from the fact that, having grasped the idea (*eidos*) of a "triangle," I am able to repeat the operation of recognizing triangles—as closed, three-sided, rectilinear figures—in an indefinite number of empirical figures. From my perceptual grasp of this *eidos* I can proceed to a conceptual (i.e., linguistic) explication of what this essence implies for objective thought, such as, for instance, proving that the sum of its angles equals two right angles.

> The necessity of the proof [writes Merleau-Ponty] is not an analytic necessity: the construction which enables the conclusion [namely, that the angles of a triangle are equal to two right angles] is not really contained in the essence of the triangle, but merely possible when that essence serves as a starting point. There is no definition of a triangle [such as a "closed, three-sided, rectilinear figure"] which includes in advance the properties subsequently to be demonstrated and the intermediate steps leading to that demonstration. Extending one side, introducing the theorem relating to parallels and their secant, these steps are possible only if I consider the triangle itself as it is drawn on the paper, on the blackboard or in the imagination, with its physiognomy, the concrete arrangement of its lines, in short its *Gestalt*.[47]

In short, the formalization of this proof is always a "retrospective" drawing out of the relationships which are already given dumbly in perceptual intuition. "Formal thought feeds on intuitive thought" he says, and in reality true certainty arises from intuitive experience, "even though, or rather *precisely because*, the principles [made explicit by formal thought] are tacitly assumed there." Without the primordial intuition there would be "no experience of truth," nor would there be any possibility of thinking formally "*vi formae* . . . if formal relations were not first presented to us crystallized in some particular thing." The ability to think out the categorial implications of the truth already given in perceptual experience issues in linguistic statements which mutually implicate each other and thus have the demonstrative value of deduced truths "because I cause [this demonstration] to emerge from the dynamic formula of the triangle." It expresses my power *to think* no less than *to perceive* the triangle's structure.

I "consider" the triangle, which is for me a set of lines with a certain orientation, and if words such as "angle" or "direction" have any meaning for me, it is in so far as I place myself at a point, in so far as the system of spatial positions provides me with a field of possible movements. . . . In so far as the triangle [is] implied in my hold on the world, it [is] bursting with indefinite possibilities of which the construction actually drawn was merely one. . . . Far from its being the case that geometrical thinking transcends perceptual consciousness, it is from the world of perception that I get the notion of essence. *I believe* that the triangle *has always had*, and *always will have*, angles, the sum of which equals two right angles, as well as all the other less obvious properties which geometry attributes to it, because I have had the experience of a real triangle, and because, as a physical thing, it necessarily has within itself everything that it has ever been able, or ever will be able, to display. Unless the perceived thing had forever implanted within us the ideal notion of being which is what it is, there would be no phenomenon of being. . . . What I call the essence of the triangle is nothing but this presumption of a completed synthesis, in terms of which we have defined the thing.[48]

These reflections enable us to see how certain supposedly atemporal truths and relationships can later be fitted into new contexts and new horizons of thought and explanation in which they will take on new significance, and it also shows that even in a purely eidetic science like geometry, the content of this science, at any one particular historical period, differs from others in function of the questions which are asked, the particular possibilities which are chosen among those present within the whole field of "infinite possibilities" implied in originary experience.

But the mere fact that "linguistic truth,"[49] if we can call it that, originates from experience and *can* refer back to experience does not seem to be sufficient to account for the radical distinction between meaning and referentiality which language introduces into experience, and therefore into the articulation of the experienced world. The problems of the interrelations of speech and perception are not *all* solved simply by showing that language-using-consciousness is a logically posterior explication of what perception has already accomplished, because, even if this be the case, it may be that we have the articulated world of perception which we have precisely because of the potentialities which the linguistic expression of meaning introduces into experience. Merleau-Ponty, in the last pages of his chapter on "*The Cogito*" in the *Phenomenology of Perception*, clearly began to wonder whether this might not be the case, and this unsettling premonition seems to have been the vital impetus behind his more and more exclusive turn to the study of language. His impatience at not being able to find the key to his perplexities must account for his abandoning *La prose du monde* as well as for his final attempt, after 1959, to change his mind about publishing *L'Origine de la vérité*.

From the simple historical observation that from 1949–50 onward Merleau-Ponty's writings on language begin to multiply greatly in number, we may wonder whether he was ever satisfied with the manner in which he had claimed to solve the relations between "factual truth" and "rational truth" in the *Phenomenology of Perception*. But even more pertinent evidence of his dissatisfaction with his early solution of this problem is provided by the observation that his philosophy of language grows considerably in complexity, introduces a radical reinterpretation of the "gestural" theory of language espoused in his early writings, and not only takes up the central focal point of all his later philosophical thought but also takes on the role of becoming *the essential paradigm* in terms of which we are finally asked, in *The Visible and the Invisible,* to understand even perceptual consciousness itself.

In his inaugural lecture at the Collège de France to which we have referred above, Merleau-Ponty not only credits Saussure (and linguistic structuralism generally) with providing us with a "theory of signs" which will provide a new basis for a philosophy of history (and, by implication, all the human sciences), but he also adds later that this structuralism provides us with "a new conception of reason" in its relation to the other modalities of experience.[50]

In the *Phenomenology of Perception*, his chapter on "The Body as Expression and Speech," though an important part of the whole, discusses the phenomenon of linguistic expression as but *one* aspect (integral but at the same time peripheral) of the perceptual objectification of objects. He sees—a thesis he never retracted nor ever needed to retract —that *words* have a "gestural" function and are, indeed, *like* gestures in this at least, that they express a meaning which is not objectifiable or expressible without their physical "incarnation" in bodily acts. Meanings are not "attached to" words, any more than they are to gestures; rather, words and gestures are the very lived conditions of the possibility of the expression of meaning at all. Both for this basic reason (which is full of very important implications) and also because of the preconceptual, "affective," "existential" level of meaning which phonemics introduces into the objectification of things by enabling us to grasp and express their "emotional essence" prior to conceptualization —in the very melody and intonations of the phonemic modulations of this particular language—the study of language has a place, though a limited and subordinate place, within the archetectonic of the *Phenomenology of Perception* as a whole.

In his later writings, primarily under the influence of Saussure and structural linguistics, he greatly extends the role of language in his theoretical explanation of the various objectifications which constitute the world of objects among which we live.

The first step in this development was to elaborate a theory of the relationship of language and speech to "silence." This he accomplished in the writings which date from the period of his assuming his new chair at the Collège de France.[51] What Merleau-Ponty means here by the "silence" which surrounds language and enables language *to occur as speech* involves the distinction between *la langue* and *la parole* which he was elaborating at this time. On the one hand, speech-acts, exercises of *la parole*, institute *la langue* and make it live, but on the other hand, speech itself is possible only on the background of all the subunderstood phonological, morphological, and syntactical rules, as well as within the context of the particular lexicon, of our *langue*. We use *la langue* in the way we use our bodies, without thought and without explicit consciousness of the structures which we are bringing into action at any one point.

The first meaning of the "silence" which makes speech possible is that of *la langue,* which itself does not speak, but which is the *ground* of all speech; this "silence" is not unstructured; it is highly determinate. Moreover, and this is even more important in our actual acts of speaking, the speech-acts of *la parole* (our particular usages of our common language in each particular case) result in a kind of "coherent deformation" of the already sedimented meanings and which is constituted of all the forms, all the linguistic institutions of the historical tradition of our distinctive linguistic culture. We speak, in short, on the background of a complex, determinate, and already articulated matrix of linguistic structures which at each instant enable our speech-acts to take place, and thus enable us to break silence and to say something new in authentic and original acts of meaning. Thus *la parole* brings about a constant dislocation and continuing change in *la langue.* We may use the same words we have used on previous occasions, or words the great thinkers and philosophers, the classical writers of our literary tradition have used, but the meaning of these words is never fully grasped and transmitted once and for all; the very *meaning* of our words is itself a limit-concept which eludes speech by always escaping beyond it into the transcendental silence of the realm of conceptual thought, which, while polarizing our attempts at expression, always escapes us to some extent, and thus always leaves room for more to be said, for our *langue* to be used by countless other speakers and writers for *their* purposes and for *their* intentions, which will, in turn, introduce us into *new* realms of linguistic meaning, which are nevertheless comprehensible and communicable to all on the basis of a common understanding and acceptance of the structures of *this* language, an acceptance of common rules which is *sufficient* for all purposes of communication but which is never fully *adequate* to bring expression to completion.

Merleau-Ponty's entire study of language is centered almost exclusively on *one* of the capital functions of speech, namely, the manner in which an act of expression enables the speaker to tear forth from a hitherto undifferentiated field of experience a new meaning and to fix it in the intersubjective mental space of his linguistic (and cultural) community as a common possession by giving it a name, by producing its *word.*

> The spoken word is a gesture, and its meaning, a world . . . . It is impossible to draw up an inventory of this irrational power which creates meanings and conveys them. Speech is merely one particular case of it.[52]

Like Heidegger and Hegel, Merleau-Ponty is most fascinated by the fact that our linguistic ability enables us to descend into the prelingual world of perceptual and emotional experience and to tear forth from the meanings which are there dumbly "bound" to this level of experience in order to discover and thematize them linguistically in "concepts" which enable us to *think* experience and not just to live it.

Unfortunately, Merleau-Ponty neither published nor even finished the final systematic development of these theses about language and thus did not achieve in any finished theoretical form the unification of his incipient thoughts on the philosophy of language (which we find in the plethora of essays he wrote during those "middle" years on various isolated aspects of linguistic meaning, linguistic expression, and on the philosophy of language in general).

Finally, we must observe that from 1959 onward he attempted to incorporate these incipient reflections on a theory of "Speech and Silence" into the much broader framework of "The Visible and the Invisible." The background silence of *la langue,* and the context of discourse which enables authentic acts of new speaking to take place, is but *one* of the structures of what, in his final work, he called "the invisible." The final significance of this thought, particularly as a philosopher of language concerned with the relationship of language to perception and of language to truth, lies in the working out of the theory of speech and perception which he sketched in this final, posthumously published volume.

We can do no more here than delineate his general problematic and relate the theory presented in *The Visible and the Invisible* to his central problem of the relationship between thought (or language) on the one hand and perception on the other. Let me sketch very briefly the final proposal he made on this matter in the final pages of *The Visible and the Invisible*.[53] Merleau-Ponty here attempts to show that the human body, as a system of structured possibilities for future action, possibilities which are realized in the "objectification" and in the very "discovery" of perceptual objects, is "structured like language." Language, as he saw it, following Saussure, is a "diacritical, relative, oppositional system" of elements which are not "absolute" bits of meaning but rather only "divergencies" (*écarts*) sufficient to enable us to establish a system of linguistic signs or *words* (in which all the phonological, morphological, and syntactical structures of our language terminate—because, after all, language is constituted only of *words*), which themselves have meaning for us only because they are opposable, according to rule, to all the other linguistic signs (or *words*) of the same category and level which our language permits. The ultimate task of the philosopher of language is to show how linguistic structures mirror and analogize the structures of perception and thus enable us to understand the structures of action which give us our primordial motives for distinguishing one object, and any aspect of any object, from any other, and thus produce, emanating from the active subject (as an embodied consciousness), the actual lived-world of our perceptual experience.

Just as we say that it is *a part of the meaning* of a color adjective in the English language (such as, for instance, "red" or "brown") that *any other* color adjective recognized and discriminated in the lexicon of that language *could* (from the point of view of purely syntactical analysis) take its place, according to rule, in a given linguistic string, so Merleau-Ponty wants to say that colors themselves, as perceived, are not so much "things" as they are "a difference between things." Let me refer briefly to his analysis of the perception of the color "red":

> A punctuation in the field of red things which includes the tiles of roof tops, the flags of gatekeepers and of the Revolution, certain terrains near Aix or Madagascar, is also a punctuation in the field of red garments, which includes along with the dresses of women, robes of professors, bishops, and advocate generals, and also in the field of adornments and that of uniforms. And its red literally is not the

same as it appears in one constellation or in the other, as the pure essence of the Revolution of 1917 precipitates in it, or that of the eternal feminine, or that of the public prosecutor, or that of the gypsies dressed like hussars who reigned twenty-five years ago over an inn on the Champs-Elysees. A certain red is also a fossil drawn up from the depths of imaginary worlds. If we took all these participations into account we would recognize that a naked color, and in general a visible, is not a chunk of absolutely hard, indivisible being, offered all naked to a vision which could be only total or null, but is rather a sort of straits between exterior horizons and interior horizons ever gaping open, something that comes to touch lightly and makes diverse regions of the colored or visible world resound at the distances, a certain differentiation, an ephemeral modulation of this world—*less a color or a thing, therefore, than a difference between things and colors. . . .*[54]

One conclusion of this analysis would be that the *ideality* which philosophers of language attribute to *the word* is mirrored in the ideality (or "invisibility," in one of the many imperfectly distinguished senses which Merleau-Ponty gives to this term) of what words themselves *refer to*. There simply is no such thing as an experience of "red" itself; every experience is of a "particular red thing" which is opposable to every other (qualitatively distinguishable) instance of what we would be disposed to take (for cultural reasons we hardly understand) as another "red" thing. In short, the experience of "red" (and of any other color) is always the experience of an instance or an example of "red" and thus always implies the subunderstood rules which determine what is to count for us as an example of "red" and what is to be rejected as being "of another color." However fine the discriminations of the color adjectives of our natural language or of our private idiolect of that language, we will never escape the component of ideality involved in our (cultural and intersubjectively determined) selective, perceptual perceiving of colors.

In short, the structures of perception are, for Merleau-Ponty, strict analogues of the structures of language. Colors are as "ideal" as phonemes; that is, the actual experiences of what we call red objects are to the color "red" what raw phonetics is to the ideal laws of phonemics. The phonemes

(and the syntagmatic and paradigmatic rules of their opposability) which constitute the phonological system of any
given natural language are, strictly *as phonemes,* not sounds
at all. They are not the raw phonetic material which given
historical speakers actually produce; they are, in fact, *never
actually spoken, but only meant.*

That a similar structure of diacritical, relative, oppositional rules governs perception, and all other forms of
objectification, was Merleau-Ponty's final belief and underlies his final and most mature attempt to relate the various
orders of intentionality to one another. Whereas he had
originally begun with the very Husserlian thesis that linguistic meaning is "founded" in the perceptual articulation
of objects, he was, in his final work, attempting to understand the perceptual articulation of the world on the
analogy of linguistic structure. Nobody—not even himself
—could *know* whether this new and vastly more comprehensive investigation would provide us with a definitive
theory of the proper way in which to interrelate the structures of "perceptual consciousness" and "linguistic consciousness," because he left us while still in the midst of
thinking out his own first systematic statement of what
such a task would involve.

3. Linguistic Structure and Speaking

It is, then, in what we can (from the perspective of his
philosophy of language) call his second or *middle period*
that Merleau-Ponty was primarily concerned with structuralism and developing his own attitude toward it. And it is
necessary to remark at once, from the beginning, that he
interprets Saussure very much to his own purposes.[55]

His attitude becomes less that of one who fully accepts
structuralism than of one who wants to attempt a dialectical
reconciliation between a phenomenology of the speech-act
and a structuralism of the linguistic rules which are realized
in speaking. In recent French Structuralism, as in classical
linguistic structuralism, there has grown up a more or less
standard, though very vague, sense in which the distinction
Saussure inaugurated between *la parole* and *la langue* is to
be understood, and this has now been extended to cover all

the recent structuralisms that have followed upon it insofar as these various "sciences" deal with subliminal, unconscious, or preunderstood structures that can be related to surface experience as Saussure related *la langue* to *la parole*.

Saussure distinguished *la parole,* the actual experience of speaking, the speech-act, from *la langue,* the system of phonological rules that permits the construction of words in a given language through the distinctive, oppositive traits of their component sounds. He devoted an entire chapter of his famous *Cours de linguistique générale* to arguing that *la langue* is the unique object of study for linguistics and that *la parole,* though not without significance in itself, falls outside the purview of scientific linguistics. For a scientific study of language, it is *la langue* that is, he says, "the essential," whereas *la parole* is "the accessory" or accidental.[56] Structuralism, which is based on a generalization of this distinction, can easily appear to be nothing other than a new and more sophisticated (i.e., French) version of positivism.

Since the direct study of consciousness, of historical origins, of functions and processes, of the individual act itself, the existentially real and concrete experience, leads us into the realm of the subjective, the unique, the nonrepeatable, the uncontrollable irruptions of free choice, which can be neither predicted nor accounted for *in theory,* Structuralism directs its "scientific" attention toward the analysis of the macroscopic and intersubjective structures, the statistical regularities, the nontemporal and nonparticular *synchronic* forms to which behavior can be found to conform. In psychiatry, individual experience is replaced by the study of the structures of an unconscious that, we are told by Jacques Lacan, is structured like language. In anthropology, sociology, linguistics, and other human sciences, the focus is shifted away from the study of man as the *subject* of experience, as the *cogito* in whom and for whom the world is constituted as meaningful, toward the objective structures of thought (and language). It is no longer a study of man who thinks or speaks but of the language that speaks in and through him. It is not that individual experience or consciousness is denied, but rather that the focus is shifted away from the "heroic" vision of man as the source and creator of his own history and of his social institutions to the supposedly infrahuman and "automatic" rules governing his behavior. Attempts to account for the structure of thought by accounting either for its historical genesis through a diachronic study of the processes of its development or for its transcendental conditions through the logical analysis of the contents of consciousness *as such* are abandoned in favor of a purely descriptive, nonhistorical, *synchronic* study of its objectified forms. The methods of Kant and Husserl, no less than those of Hegel and Dilthey, are to be completely bypassed.

There is, of course, in attempting to characterize a style of thought that embraces as many disciplines as does contemporary Structuralism, the danger of becoming altogether too vague. Merleau-Ponty warns of this in his discussion of Lévi-Strauss, where he also succinctly gives his own understanding of the term "structure."

> Social facts are neither things nor ideas; they are structures. Overused today, this term had a precise meaning to begin with. . . . In linguistics . . . structure is a concrete, incarnate system. When Saussure used to say that linguistic signs are diacritical—they function only through their differences, through a certain spread between themselves and other signs and not, to begin with, by evoking a positive signification—he was making us see the unity which lies beneath a language's explicit signification, a systematization which is achieved in a language before its conceptual principle is known. For social anthropology, society is composed of systems of this type. . . . The subjects living in a society do not necessarily know about the principle of exchange which governs them, any more than the speaking subject needs to go through a linguistic analysis of his language in order to speak. They ordinarily make use of the structure as a matter of course. Rather than their possessing it, it possesses them.[57]

If one were to take Merleau-Ponty's numerous professions of discipleship to Saussure at face value, one would say that he begins with a total acceptance of Saussure's semeiology. His interpretation of this semeiology enables him to bring his earlier reflections on speech as linguistic gesticulation together with Saussure's theory of the linguistic sign and to interpret Saussure philosophically:

> What we have learned from Saussure is that, taken singly, signs do not signify anything, and that each one of them does not so much express a meaning as mark a divergence of meaning between itself and other signs.[58]
>
> The well-known definition of the sign as "diacritical, oppositive, and negative" means that language is present in the speaking subject as a system of intervals between signs and signification, and that, as a unity, the act of speech simultaneously operates the differentiation of these two orders.[59]

Prior to Saussure, it was usual to define the word-sound (what he calls the "acoustic image") as the *sign* (*signifiant*) of its meaning or of its reference. Thus the sound of the word "tree" would evoke, because of a conventional association, the concept (*signifié*) and, through the concept, the actual individuals of the class of beings called "trees." The earlier semeiologies, which went back to Aristotle and Ockham, made no essential semeiological distinction between so-called "natural" signs (smoke as the sign of fire) and "linguistic" signs. In opposition to the tradition that treated all signs as belonging to the same genus, Saussure based his semeiology on the recognition that, in language, the interpenetration of the *signifiant* by the *signifié* does not permit this artificial separation of the one from the other. The word-sound does not *merely remind us* of the idea with which it is associated. Saussure thus gives the linguistic *sign* a technical sense; he reserves the word *sign* to designate the combination of the concept (*signifié*) and the acoustic image (*signifiant*) into a unity. "We propose," he wrote, "to keep the word *sign* to designate the totality [i.e., the word as meaningful] and to replace the words *concept* and *acoustic image* by *signifié* and *signifiant* respectively."[60]

As we have seen above, Merleau-Ponty had argued, even before reading Saussure, that the meaning of a word and *its* sound could not be completely arbitrary. But this acceptance (or this interpretation) of Saussure forces Merleau-Ponty into an uncomfortable position in regard to the purely structural aspects of speech and the possibility of a universal grammar. In his linguistic writings, Merleau-Ponty orchestrates the Saussurian doctrine of "opposability": Just as phonemes are able to become distinctive and thus "meaningful" signs only because they can be "opposed" according to rule to others, so all the semantemes and words, all units of meaningful sound in a given language, have meaning only thanks to their possible opposition (in the same place in a given linguistic string) to others that *could* take their place. For instance, a color adjective, in this view, would take its meaning from the fact that it is opposable to the other color adjectives of that given language and it is only as a part of this "system" as a whole that it carries its own distinctive meaning. Merleau-Ponty likes to cite and refer to the following passage from Saussure above all others:

> In language there are only differences and no positive terms. Whether one takes the point of view of the *signifié* [concept] or of the *signifiant* [acoustic image] language contains neither ideas nor sounds which would pre-exist the linguistic system but only the conceptual differences and phonic differences which issue from the system.[61]

In short, a language as *langue,* as the system of (phonological) rules that are the necessary structural conditions for speech, is not a vocabulary of signs or words but the methodical means, the rules, a given speech community has for discriminating one sign for another. It is at any one point in time utterly impossible to fix the vocabulary of a given language, of a given speaker, of a given child who is learning the language; no dictionary or lexicon is ever complete, because new and incubating changes are forever in process of becoming actual—without, however, the language *as langue,* as system, being in the least affected. It is in this sense of language that we must conclude that the child learns the language as a whole, globally by unconsciously grasping the style of its distinctive phonemic oppositions in practice, and it is *in this sense* of language that we can and must say, for instance, that the French language preexisted all the works of French literature and is essentially untouched by whatever writers may use it to express.[62]

But here we come upon another paradox in Merleau-

Ponty's "structuralism." Namely, if words and linguistic signs have no meaning in and of themselves but only serve to mark the differences that distinguish one sign from others, we want to ask how is it that words can nevertheless be understood in isolation, independently of any awareness of those forms to which they could be opposed and which could occur in the same place in a given linguistic string?[63] Even though we can grant that all the words of a language "hold one another in place"[64] and form a synchronically closed system, it is clearly not necessary (and in any case it is impossible) to know *all* the words of a given language in order to understand just any other, or to know *all* the color adjectives in a given language to understand the one I mean just now. The answer to this question, of course, takes us away from *la langue* towards *la parole* and to questions of *referential meaning* and *semantic conditions*. This question takes us away from language as the necessary, presupposed structural condition of all speaking to the *speech-act* itself, and Merleau-Ponty, like all phenomenologists (and, one might add, Wittgensteinians as well), recognizes that meaning is actualized only in *use* and that the sentence (the assertion, the proposition, the question, and so on) is, in an existential and ontological sense, intentionally prior to its component parts (the morphemes and words, which can be discovered only by a later, formal analysis).

Though we cannot deal with this in any detail, we are here touching on one of the most delicate points in Merleau-Ponty's interpretation of Saussure. It involves the primacy of the speech-act over its formal (and logical) conditions. Here it is sufficient to emphasize what, according to Merleau-Ponty, is the crowning glory of structural linguistics, namely, to have discovered and enabled us to account for the phonological level of meaning in language, which is immanent to the linguistic system itself and which is independent of all questions of referentiality and semantics. This is a level of meaning, the meanings words have just through their ability to fit into just these combinations with just these other words of *this* language (which is essential to our understanding not only of the diverse possibilities for expression we find in different natural languages but also of the peculiar genius of the poetic and literary uses of language). This was completely ignored in all the earlier, primarily "intellectualistic" theories of language.

Noam Chomsky has pointed out that the major defect in the linguistic structuralism of Saussure and his disciples was to believe that syntax was a relatively trivial matter. Saussure was concerned with the taxonomic analysis of strings of sounds (from left to right if written, in temporal sequence when spoken), that is, with a "linear" analysis that neglected the various more abstract relations between the component parts of sentences which must be studied by any grammar that would go beneath the phonological surface to the logical relations of the "deep structure" not reflected in the surface string. Saussure believed that the system of language was restricted to groups of sounds, and the rules of their development into words and phrases; this was, for him, *la langue*. All other considerations, including not only referentiality and semantics *but even syntax*, lay outside the scope of linguistics proper and were to be assigned to the "accessory" realm of *la parole*, the speech-act. Even if a completely fair and nuanced study of his thought would require some qualification here, this was undoubtedly the thrust of his conclusions, and it is for this reason, Chomsky argues, that there was "very little work in syntax throughout the period of structural linguistics."[65] It is also why the structural linguists, before the advent of "depth grammar" and the study of the formal rules governing grammatical transformations of various types, not only neglected but *inhibited* the "philosophical" as well as the scientific study of grammar in its own right. That was a project of the seventeenth- and eighteenth-century philosophical grammarians that had to be consigned to oblivion.

In this we have to recognize Merleau-Ponty as a true disciple of Saussure. His philosophy of language gives a very small place, if any, to purely grammatical considerations. He is concerned uniquely with what we can call semeiology in a narrow sense: the study of the mechanisms of the emergence of sense within the phonological system of signs that is realized in *words*. It is almost as if, for him, grammar would be found to be nothing more than a minor subdivision of phonology, and this is, no doubt, also the reason why Merleau-Ponty was so embarrassed by Husserl's proposal for an "eidetics" of language. It is only in *La prose du monde* that Merleau-Ponty takes up the Husserlian question of grammar seriously; there he discusses the "algorithmic" aspect of language, that aspect which, once we know the rule, always enables us "to go on" (as Wittgenstein would also say) and which permits the use of language for the higher purposes of scientific and theoretical thinking.[66] Though Merleau-Ponty fully recognized that language both originates (teleologically) and culminates (existentially) in speech-acts (*la parole*), which are always grammatically formed complete units of meaning, or sentences, he did not explicitly study grammatical structures for themselves. This was, he felt, the attitude toward language specifically adopted by the logician, not the linguist or the philosopher concerned concretely with the phenomenon of expression. It was the discredited approach of the "ideal language" experimenters and of those in search of some perfectly defined and completely explicit linguistic instrument that could, for certain ideal purposes, *take the place* of ordinary language; it was an abstract and derived approach to language that would be of little service for the illumination of productive speech.

If he had been more open to syntactical considerations, he would no doubt have found that syntax is much more perfectly "translatable" from one language to another than are "words," and that the study of grammar would require the posing of a number of questions that his own theory of language avoids *in fact* if not in principle. He did recognize that *la parole* is related to *la langue* as "fact" to "essence" (in the Husserlian acceptance of these terms), not only, though perhaps primarily, in the sense that the structures of language are always *logically* already presupposed in any actual speaking, but also in the sense that the structures of *la langue* are precisely the rules of *speaking* and are, though logically presupposed in analysis, historically and ontologically generated by speech itself. The two are as inseparably united as are an instance and its type.

We have seen above that Merleau-Ponty approves of Husserl's decision to put the theory of language at the center of his philosophical investigations and that he found the "little" (!) Husserl had to say on the subject to be "original" but "enigmatic." What Merleau-Ponty found especially "enigmatic" was the whole of the *Fourth Investigation* and most of *Formal and Transcendental Logic*—hardly a minor chunk of Husserl—particularly for its theory of pure apriori grammar. On several occasions he attempted to interpret Husserl unhistorically, in his own sense, and even seemed to think that Husserl later abandoned his idea of such a universal logical grammar. Merleau-Ponty not only feared that such a universalistic, eidetic point of view would necessitate a return to the discredited attempt of the likes of Carnap and the Logical Positivists to replace natural language with some form of artificial "ideal" language, but felt that his own gestural theory of the meaning of words made it necessary that no natural language be the exact equivalent of any other—either in its actual form or in its potentialities for expression. We must, therefore, see how he was forced to answer Husserl's challenge from within the resources of his own thought.

Against the claims of "philosophical" grammarians like Husserl (and, we can well believe, like Chomsky, had he known his writings), Merleau-Ponty frequently inveighs against the conception that there are certain "universal" or "eidetic" structures of language in general of which the grammar of any particular language would be only some cloudy or imperfect realization. He does not believe, at least in the central body of his writing, either that there are universal structures underlying all grammars (that is, logically prior to any particular grammar) or that there is some *eidetic telos* of grammar toward which empirical, historical grammars can be seen to be groping.

> . . . we must understand that since synchrony is only a cross-section of diachrony the system realized in it never exists wholly in act but always involves latent or incubating changes. It is never composed of absolutely univocal meanings which can be made completely explicit beneath the gaze of transparent constituting consciousness. It will be a question not of a system of forms of signification clearly articulated in terms of one another—not of a structure of linguistic ideas built according to a strict plan—but of a cohesive whole of convergent linguistic gestures, each of which will be defined less by a signification than by a value

of usage. Far from particular languages appearing as the "confused" realization of certain ideal and universal forms of signification the possibility of such a synthesis becomes problematical. If universality is attained, it will not be through a universal language which would go back prior to the diversity of languages to provide us with the foundations of all possible languages. It will be through an oblique passage from a given language that I speak and that initiates me into the phenomenon of expression, to another given language that I learn to speak and that effects the act of expression according to a completely different style—the two languages (and ultimately all given languages) being contingently comparable only at the outcome of this passage and only as signifying wholes, without our being able to recognize in them the common elements of one single categorial structure.[67]

Thus, though Merleau-Ponty seems, frequently and explicitly, to rule out the possibility of linguistic universals, we must note that he hardly ever discusses purely grammatical or syntactical relationships as such, that he never distinguishes surface from depth grammar (as not only Chomsky but also Wittgenstein and Russell do), and that he always leaves the door open by qualifying his own assertions with phrases like "if universality is attained,"[68] "if there is such a thing as universal thought,"[69] "but even if these invariants exist,"[70] and similar locutions, which seem to express doubt and qualification rather than fully convinced denial. As always, Merleau-Ponty proceeds dialectically. At the outset we are faced, in this final paradox of language, with two quite straightforward facts about linguistic experience. On the one hand it seems to be well attested and theoretically well founded to believe that all of the empirical languages known to man are completely sufficient for all purposes of human communication, that none is privileged, that none necessarily deforms thought, that there is nothing that can be said in one language that cannot be said equally well—though, of course, using different phonological, morphological, and syntactical possibilities—in any other. This might be called the fact of the universal equivalence or translatability of each language into every other; this is particularly evident on the level of syntax but certainly extends

throughout the whole domain of semantics, at least in principle.

On the other hand, there are the kinds of considerations
we have seen Merleau-Ponty urging, to the effect that there
are practical and theoretical limits on "translatability" and
that natural languages, if only because they have diverse
phonological and morphological systems—to say nothing
of the diachronic developments of their syntax as well, the
vicissitudes and accidental historical changes to which they
are subject, and so on—are not *exhaustively* translatable
into one another. In his typical fashion Merleau-Ponty will
not take his stand on the side of either of these opposed
positions, though it is clear that he is more suspicious of the
"intellectualist" than of the "empiricist" (or "skeptical"—
he likes to think of himself as a "skeptic") framework. Precisely because the ideas or concepts that language expresses
can be neither entertained nor distinguished except through
some particular use of language, he rejects a universality
that would come "from above," so to speak, from a universal
mind, a system of "innate ideas," or a power of thought that
could think without the use of some language. But is this to
deny *all* universality? It would seem, if we read him carefully, that he does not go this far, and we can thus pose the
question more clearly. The question is not: are there some
linguistic universals? but rather: what *kind* of universality
do we find in language? And, if we pose the question in this
way, we find that Merleau-Ponty gives, though hesitatingly,
an original answer that owes a good deal both to structuralism and to phenomenology. We can briefly sketch his answer in two steps.

Let us begin with his earliest statement of the problem
from *Phenomenology of Perception:*

> If there is such a thing as universal thought, it is achieved
> by taking up the effort towards expression and communi-
> cation in *one* single language, and accepting all its am-
> biguities, all the suggestions and overtones of meaning of
> which [it] is made up, and which are the exact measure of
> its power of expression. . . . The meaning of a sentence
> appears intelligible throughout, detachable from the sen-
> tence and finitely self-subsistent in an intelligible world, be-

cause we presuppose as given all those exchanges, owed to the history of the language, which contribute to determining its sense. . . . But in fact . . . the clearness of language stands out from an obscure background, and if we carry our research far enough we shall eventually find that language is . . . uncommunicative of anything other than itself, that its meaning is inseparable from it. We need, then, to seek the first attempts at language in the emotional gesticulation whereby man superimposes on the given world the world according to man. There is here nothing resembling the famous naturalistic conceptions which equate the artificial sign with the natural one, and try to reduce language to emotional expression. . . . It would be legitimate to speak of "natural signs" only if the anatomical organization of our body produced a correspondence between specific gestures and given "states of mind." . . . It is not enough for two conscious subjects to have the same organs and nervous system for the same emotions to produce the same signs. What is important is how they use their bodies, the simultaneous patterning of body and world in emotion. . . . Behavior creates meanings which are transcendent in relation to the anatomical apparatus, and yet immanent to the behavior as such, since it communicates itself and is understood.[71]

Here we might say that we have an existential basis for the distinction between grammar and depth grammar: each man makes himself understood even though each speaks his own language; were it not for social pressures and the need to conform to the institutions of the group, there would be as many languages as there are people, and *in one sense* there already are. Is it not the case that in some areas such as New Guinea where tribes are numerous, small, hostile, and extremely suspicious of one another, one will find two or three hundred (some writers say as many as seven hundred) different languages whose speakers are mutually unintelligible to one another? And, even within our own tribe, do we not each one develop our own idiolects, our own personal versions of whatever language we agree to speak for purposes of communication? We see here the ground of Merleau-Ponty's suspicion of universal structure. Perhaps the teaching of a language to an infant is not so much an effort to give him something he could not develop for himself but an effort to prevent him from fabricating his own.

The only foundation for universality that Merleau-Ponty will accept is not the "eidetic" universality of a necessary *apriori* logical form but the comprehensibility achieved in "the oblique passage from a given language that I speak . . . to another given language that I learn."[72] The event is too hesitant and passing to imagine that some common mind or some explicit convention is responsible for it; at the same time it is too systematic, too consistent to be reducible to a series of accidents. On the one hand there is the practical impossibility of giving *one*, ideal, formal analysis of any given language that would show forth its unique rational formula, that would enable us to define its essence un-equivocally and derive all its various characteristics from a common principle, showing their proper hierarchies and derivations. It is equally impossible to account rationally for the historical relationships between languages or to pinpoint the time, for example, at which Latin irrevocably becomes French. But, at the same time, when one takes up the linguistic history of the human race, the continuous proliferation of aberrant forms in which no structure is ever fully finished or achieved and in which no innovation can be precisely dated, one sees that there is no precise break between any one language and any other, no clean line of demarcation between one idiolect and another. At this point, says Merleau-Ponty, one sees that "to be precise, *there is only one language in a state of becoming*."[73]

> If we must renounce the abstract universality of a rational grammar which would give us the common essence of all languages, we rediscover at the same time the concrete universality of a given language which is becoming different from itself while remaining the same. Because I am now speaking, my language is not for me a sum of facts but a unified instrument for a complete intention of expression. And *because it is so for me I am able to enter into other systems of expression*, at first by grasping them as variants of my own, and then by letting myself be inhabited by it until my own language becomes a variant of it. Neither the unity of language, nor the distinctions among languages, nor their historical derivations from one another cease to be understandable just because we refuse to conceive one essence of language. It is simply that they must be conceived

not from the standpoint of the concept or of essence but from the dimension of existence.[74]

There is, therefore, an experienced and "existential" foundation for universality in language, but it is not that of the "innate ideas" of the Cartesians or of the logical *aprioris* of "rational grammar." It is rather the "oblique" or "lateral" universality of incomplete but sufficient comprehensibility that we effect in actually speaking to others. We must each speak according to common rules or we would not be understood, and yet each act of speech is, in each case, a "coherent deformation" of the rules already given and accepted. In his essay on Lévi-Strauss, Merleau-Ponty applies the same conception to social structures.

> There thus appears at the base of social systems a formal infrastructure (one is tempted to say an unconscious thought), an anticipation of the human mind, as if our science were already completed in events, and the human order of culture a second order of nature dominated by other invariants. But even if these invariants exist, even if social science were to find beneath structures a metastructure to which they conformed (as phonology does beneath phonemes), the universal we would thus arrive at could no more be substituted for the particular than general geometry annuls the local truth of Euclidean spatial relations. . . . The implications of a formal structure may well bring out the internal necessity of a given genetic sequence. *But it is not these implications which make men, society, and history exist. . . .* This process of joining objective analysis to lived experience is perhaps the most proper task of anthropology. . . . This provides *a second way to the universal;* no longer the overarching universal of a strictly objective method, but a sort of *lateral universal* which we acquire through ethnological experience and its incessant testing of the self through the other person and the other person through the self.[75]

We are thus brought, in our schematic analysis of Merleau-Ponty's thought on this subject, to the final step in his argument. It is one that preoccupied him throughout his writings and that ties his own phenomenological method to Husserl's, namely, his attempt to understand the relationship between "fact" and "essence," the instance and the type, induction and eidetic intuition (*Wesenschau*). In this same essay on Lévi-Strauss he refers to "the old prejudice which opposes deduction to induction." He had examined this in some detail in his essay on *Phenomenology and the Sciences of Man,* and he returned to it especially in the methodological sections of *The Visible and the Invisible.*

To be brief, Merleau-Ponty argues that not only in the human but in *all* the sciences "pure inductivity is a myth," that there is no fruitful research that is "a pure inventorying of constants in themselves."[76] Actual thinking moves back and forth between experiencing and intellectual construction.[77] When one brings a particular instance under a general law, one "reads its essence" by adopting an "idealizing fiction" that is founded on the facts, and in terms of which the facts make sense. Such a structure or "essence," thanks to the comprehensive and interpretive imagination of the scientific investigator, is not a natural or cultural force in its own right, but a "light" that enables us to clarify concrete experience. It is no insight into an essence if one cannot turn to the corresponding individual, the set of examples of which it is the "essence," and we know that Husserl himself "never obtained one sole *Wesenschau* that he did not subsequently take up again and rework, not to disown it, but in order to make it say what at first it had not quite said."[78] This is because there can be no knowledge of facts that does not involve some insight into their invariant structures, but at the same time these "invariant" structures are nothing at all but the structures the facts themselves exhibit as they are situated and organized from the point of view of the reflective scientist. One never just collects facts, and even when one has collected a large number for some purpose, one selects from among them a finite number through a "free variation" in imagination in order to construct the "idea" that will render them comprehensible: "that which cannot be varied without the object itself disappearing is the essence."[79]

> ... philosophy does not possess the truth about language and the world from the start, but is rather the recuperation and first formulation of a Logos scattered out in our world and our life and bound to their concrete structures ... the contrast between fact and essence [is] explicitly mediated by the

idea that the purest reflection discloses a "genesis of meaning" [*Sinngenesis*] immanent in its objects—the need for each manifestation of its objects to have a "before" and an "after" and to develop through a series of steps or stages in which each step anticipates and is taken up in a subsequent one. . . . Of course this intentional history is not simply the sum of all manifestations taken one by one. *It takes them up again and puts them in order;* in the actuality of a present it reanimates and rectifies a genesis which could miscarry without it. But it can do so only in contact with what is given, *by seeking its motives within it.* It is not just an unfortunate accident that the study of significations and the study of facts encroach upon one another. If it did not condense a certain development of *truth,* a signification would be empty. . . . Superficially considered, our inherence [in history] destroys all truth; considered radically, it founds a new idea of truth. As long as I cling to the ideal of an absolute spectator, or knowledge with no point of view, I can see my situation as nothing but a source of error. But if I have once recognized that through it I am grafted onto every action and all knowledge which can have a meaning for me, and that step by step it contains everything which can *exist* for me, then my contact with the social in the finitude of my situation is revealed to me as the point of origin of all truth, including scientific truth. And since we have an idea of truth, since we are in truth and cannot escape it, the only thing left for me to do is to define a truth in the situation. . . . Ultimately, our situation is what links us to the whole of human experience. . . . "*Science*" . . . *designates the effort to construct ideal variables which objectify and schematize the functioning of this effective communication.*[80]

Husserl and Merleau-Ponty developed a phenomenological method that was neither deductive nor purely empirical.[81] Merleau-Ponty became, while writing *Phenomenology and the Sciences of Man,* interested in structural linguistics primarily, I think, because it presented him with the best example, and the *only* example at that time, of a science that could formulate "essential" or structural laws that still clearly participated in the historicity, contingency, and open-endedness of the primary data they themselves thematized. It showed how essential laws, which ordinarily lie beneath the threshold of experience, can nevertheless be shown to be the necessary structural conditions of the experience of which they are the laws. It gave him one of the clearest illustrations of the correlativity of fact and essence in experience and thus the means of bringing structuralism and phenomenology together and of reconciling them in a higher synthesis. All the phonological, morphological, syntactic, and other laws that govern the speech act and make it possible can clearly be shown to be *necessary* (and "invariant") laws, that is, insofar as they thematize conditions without which speaking would be impossible, and yet these laws are themselves generated by historical, contingent acts of speech, which they serve and which they are *of*. They have no "substantiality" in themselves. (In the words of Saussure, "language is not a substance but a form.") The ultimate unity of *la langue* and *la parole,* that is, of the structural conditions and of their actualizations in the experiences that confer on them their ontological validity, is what Merleau-Ponty was striving to understand and account for on the structuralist basis provided by Saussure—the first sustained, powerful, coherent attempt to integrate the discoveries of linguistic structuralism into a phenomenological perspective.

IV   The Levels of Meaning in Language

The term "meaning" is one of the most vague and capacious which we find in any natural language. Like "time," "home," "being," "seeing," "understanding," "knowledge," "perception," "good," "true," "beautiful," "order," "unity,"—and all the other "transcendentals"—it requires a systematic and detailed analysis, which we can do no more than sketch out in our present status of ignorance of the laws which relate thought to experience. Sartre once wrote that "we are condemned to freedom," but Merleau-Ponty replied, more fundamentally, that "we are condemned to meaning." The very root of human freedom, the root of that which makes us the "transcendental" species on this planet—in which we live in such uncomfortable and graceless relationships with our ecological environment and other creatures systematically—is that of all the creatures involved in our common fate, we alone experience the world as meaningful, humorous, beautiful, orderly, and so on. Though "meaning" extends far beyond the usages of language, it is within the study of our unique linguistic competence—our ability to understand, to operate *according to*, and to thematize the laws of formal thought—that we can pose the question of the meaningfulness of experience in any disciplined manner and thus produce its "theory." As a preliminary attempt, inspired by the phenomenology of Husserl and Merleau-Ponty in particular, our discussion of the

124

levels of meaning in linguistic experience will be based on distinguishing four levels of such meaning.

1. IMMANENT MEANING: LANGUAGE AS A PHONOLOGICAL SYSTEM

MERLEAU-PONTY HAS, more clearly than any other phenomenologist, and certainly better than Husserl, orchestrated the first level. His philosophy of language was, in this respect, inspired by Saussure and structural linguistics, and to some extent shares its defects.[1] The great achievement of structural linguistics (in the work of persons like Saussure, Jacobson, Trubetskoy, Hjelmslev, Martinet, and others) was to discover, just on the surface level of the taxonomic analysis of language, that a given linguistic system (*langue*) follows strict syntactic and paradigmatic regularities which can be formulated in terms of phonological and morphological rules distinctive of that language. These rules are more basic, more "automatic," and more "impersonal" than the syntactical rules which govern the use of language for the purposes of representing meanings, expressing attitudes, or addressing oneself to another. They are discovered simply by the analysis of empirically given languages taken just in their "objective" aspect of historically given data, as something to be described, as it is, without reference to any higher function or purpose it may have (such as, for instance, in the *intention to speak*).

To take language in this empirically neutral way as a "natural" object is to take it, in the words of Saussure, as *langue* and not as *parole* (not as the actual utilization of a given language by a speaker for the purposes of signifying, naming, expressing something, and so on). *La parole* is a speaker's *use* of a given language here and now for purposes of expression. But, in order to speak, the speaker must be in possession of a *langue,* and this language is an already instituted and available system of phonological, morphological, and syntactical rules which (logically) preexist any present and actual use of the language by an individual speaker.

If we isolate *language*, then, as a finite and closed system of phonetic elements (phonemes, sound segments) which follow certain highly restrictive phonological rules (according to sequence patterns, complex plays of oppositions, arrangements into forms or morphemes, and so on), we find that language exists, in the first instance, beneath the level of speech as a highly organized system independently of its use to signify anything other than itself. The phonemes which constitute the various restricted phonological systems permitted in any given natural language have no meaning in themselves. This is to say that they are not truly *signs*, and, *on this level,* the ancient Aristotelian definition of language in terms of the *sign-meaning* or *sign-thing signified* dichotomy has no application.

The phonemes which constitute a linguistic system refer to nothing extralinguistic; they signify only themselves and their relationship to all the other elements of the given language. Each phoneme takes its place in the phonological system as an element sufficiently distinct to be distinguished from all others in the same system and capable of being related to others according to a system of phonological rules which apply only within the system and refer to nothing outside the system itself. In other words, each phoneme takes its place in the phonetic system as the *diacritical element* necessary, according to rule, to distinguish each "form" and eventually, in combinations, each word from another.

The morphological rules according to which morphemes and words distinguish themselves from one another as arrangements of sound segments constitute the "structural system," which defines a given language and distinguishes it from any other. Each element in the system, and ultimately each word, must be defined in terms of its relation to all the other elements of the system, and this is why it is unnecessary to look for the meaning of words—on this level —in anything transcendent to the system itself. The linguistic convention which defines a given language institutes itself as a meaning insofar as meaning is understood "structurally," that is, as a system of phonological and morphological rules. This is also why a language cannot be learned "by parts" but must in some sense be learned "as a whole," that is, because the elements of a language have no sense (and make no sense) when separated from the distinctive rules of combination which hold throughout the language globally.

A language, as *langue,* is, then, a finite system of word-sounds arranged according to "diacritical" variations and regularities necessary and sufficient to distinguish each word from every other and permit it a place in the system. The only *meaning* of language, on this level of analysis, is contained within itself. As Saussure said repeatedly, language is *"un système où tout se tient."* Approached just as a morphological system based on phonological rules, language carries its meaning wholly within it; it has an *immanent* meaning distinctive of its own style, of its own intonation, of the peculiar play of distinctive oppositions which distinguish it from every other.

There is here no "deep structure" of language; we are on the phonological surface which distinguishes each natural language from every other as a highly selective and restrictive use of sounds (chosen arbitrarily from among the much vaster phonetic possibilities of our natural speech mechanisms as such, that is, all the sounds the human organism *can* produce), all of which refer to themselves and to one another through their value in use (*valeur d'emploi*) in a systematic manner. Thus, although sometimes very great in number, the words which constitute the lexicon of any natural language are a finite system of words formed according to the "closed" phonological rules of that particular language, all of which are definable in terms of other words taken from the same lexicon. Though the number of words capable of being formed in accord with the phonological style of a given language is indefinite, and may appear as an "infinity" with respect to the two or three score phonemes used for their production,[2] we know that the vocabulary of no natural language is actually infinite and that it is "closed" in a manner analogous to and determined by the phonological system. Both on the level of morphemes and on the level of words all the forms of a given language refer to and presuppose one another in fixed ways.

It is this aspect of language which enables us to understand the intralinguistic or "syncategorematic" functions of words.[3] Taken categorematically, a word is "paired with" and refers to something other than itself, that is, a meaning, a thing, a mood, a state of affairs, and so on. But there seem to be many words which do not refer to anything, as, for instance, the word "to" in the sentence *She stoops to conquer*,[4] or the interrogative particle *ne* in Latin,[5] or the syncategorematic words for conjunction, negation, disjunction, and so on. Some linguists say simply that such words have no meaning,[6] but it would be better to say that their meaning is "immanent" to the linguistic system itself. They *do* have meaning insofar as there are clear grammatical rules for their use, and their omission results, in a given language, in ungrammatical sentences. But it is not only that such words have an intralinguistic function, that is, that they take their meaning from the place they hold in the system as a whole, but that *all* words have something of this immanent function of deriving their meaning from the positions they are *able* to occupy according to the rules of the given language. Thus Merleau-Ponty can write: "Each word *has* meaning only insofar as it is sustained in this meaning-function by all the others. . . . For a word to keep its sense it has to be held in place by all the others. . . ."[7] We reach here the most important contribution of structural linguistics to the theory of meaning. Merleau-Ponty has, perhaps better than anyone else, brought this aspect of language to the fore in his studies on the learning of language and in his argument for the "immanent," "gestural," and "affective" meanings of words (which are, at the same time, as he sees it, arguments *against* the possibility of a universal and eidetic grammar for all languages).[8]

Both Saussure and Merleau-Ponty like to say that words are defined less in terms of their "meaning" (which would require taking them as signs) than by their "value" in usage (*valeur d'emploi*).[9] In his remarks on babbling in children, and on the "inner speech" of adults (which is but a continuation of childish babbling),[10] Merleau-Ponty is especially sensitive to what we might call the sound-sensuous meanings of words, the meanings which are not yet distinguished from the phonological patterns themselves but which are realized precisely in the verbal gesticulation of uttering sounds and noises in rhythmic and patterned forms. This is perhaps similar to what mystics like Boehme referred to as "the language of Adam"—the "sensual speech" (*die sen-*

sualische Sprache) of self-expression which takes place beneath the level of the concept and the idea.[11]

Now, the point here is that these natural signs, employed as phonemes according to strict phonological laws, do not *in themselves mean anything* other than themselves: it is their combinations, according to phonological rules, which enable the speaker to form *words* which *do* mean something, in that they refer beyond themselves to things, events, and contexts of real, nonverbal experience. But, Merleau-Ponty's essential point is that words, even when they finally achieve the ability to carry referential and, eventually, conceptual levels of meaning, never completely lose that primitive, strictly phonemic, level of "affective" meaning which is not translatable into their conceptual definitions. There is, he argues, an affective tonality, a mode of conveying meaning beneath the level of thought, beneath the level of the words themselves (which the phonological patterns permit to come into existence), which is contained in the words *just insofar as they are patterned sounds*, just as the sounds which this particular historical language uniquely uses, and which is much more like a melody—a "singing of the world"—than fully translatable, conceptual thought. This is a level of meaning which Merleau-Ponty, almost alone among philosophers of language, seems sensitive to. It is a level of affective communication which seems to belong to processes that, in themselves, are nonverbal, but that are a necessary part of the formation and production of words.[12]

There is a meaning immanent to language, writes Merleau-Ponty, of which conceptualism and intellectualism know nothing (or which they have forgotten): "The meaning of words must be finally induced by the words themselves, or more exactly, their conceptual meaning must be formed by a kind of subtraction from a *gestural meaning* which is immanent to the word. . . ."[13]

> And elsewhere: There is a languagely (*langagière*) meaning of language which effects the mediation between my as yet unspeaking intention and words, and in such a way that my spoken words surprise me myself and teach me my thought. Organized signs have their *immanent meaning*, which does not arise from the "I think" but from the "I am able to."[14]

The word, taken just as an element within the language of which it is an integral part, is a "sign" not of *something else* but of all the other "signs" which constitute the language as a whole, and, if they are then taken to allude to the world, it is as a global whole, all together, that they serve to make the whole present to our thought. On this level, but only on this level, the cultural relativism of a Benjamin Whorf makes sense and we can agree with Merleau-Ponty that no language is completely translatable into another because at least one thing, the meanings of the phonological system itself, must be left behind in any translation. This discovery of the importance of the "immanent," "affective," or "existential" meaning of words—a meaning which is not "rendered by" but which "inhabits" words[15]—is at once one of the greatest originalities in Merleau-Ponty's contributions to the phenomenology of language and the source of his misunderstanding and denigration of the more "logical" and "grammatical" discussions of language by Husserl, particularly insofar as these involved the project of discovering "grammatical universals" common to all languages. It led him into the kind of exaggeration we are accustomed to associate with Wittgenstein on another level: "The word is a *tool, defined by a certain use,* without our being capable of formulating this use in an exact conceptual formula."[16] Merleau-Ponty is, on the whole, more concerned with the process of learning a language and with what Chomsky calls "linguistic competence" in its dumb, prereflexive sense than with describing and distinguishing levels of meaning; he is more concerned with the "miraculous" emergence of words within a preverbal and even nonverbal process of oral gesticulation (governed by rules unconcerned with and insufficient to account for meaning in any categorial sense), that is to say, with the primary phonological systems of speech, than with the syntactic and semantic structures which endow words with "objective" and "ideal" meaning. He writes:

> . . . we can no longer consider the learning of language as an intellectual operation of reconstituting meaning. We are no longer in the presence of two entities (the expression and its sense) the second of which would be hidden behind the first. Language as the phenomenon of expression is consti-

tutive of consciousness. To learn to speak, in this perspective, is to coexist more and more with the surrounding world. To live within this milieu, for the child, is an incitement to appropriate language and thought as its own. . . .[17]

But precisely because the primary phonological systems according to which we speak necessarily reach their culmination in *words*, it is impossible to limit the discussion of what language *means* to the immanent and intralinguistic structures of phonology. With the emergence of words, meaning becomes dependent on syntactic (and semantic) rules and structures which are not accounted for by phonology and morphology. With the word, language becomes a semeiological system, which is to say that it is endowed with the function of standing for, indicating, or referring to something other than itself. What the higher systems of syntax and semantics bring into play is another "miraculous" human ability, the ability to take something for something else, to analogize (the elemental and all-pervasive function of higher intelligence which the associationists spoke of in terms of "association" and which Husserl called simply "pairing," *Paarung*). It is, we hope, unnecessary here to vindicate once again the distinction between "meaning" and "reference," which has so often, beginning with Saint Anselm's dialogue *De Veritate,* been discovered and then forgotten by philosophers. We accept the distinction in the Fregean (*Sinn, Bedeutung*) and Husserlian (*Bedeutung, Erfüllung*) sense.[18] To say that language is a semeiological system is to say, in the most general way possible (so as to avoid otiose controversies), that words are "paired" with meanings (or "carry" meanings) and may refer to things in the real world which would instantiate or verify such meanings. We find, then, a double transcendence of language as "sign" of something else, and we *ipso facto* distinguish the word-sound (or the written mark) from what it *means* as well as from what it denotes, "names," or refers to.

2. Transcendent Meaning: From the Semeiotic to the Semantic

WITH THE recognition that word-sounds carry (are "paired" with) meanings, we necessarily operate the passage from the conception of linguistics as a science of elements interrelated in a closed system to the conception of linguistics as a science of usage according to rules of syntax for the purpose of signifying something transcendent to the semeiological system itself. The primary, although incomplete, elements of syntax are *words* which must be arranged according to strict syntactical rules *in order to* make sense. Such rules are the necessary, although insufficient, rules of sense. All this is hardly new and hardly worth restating. But I would like to make here two remarks concerning *words* inspired by Paul Ricoeur's now fairly celebrated polemic with the structuralists, which is one of his recent contributions to the phenomenology of language.[19] He says that "the word" is both "much more and much less than the sentence." Both remarks are important for our purposes. The word is evidently "less" than the sentence (and this is *the* fact about "mere words" which has been recognized since the earliest philosophies of language), because it is destined to take its place in a sentence. The only complete unit of meaning is the sentence within which words are syntactically ordered. Even in cases where men seem to speak in words rather than in sentences, such as the first words uttered by the child,[20] or ejaculations (like "Splendid!" "Bravo!" "Fire!" and so on),[21] or other shorthand and elliptical forms, such words are *understood* as sentences. Words, as such, have no functions apart from their functions within sentences, and the incomplete grammar of the "parts of speech" (of the verb, the noun, the adjective, and so on) which we find in grammars has meaning only in function of the *only complete* syntactical unit—which is the complete sentence. Nevertheless, the word, the compound word, and the subordinate phrase have meaning, although always incomplete meaning, independently of sentences, which is to say that they are "signs" (of meanings, of things), and thus, as opposed to the elements which compose them, they carry meanings which point beyond themselves, meanings of which they are only arbitrary and conventional symbols, which appeal to the usage of language with the intention *to speak* (*la parole*). They are, as Ricoeur rightly says, at the "juncture of language and speech" (*au carrefour de la langue et de la parole*).[22]

It is just here that the word, although less than the sentence as a constitutive part of the sentence, is "more" than the sentence in its ability to fix meaning and to "outlive" the sentence. The only complete and unitary expression of meaning is achieved in the properly formed sentence (as a grammatical agreement of words); the sentence is thus normally the only full unit of thought and, as such, as we shall see, enjoys a certain independence from the words which compose it. But, at the same time, our sentences are highly transitory, passing, rapid happenings or events. They are what happen to words. We scarcely ever fix our sentences permanently in our minds or remember them. If we wish to remember them, we must deliberately "memorize" them. We learn vocabularies of words but not vocabularies of sentences (except for the most standard and stock phrases of a language). Words, on the contrary, represent sedimentations of more incomplete but more readily available meanings; they outlive the sentence, which quickly dies (and as Ricoeur says: "means to die"); they get defined in dictionaries and can be stored in our cultural space in a way sentences (with exceptions perhaps for some of the very greatest) are not.[23] The most illiterate peasant cannot speak without some explicit awareness of the words he is using, but he can and does speak without any thematic awareness of the rules of grammar according to which he is using his words in sentences. Words provide us with the sedimented lexicographical possibilities of our language and put the whole past history of our language at our present disposal. Ricoeur argues, in an interesting way, that the word is the primary instrument (though of itself it is incomplete for the expression of meaning) of the passage from the semeiotic level to the semantic level. For, just like the phonemic "sign" in a given linguistic system, the "word," as such, has no meaning; it is a "sign" differentiated by a conventional rule from all the others and, as "sign," that is all it is. It does not tell us, of itself, of what it is the "sign." So far as the linguistic system itself is concerned (as *langue*), its "meaning" is wholly outside it, arbitrary; it is but one more phonetically and morphologically distinct element in a closed system of mutually interrelated elements which holds its distinctive value in the system from the fact that there are clear (infrasemantic) rules which differentiate it from all the other "signs" or elements of the system. As an element in the semeiotic system, the word is only "virtually" meaningful; it must be animated by an intention which comes from outside the sound-system as such to take on meaning. But, at the same time, it is the word which can be "paired" with meaning, which can be thought and uttered and thus take on semantic value within the actual production of a meaningful sentence, because all sentences are composed of nothing but words. It is in this operation that its ambiguity is revealed: that which was a "mere sign" becomes the vehicle of "meaning." We owe new and great words, charged with new meanings which enrich the possibilities of our language and our thought, to the original and "new" uses of words by poets, philosophers, creative and inspired minds. The sense of the word "belief," for instance, will never again be the same for a literary man as it was before Hume made it a fundamental category of philosophical discourse; a great mind impresses itself on us through giving words distinctive and new senses. But, at the same time, these senses and these words remain without effect on the laws of syntax and grammar as such; the laws of syntax can swallow up and accommodate any words which have been and may be invented; these laws remain on a higher and different plane of abstraction and generative power. We can pose problems of "universals of grammar" and an "eidetic of language" on the level of syntax which we cannot pose on the level of the word.

And let us add further that it is our experience of words in their isolability which leads us to question the equivalences of experience between different linguistic cultures and the translatability of languages into one another. Words, just as such (whether as opposable elements of *la langue* collected in dictionaries or in acts of actual usage in *la parole*), are hardly ever exact equivalents of one another as we move from one natural language to another. On the other hand, the purely syncategorematic or syntactical elements in various languages, particularly when formalized into the rules of pure logical grammar, approach and even reach the perfect unity (and translatability) of mathematical and other purely formal systems. It is for this reason that syntax must be the basis for the translatability of languages and that it is only on the level of syntax that one will find the kind of universals of language which the existence of words—and their insistent phenomenal presence on the surface-level of experience—makes. For, with its words, different linguistic cultures divide and thematize the world in many different ways. As Erich Fromm writes, for instance:

> Whether or not subtle affective experiences can arrive at awareness depends on the degree to which a given language has no word, while another . . . may be rich in words which express these feelings. In English . . . we have one word, "love," which covers experience ranging from liking to erotic passion to brotherly and motherly love. In a language in which different affective experiences are not expressed by different words, it is almost impossible for one's experiences to come to awareness. . . . Generally speaking, it may be said that an experience rarely comes to awareness for which the language has no word. . . Every society excludes certain thoughts and feelings from being thought, felt, and expressed. There are things which are not only "not done" but which are not even thought. In a tribe of warriors . . . there might be an individual who feels revulsion against killing and robbing. Yet it is most unlikely that he will be aware of this feeling. . . .[24]

3. Syntax and Semantics

THE SENTENCE IS, then, what we do with the words we have learned; it is our attempt to grasp and express a meaning which has been left to us in the words of our language, and ultimately to use these words in new ways and give them new senses. The uttered sentence is the creative moment which never employs just the same words in just the same combinations and with just the same sense twice. Sartre, with his fine sensitivity to the nuances of verbal creativity, writes:

> It is within the sentence, in fact, that the word can receive a real function as a designation; outside the sentence the word is just a propositional function . . . entire sentences, commonplaces, do not, any more than words, pre-exist the use which is made of them. . . . To understand the word

in the light of the sentence is *very exactly* to understand any given whatsoever in terms of the situation and to understand the situation in the light of the original ends. . . . In order for words to enter into relations with one another, in order for them to latch on to one another or repulse one another, it is necessary that they be united in a synthesis which does not come from them. Suppress this synthetic unity and the block which is called speech disintegrates; each word returns to its solitude and at the same time loses its unity, being parcelled out among various incommunicable meanings.[25]

And Merleau-Ponty writes in the same vein:

I understand or think I understand the words and forms of French; I have a certain experience of the literary and philosophical modes of expression offered me by a given culture. I express myself when, utilizing all these already speaking instruments, I make them say something they have never said. We begin reading a philosopher by giving the words he makes use of their "common" meaning; and little by little, through what is at first an imperceptible reversal, his speech comes to dominate his language, and it is his use of words which ends up assigning them a new and characteristic signification. . . . I say *I know an idea* when the power to organize discourses which make coherent sense around it has been established in me; and this power itself does not depend upon my alleged face-to-face contemplation of it, but upon my having acquired a certain style of thinking, I say that a signification is acquired and henceforth available when I have succeeded in making it dwell in a speech apparatus which was not originally destined for it. Of course the elements of this expressive apparatus did not really contain it—the French language did not from the moment it was established, contain French literature. . . .[26]

We may oversimplify somewhat, but I believe we will not falsify the central insight contained in these passages if we locate the central phenomenon of language *as speech* (that is, in its *actuality* as opposed to its *virtuality* as a *system*) by saying that language is *a speaking to someone about something.* This tripartite Husserlian schema, although in need of interpretation as a formal invariant of language, has taken on a new importance in the debates between structuralists and phenomenologists at the present time. Language cannot be exhaustively accounted for as a closed structural system of rules, precisely because it involves the intention and the need to apply such rules in a movement which points beyond them (1) toward the ideality of meaning, of what we use language to say, of "the meant," and (2) toward the things in the world about which we are speaking, toward those realities to which our meanings apply and which verify them. Moreover, language is the means by which we address ourselves to others and express our moods, feelings, desires, commands, prayers, whims, and so on (in what Husserl called "non-objectivating" or "non-presentational" acts). Thus language, which can be considered as a closed system of signs or symbols governed by fixed rules on the semeiotic level, on the semantic level necessarily refers to something other than itself (and thus, in a peculiar way, participates in the self-transcendence and reflexivity of consciousness itself). This is true of language not as an inert, cultural institution (*langue*) but as the act of speaking (*la parole*), the "speech-act." The level of semantics, or meaning in the proper sense of the term, is reached at the moment when what was a virtual possibility of expression, when a choice among all the possibilities of the system has been made and others thereby excluded, when a new and actual combination of words takes place a sentence.[27] Language in this sense is the means used by the subject to come to himself and to direct himself toward something beyond himself. Moved to the semantic level, the semeiotic system becomes a subject who speaks to another. This is the level of the institution of meaning as such, of creation and actualization, when hitherto unused possibilities of discourse are uttered and understood. The originality and importance of Noam Chomsky's "transformational generative grammar" are rooted in this discovery: that the only role of the "system" is to serve creative speech, that *langue* is subservient to *parole* and is absorbed in it, that what must be explained by a linguistic theory is the possibility of forming new sentences within the fixed rules of syntax. This creativity alone will give us *sufficient* explanation of "linguistic *competence*."

> The central fact to which any significant linguistic theory must address itself is this: a mature speaker can produce a new sentence of his language on the appropriate occasion,

and other speakers can understand it immediately, though it is equally new to them. Most of our linguistic experience, both as speakers and as hearers, is with new sentences; . . . the class of sentences with which we can operate fluently and without difficulty or hesitation is so vast that . . . we may regard it as infinite. Normal mastery of a language involves not only the ability to understand immediately an indefinite number of entirely new sentences, but also the ability to identify deviant sentences and, on occasion, to impose an interpretation on them. . . . It is clear that any theory of language that neglects this "creative" aspect is of only marginal interest.[28]

The originality of "generative grammar" is that it goes beneath the surface-level phonological analyses of the structural-linguistic conception of language to an examination of the more abstract rules of syntax, which alone allow us to pose the question of "meaning" in a full and complete sense—on the level of the sentence.[29] By posing the question of "universals of grammar," Chomsky gives a new sense, although he nowhere takes cognizance of this, to Husserl's phenomenological project of a pure logical grammar. Whether he can ultimately do more than this is not certain, because in its very program "transformational generative grammar" encounters a *paradox* of language which cannot be solved on the level of syntax; that is, language is able to incarnate the living meaning-intentions of original speakers in their creative production of ever-new sentences according to syntactic rules which themselves remain invariant and "universal" (deep-structures) beneath the surface of ordinary speech.

We may well sympathize with Chomsky and others who find it impossible, at least in the present state of human nature, to distinguish the borderlines which separate the syntactic from the semantic rules which govern the constitution of meaning.[30] One way to settle the question, at least for purposes of discussion, would be to follow the distinction which Husserl elaborated in *Formal and Transcendental Logic,* namely, that the laws of syntax which formulate the *formal* aprioris which govern the possibility of the formation of sentences are not sufficient to enable us to produce meaningful sentences. The *formal* apriori laws of "pure logical grammar" provide us with *necessary* and universal, but not *sufficient,* conditions for the sense and meaning of sentences; these laws of pure grammar (*reine Formenlehre der Bedeutungen*) must be supplemented by more particular rules specific to the various "material regions" of meanings, which enunciate *material* aprioris governing the contextual relevance of the words within a sentence to one another. As is well known, Husserl discussed this problem with reference to his distinction between nonsensical propositions and countersensical propositions (*Unsinn—Wiedersinn*). For instance, if the formal laws of grammar are not observed (according to which, for instance, only predicates can be predicated of a substantive), we get such strings of words as: "Brown squirrel is and," "If however wants tomorrow," "King but where seems anyway," and so on. Such "heaps" of words are meaningless because they violate purely formal laws of syntax. But the strict observance of the formal rules of syntax is not, just of itself, sufficient to guarantee that the sentences formed in accord with them will be meaningful. Pure grammar does not rule out such formulations as: "All squares have five corners," "This algebraic number is blue," "Blue plus one equals three," "Portugal is not diatonic," and so on. Such formulations violate no law of formal logic or grammar; the substantives are substantives and the predicates are predicates, but these expressions are nevertheless countersensical because they violate laws of material or "regional" relevance which require that the words which are put together in sentences must, at the very least, be intrinsically related as belonging to the same region of discourse. A sentence like "Portugal is not diatonic" is devoid of meaning because one cannot legitimately affirm or deny of a country a musical status of this sort.[31] The laws which would enunciate the *sufficient* conditions for a sentence to have meaning must, therefore, be more than merely "formal"; they must take into account the material meaning-content of the words used, and this can only be done by distinguishing "contexts" or "regions" of meaning, each with its own specific "synthetic" aprioris. This alone, to be sure, does not tell us very much. It tells us only that there are semantic laws of "context" which cannot be reduced to the purely formal structures of syntax.

But, nevertheless, such a distinction does at least enable us to isolate "the syntactical" (*das Grammatische selbst*) from all other meaning-conditions and thus to situate the project of a "pure logical grammar." Insofar as the transformational grammar, which is being elaborated by Chomsky and his school, is concerned with "universals of grammar," even if it should succeed in its task, it will not be able to provide us with the sufficient conditions of meaningfulness. Precisely because grammar is concerned with "the universal" structures according to which sentences are formed, it cannot govern the particular contexts within which words are used in living and new ways in the act of speaking.[32] In order to do *this*, semantic (as opposed to merely syntactical) considerations must be brought into play.[33]

One could, without injustice, interpret the whole progression of Husserl's philosophy of language, from the *Logische Untersuchungen* to *Erfahrung und Urteil*, as an attempt to articulate this distinction. The fundamental correlation in his thought is that between "categories of meaning" (or signification) and "categories of objects," between judgments about experience and their foundations in experience. In his studies on pure logical grammar he posed the question of the necessary conditions of the possibility of propositions and elaborated the formal apriori conditions of judgment; in his studies on transcendental (that is, phenomenological) logic he attempted to provide examples of the material or "synthetic" apriori conditions of meaningfulness (within the various regional ontologies) which, through experience, specify the purely formal study of "objectivity in general."

4. THE HIGHER UNIT OF "TEXTS"

BEFORE PROCEEDING, let us briefly summarize a few widely accepted Husserlian theses about linguistic meaning. (1) The *meaning* of a sentence must be distinguished from the words which compose it taken in isolation. The same meaning can be expressed in any number of different verbal forms, in the same or other natural languages, and the translatability of languages into one another (through transformational rules of various kinds) shows that sentences enjoy a specific distinctness, as units of meaning, from the words that compose them. In translating from one language to another we do not isomorphically render each element of one language into another. (2) This *meaning* must, furthermore, be distinguished from my own psychological acts which accompany its expression; my sentences may *convey* my inner psychological states to another but they do not *mean* them, since the same meaning can be expressed at other times, when I am contented and pleased with myself and not only when I am gloomy and depressed as at the present moment, and so on. Meaning is essentially free of all the indexical, egocentric, or, as Husserl would say, "occasional" circumstances which escort and accompany it. (3) Furthermore, this meaning of my sentences may produce external effects on my milieu and on other persons, but the *meaning* of a sentence is not exhausted in the effects it may cause; the same meaning may at one time be causally very potent and at another without any effect ("overt response") at all (if, for instance, I am addressing an idiot). Ideas "whose time has not come" are without effect. (4) We are, furthermore, assuming that it is unnecessary to repeat in this context that meanings are not simply things referred to or the act of reference, and that they are not mental images or clear and distinct ideas open to introspective inspection "within" the mind. (5) Finally, we know that, although the expression of meaning requires a phonological system and a syntactical system as its necessary condition (and that there *are* purely phonological and syntactical levels of meaning), these are not sufficient to account for meaning, for, otherwise, we would not be able to explain how the normal speaker is able to understand perfectly well the *meaning* of ungrammatical sentences garbled on the tongues of illiterates or foreigners who have not yet learned all our linguistic conventions. There seems to be no meaning-ambiguity in such sentences as "We was robbed," "He don't live here no more," "Boss-man likeum Turkey-shoot," "There ain't no hoss that can't be rode," "Thank you for let me be myself" (and other such common examples of popular, everyday speech) on the semantic level even though such expressions clearly violate syntactical and morphological rules.

Thus the relationship of grammaticality to semantics raises many interesting questions. One of them is the relationship of sentences to their linguistic contexts, and, secondly, the displacement introduced into reflection on language by the institution of writing. We do not really speak or think grammatically; any taped example of unedited speech will show many false starts, half sentences, changes of tense and verb sequence which are ungrammatical. It is only the edited, printed text which is fully "grammatical" and from which we can learn the rules of language. Thus writing introduces an "idealization" of a second power into the investigation of "speech-acts."[34] And it is this fact above all which has led contemporary structuralists to the conclusion that there is a higher organizing semantic principle in the production of meaningful discourse than the rules which govern the production of sentences.

One of the most philosophical of recent linguistic structuralists, Émile Benveniste, argues that the recognition of the *meaning* of the various constituent parts of linguistic strings is essential to distinguishing them. He argues that the ultimate reason certain phonemic sequences are permitted and others are not permitted in a given language is that they *can be* incorporated into just those morphemes (bound forms) or words (free forms) which *can make sense* in a given phonological system. *Meaning* is thus recognized (heretically for a "linguist") as the fundamental condition which any linguistic unit must have if it is to have linguistic status. Rather than imagine complicated, and inoperative, procedures for leaving "sense" out of phonological and morphological analysis in order to give just the "formal traits" of the elements which constitute a linguistic string, Benveniste holds that we should admit that "meaning" or "sense" is an indispensable condition of all linguistic analysis. We must only distinguish the ways in which it operates on various levels. The only linguistic "value" of infraphonemic traits is to discriminate phonemes. But it would be ultimately impossible to define the distribution of any given phoneme, its possible syntagmatic and paradigmatic combinations, unless it were itself referred to some particular unity of a higher level which contains it and in which it is integrated as a constitutive element. Thus, the phoneme can only be defined as a *constituent* of a higher level, the morpheme or word, and this is the only proper basis for distinguishing phonemes in any given language. In short, a given linguistic unit can be accepted in a given language only if it can be identified in a higher unity: strings of phonemes *can* become morphemes; morphemes *can* become words; a word *can* become a sentence. But it is because the higher *linguistic sign* always already has a meaning or makes sense prior to this analysis that the analysis itself is possible. All the so-called purely "formal" procedures which set out to analyze the structures of language without any resource to "sense" or "meaning" are in reality only complicated exercises of the imagination, legitimate no doubt for purposes of formalization, but which add nothing to the rigor of our analysis of language. The fundamental linguistic fact is that the words of a given language have a meaning and that their combinations make sense.[35]

Yet, Benveniste stops with sentences, which he considers to be the highest distinct unit of discourse. He believes that all sentences have basically the same form, namely that of the predicative proposition (all other forms being modalizations of this basic form), and that sentences (unlike phonemes, morphemes, and words) are not "oppositive" to one another—that there are classes of words but no classes of sentences. Thus the linguistic study of the rules of meaningfulness, whether syntactic or semantic, must terminate in the analysis of sentences.

It is this which the contemporary structuralist hermeneutics of Derrida, Ricoeur, Gadamer, and others feels it must contest. We do not think merely in words, but in sentences; but, by the same token, we do not think simply in sentences either, but in paragraphs, in whole stories, in myths —in what can be written down (or memorized) as "texts." There has to be an organizing principle of meaningfulness in language higher than the sentence simply because, to be meaningful, sentences cannot follow one another in random order. Not just any sentence can follow any other. Rules of contextuality, broader even than simple logical laws of noncontradiction, compatibility, and implication, come into play.[36]

At any given moment, our language—as an objective

linguistic system, as *langue*—is, for us, much more virtual than actual; in expressing ourselves we seldom advert to our language as such. As we speak, our language is almost never at the primary focal point of consciousness; rather, it is those things (events, thoughts, arguments) which we use language to think or speak about which are at the center of our attention. We attend primarily to what we mean to say, to what we are trying to say, to what we are talking about, sometimes to the person to whom we are speaking, or to the purposes for which we are speaking—these are what guide our speech. When the child begins to respond linguistically to its mother, it does not concentrate its attention on her lips, from which the sounds to be imitated emerge, but fixes her gaze with its eyes. Neither the orator nor the ordinary speaker has much reflexive awareness of the words and syntax he is using; like acts of consciousness, acts of speaking require a second, deliberate act of reflection to objectify them as such. This is why it happens that when we have engaged in a train of thought or attempted to present an argument, we seldom remember, a few minutes later, just which words we used to do so, though we could express the same argument again, in other words, any number of times. "Thus it often happens that we find ourselves knowing something which we have learnt by means of words without being able to remember a single one of the words which conveyed it to us."[37] This shows the evanescent, fleeting character of our sentences, which are nevertheless always composed of words with more or less solidly fixed dictionary definitions. We can always repeat an argument, but if we had to use again just the same concatenation of words, just the same sentence structures, just the same verbal images, just the same turns of phrase, we would normally be at a loss. Moreover, we frequently have the experience of knowing more or less clearly what we *want* to say without being able to find just the words necessary to express what we mean. We experience an impatience with ourselves and with our interlocutors; we experience ourselves being misunderstood. The exclamation: "That is not what I mean!" is followed by further words to make our meaning more clear. We try various linguistic alternatives; if we are brought to a stop, our interlocutor may suggest words or phrases (which we reject or accept as more or less satisfactory, more or less equivalent, or the best available, vehicles of what we mean to convey). Thus the relation of our psychological intentions, of what we *mean* to say, to the words we are able to use at any given moment becomes problematic. There is no one-to-one isomorphic correspondence between words and thoughts; there is clearly a certain independence of the one with respect to the other which must be accounted for.

On the one hand, we cannot think without words; words are the embodiment and concrete actual realization of thought. Yet on the other hand, what we mean to say by means of words somehow transcends any particular verbal formulation of it. The irreducibility of thought and intention to words is at least part of the phenomenon of language which led earlier "intellectualistic" philosophers to locate meanings (as concepts) outside of language altogether as transcendent ideas, existing prior to and logically independent of any actual speaking. Merleau-Ponty attempts to account for the illusion that "thought" appears to enjoy priority and independence with respect to language by distinguishing the already objectified ("sedimented") meanings and forms of expression available to us in our maternal tongue prior to any actual use of these possibilities for expression from the actual utilization of these means of expression in speech (*parole*). That our language is an historical and cultural instrument that was forged prior to our own use of it, that the world of thought was already instituted and structured when we came on the scene, and that this language is the *medium* through which we communicate with the thoughts of others, gives us the illusion of there being somewhere a realm of "fixed" meanings that preexist present and actual thought about them. This is the theory of language as the "instrument" of thought, and since language is clearly "instrumental," there is a truth of intellectualism. But it is not the whole truth; language is more than an instrument.

> Available meanings, in other words former acts of expression, establish between speaking subjects a common world, to which new words actually being uttered refer, as gestures refer to the sensible world.[38]

Sartre and Merleau-Ponty join forces in bringing forth arguments against the possibility of thoughts existing independently of any actual use of language, though none of these arguments fully demonstrates that thought is not *logically prior* to its verbal expression. To say that thoughts are experientially *inseparable* from words, that the use of words is an absolutely *necessary condition* for thought, that we must express what we mean in words, even to ourselves, in order to know what we mean, even to deny that there is anything such as a thought or experience which is verbally ineffable,[39] is not *sufficient* to demonstrate, by strict implication, that the intention to speak and the conceptual purposes concretized and actualized in language do not enjoy a *logical* (and *ontological*) priority over their expression.[40]

Moreover, it is essential to the grammatical forms of any language to permit the new and spontaneous expression of meanings which have never been uttered before. Linguistic experience and grammar can be coextensive, perhaps, but *not identical*, precisely because there can be no rules for applying the rules of grammar. Merleau-Ponty calls this the "paradox" or "contradiction" of language:[41] it must proceed according to fixed rules, or understanding would be impossible; yet the rules themselves must permit the expression of what is as yet unexpressed, what has never before been said. In other words, we necessarily speak according to certain rules or we would not be understood, and in some sense we *know how* to apply correctly and effortlessly ("without thought") all the complex phonetic, morphological, syntactic rules which govern our native language. If we know how to speak, we know how to apply these rules at will, because that is what knowing how to speak means. But to apply a rule correctly is not itself a behavior which can be explained in terms of further, higher-order rules *ad infinitum*. This infinite regress must stop somewhere and it stops in the act of speaking. He who knows how to speak is one who is skilled in applying grammatical rules; he is not one who knows more rules for applying these, because there can be no rules for something which has not been done before, and to speak is to say what has not been said before. It is of the essence of grammatical rules that they be "generative" (in Chomsky's language), that is, that they permit us to express what has never before been uttered. It is here that we come, then, to the threshold of the *crucial phenomenon* of language.

Maine de Biran in the eighteenth century wrote a celebrated paper, *Sur la décomposition de la pensée,* which Condillac took up with great enthusiasm—comparable to the enthusiasms of contemporary linguists in attempting to discover the minimal number of elements of which thoughts are composed and to elaborate the laws of their various combinations. In his work on grammar Condillac came to believe that language is not *only,* or even principally, a question of *communication,* but that it is primarily an instrument for the analysis of thought, of the articulation of meaning. If, for example, I fix my eyes on an edible object, such as an orange, and make a sign that I would like to eat it, a gesture is sufficient to express my intention; if, on the contrary, I wish to articulate and express this intention in language, an indefinite number of sentences will be required to make my meaning clear. The original "thought" which was prior to speech, "simple," and all given at once, without any temporal and linear juxtaposition of discrete elements, requires, in language, a long discourse. Its "parts" must be laid out in succession, and this takes time. In short, there is no reason to suppose that the laws which govern the *linguistic* articulation of a thought are to be isomorphically read back into the primary thought which they analyze and express.

If we turn our attention away from *the text* to the "intention to speak" (which most preoccupied a James or a Sartre), we will be impressed by the fact that the rules of linguistic usage are a necessary condition of the expression of thought, but that they are, in any given instance, inadequate to the thought which any given speaker is trying to express. The meaning of a word may well be its grammatical use, but the rules of grammatical usage are hardly ever perfectly respected, nor is their strict observance necessary for the expression of meaning. It is because "usage is free" that the very idea of a *complete* dictionary or a *complete* grammar of any natural language is a countersense, and also why a purely synchronic description can never replace the diachronic study of language. A given word may indicate or suggest its *concept,* but words and concepts cannot be strictly correlated and to explain or define what any given word *means* (i.e., its concept) requires an indefinite number of other words, all equally imperfectly adapted to their own senses.

Anyone who has ever had the temptation to stand before an audience to make a speech or to sit down before a typewriter to write a book recognizes within himself the presence of something which has to be said, which he knows he wants to say, and which he effectively begins to say when he begins to speak or write. If not *thought* itself, *the intention to speak* is both causally and temporally prior to the words which one uses to articulate a given thought. All parents know, and no linguist would deny, that children can think before they can speak. This unexpressed thought is experienced as something given all-at-once, something which must be articulated in fragments, temporally laid out bit by bit. Without language, thought would remain indistinct and incomprehensible even to the thinker himself; but no speaker or author has ever been satisfied that the *language* in which he has expressed what he had to say was perfectly adequate to his intention, though he would always be able to reject foreign suggestions and interpretations as *not* what he intended, as contrary to his meaning. An author or speaker can always give the *same* argument in different words; in fact, nobody ever expresses what he means to be the same development of his thought in just the same words as those he used on an earlier occasion. Yet, if you ask an author to summarize or revise what he has said, he will find it impossible to be completely faithful to what he meant to say.

Ultimately, what one means to say will always remain incomplete and unsatisfactory when articulated in language. The more important his message the more an author has the feeling of having inadequately expressed it. There is always something *more* and something *different* to say in our attempts to say the *same* thing. That is why it is dangerous to let an author correct his own proofs; he always wants to rewrite the book. The finished product is always a compromise between what he really meant to say, what he thought he was saying, and what he actually expresses. If one wants a concrete example, there is none better than that of Ludwig Wittgenstein before his philosophy classes (on Norman Malcolm's account): here was a professor who was always discontented with what he said, who often stopped himself in midsentence, referring to his just enunciated words as stupid, idiotic, impossible, and who was often so exhausted by the experience of not having been able to say what he meant to say to his own satisfaction that, at the end of the hour, he would race out to a cinema in an attempt to forget the whole debacle.[42]

But if, on the other hand, we turn our attention away from the intention of the "author" (as such structuralists as Derrida and Lévi-Strauss would prefer) to the *text* itself, we will find that the text, as text, once it has been written down and "published," *has no author.* Structuralists prefer such "texts" as myths because they manifestly have no one author and arise from the common, subconscious experience of a cultural group; but if you give a text of Shakespeare or of Jean Genet to Freud, you will get an interpretation in terms of oedipal guilt; if you give the same text to Lucien Goldmann, you will get a Marxist-economic interpretation; if you give the same text to Lévi-Strauss, you will get an interpretation in terms of kinship structures, and so on. And, obviously, all these interpretations are legitimate, and both Shakespeare and Genet wrote more than they *knew* they were writing. There is *a meaning in the text* which not only transcends the rules and elements of linguistic usage, which were always contingent and could have been replaced by others equally capable of conveying their message, but also transcends the psychological and deliberate intentions of the authors themselves. This is the ultimate truth of structuralism and the basis of the strength of its challenge to the contemporary philosophy of language; we must discover those principles of organization of linguistic meaning which transcend sentences and govern the creation of literary units of a higher order, not in the intentions of the author or narrator but in the formal structure of the text itself. The danger of this structuralist approach is that it will eliminate both the author (the subject who thinks and intends) and the referent (the world about which he is speaking); but the necessity of taking texts, that is, strings of coherent, mutually implicating series and paragraphs of sentences, *just as such*—just as linguistic units of a specific level and kind—is demanded by our present lack of knowledge of their formal structure(s).

Thus, in a sense, we have seen the search for the "transcendental" foundation of meaning in the last generation graduated into three different levels. With the Husserl of the *Cartesian Meditations* in particular, but in Husserl generally, the transcendental foundation is to be found by a meaning analysis of the egological center of experience, the sole, individual, constituting consciousness. Husserl speaks most of the time as if transcendental consciousness were perfectly silent, above and beyond any particular language, the absolutely sovereign "observer" and "constitutor" of all objects.

With Merleau-Ponty and the existentialist interpretation of phenomenology it is the plural we-consciousness which is foundational ("transcendental subjectivity is intersubjectivity") and the problem is not to understand how the individual transcendental ego constitutes the world of objects but rather how—given a world of objects in which it is immersed from the beginning—the ego can find itself and distinguish itself from the collective, social life of the intersubjective, historical, cultural constitution of meaning. But, in Merleau-Ponty, language was never more than one —though perhaps the central one—of the instruments available for the analysis of the constitution of meaning.

Now, a third step has been taken. In investigating meaning in its specificity, the structuralists have claimed to discover a transcendental foundation for meaning which is independent of any particular consciousness as such, but also independent of society and history as well. It will consist of just those objective semantic conditions which render meaningful any string of words, any string of sentences, any text, intelligible just as such, and in themselves. Linguistics is, in this view, not a part of the social sciences, but its foundation; it will provide us with the new methodology which will finally make the social and human sciences *scientific.*

V   Metaphorical Expressions

THE PROBLEM OF the metaphorical ("polysemic" or "plurisignative") aspect of language is perhaps the most perplexing, vexed, and intractable question in the whole of the philosophy of language. It brings us to the pivotal center of the distinction between language as a "system" and language as "speech-act," language as "illocutionary" and "perlocutionary," as "logic" and "rhetoric." Here we are getting into deep water; everything up to now—even in the quarrels we have had with our adversaries—has been comparatively easy. Once we enter the realm of "metaphor" we no longer have any true "adversaries" for the simple reason that there are no theories of metaphor sufficiently developed to be opposed to one another for more than a few minutes of reflection at a time. *Here*, finally, all philosophers of language become bewildered friends seeking a common shelter simply because no one dares to say outright "I'm right and you are wrong." We are clearly closer to the basic reality of language—something so complex, so rich, so variegated, so subtle, so capable of infinite variations and resources for expression that no single mind, no single school, can hope to teach us definitive lessons. Nor do I hope to teach anyone definitive lessons; my purpose in this chapter is only to locate the essential point of divergence which separates the contemporary combatants into two camps.

The most general locutions currently used to designate a complete unit of meaning are "expression" and "utterance." We prefer the Husserlian term "expression" because

151

it is the more general one and thus is not restricted to either written or spoken meanings and, indeed, is broader than speech itself—since an *expression* of meaning need not (but always can) be linguistically formed.

1. THE PHENOMENON OF EXPRESSION

FROM THE point of view of phenomenological analysis, language appears as one aspect of a total, contextual, human activity of "expressing" which cannot be studied in isolation from man's existential insertion in his life-world. If man *as a unitary whole* is intentional of the world, it is impossible to isolate the study of language from the study of man as a world-intending organism, a dynamic experiencer who structures his experience by *expressing* its *meaning*. According to phenomenology, the relation of man to the world is not static and juxtapositional but dynamic and dialectical. An intentional consciousness is a consciousness strictly correlative to its life-world and can be defined and analyzed only in terms of this "ecological" correlativity.

Secondly, according to the phenomenological view defended here, any theory which would analyze human reality into "pure" disembodied consciousness on the one hand and a body as its corporeal "instrument" on the other is excluded. Any division of subject and object which would make a lived-corporeality just another "object" of consciousness is likewise excluded. Human reality as a unitary whole is intentional of the world.[1]

Another way of saying the same thing is to say that man is essentially *expressive*. Man is expressive even before he speaks: in his corporeal attitudes, in behavior, in gestures, in rhythmic movements and tonal utterances, in the creation of artifacts, works of art, and social institutions of all kinds. Man is expressive by his very existence; as Merleau-Ponty observes, for instance, a man's face is condemned to express *something* even in sleep, even in death. Speech is but one form, doubtless a late and derived form, of expression, and persons who have lost the ability to speak have not for all that lost the ability to express themselves. The schizophrenic all rolled up in a ball with his face in his hands and unable to utter a sound is still "speaking" in the only way he can. In fact, he shouts. Or to take another example, most friendships are inarticulate. Authentic kindness and sympathy for another are seldom "spoken about"; they are simply *done* and *accepted* on a level of subunderstood, implicit, mutual comprehension, which is the more *expressive* the less is "said" about it. No man can rely on language alone to say what he *means*.

Expression is thus a more basic and a much wider category of lived experience than linguistic communication. Expression precedes and pervades all efforts at communication with others, and communication itself greatly exceeds the area of linguistically expressed meanings, feelings, desires, purposes, judgments, and so on. The man who attempts to say all that he knows or all that he feels is condemned to failure. Logicians like to tell us that there are meanings ("propositions") which are the same for all men and which can be communicated by various empirical linguistic expressions, uttered in various places and at different moments of history. This is partially true and it is evident from what we have argued above that we would be the last to question this aspect of language.

In the extremely simplified and abstract language of mathematics and formal logic it is possible to express such meanings and to communicate them in an almost completely adequate manner. However, when one says *communication* one enters the world of the intersubjective constitution of meaning and it is necessary to suppose that even in the communication of mathematical concepts or logical "truths" there lies beneath the threshold of what is, strictly speaking, communicated differences of meaning both for the "communicator" and for the "receiver" that are remarkable. In the highly formalized and abstract forms of communication with which formal logicians are content, such differences of meaning are "negligible," but in other forms of communication they become less and less negligible as we proceed from the derived and abstract schemata of mathematics to the lived experience which is their source. Men speak and think and act before they can reflexively analyze and systematize *what* they have said and thought and done. Our insertion in the world of lived experience precedes any thought about experience. It is possible to ascend to fully communicable meanings which will be *the same for all* only by leaving behind, by abstracting from, every element of concrete, particular individuality that makes a given "expression" expressive.[2]

2. THE APPRESENTATIONAL STRUCTURE OF LANGUAGE

IT IS BECAUSE man is involved in the world and interested in the world in the company of other men that he speaks. Uttered sounds become instruments for conveying meaning. The essentially *referential* character of gestures, words, signs, and symbols is frequently indicated by saying that words and signs are *arbitrary conventions*. But we must reject the "rationalism" inherent in this statement. Men did not (and do not) sit down and reflexively excogitate meanings and then agree on conventions for expressing them—any more than they founded civilized society on an explicit "social contract" as rationalistic social theory prescribed. Thought and meaning are fully incarnate in language; the thematization of meaning does not precede language, but rather, language makes such thematization possible. "For the speaking subject, expression is a *coming to awareness;* man does not express himself only to others; he expresses himself in order to discover what he means himself."[3] The rationalistic separation of thought from expression is based on the presupposition that thought can exist *of itself* before its bodily, fleshly expression in gestures, signs, and language. But if gestural and verbal expression is a "localization" and a "temporalization"—an *incarnation* —of meaning, the possibility of its corporeal expression in words is an essential condition of the constitution of meaning.

According to Husserl all forms of symbolic expression (in the widest sense) are marked by their *appresentational structure.* Here we are concerned only with language, though it must be borne in mind that much of what is said concerning language also applies to other forms of experience and expression.

Husserl developed his theory of "appresentation" primarily for two purposes: (1) for the purposes of his phenomenology of perception and, within this phenomenology,

(2) to explain our perception of other persons. In a given intuitional or perceptual experience much more is "apperceived" than the particular angle or perspective of the given perceptual object which is directly in front of us in this present perceptual experience. All of our experience presupposes at each instant its temporal, flowing character, it presupposes the fact that we have perceived before and will perceive again, that we fatally know more both by retention and by protension about any given object of experience than this immediate, present experience gives us. If we are "presented" with a physical object, the fact that it has other sides congruent with the perspective before us, the fact that it fits into a texture of the other sense-modalities under which it could also be perceived, the fact that it can be experienced by others and by ourselves again in innumerable open and unfinished future experiences, the fact that this object organizes itself in our experience according to its perceptual "type"—all these aspects of the object are "appresented" as being "given-with," as being "co-present" with the primarily and immediately intuited object. The first law of the analysis of perception is always to distinguish what is strictly "given" in experience from what is "given with" this experience. When we turn to the experience of other persons, which Husserl dealt with primarily in the *Fifth Cartesian Meditation*, we see that what is primarily given is the "living" material body of the other; his internal psychological life, on the other hand, his existence as another center of the experienced world, as a personal stream of ego experiences, is and can be only "appresented" in what Husserl calls an "associative, analogical apperception." To say that an object, or aspects of an object, is "appresented," rather than directly intuited in the present instance of experience, is not to deny that it is also properly "given" but rather to distinguish the mode of its givenness.

These few remarks will suffice to recall Husserl's important doctrine of appresentation and to allude to some of its numerous ramifications. Here, I am using Husserl's theory of appresentation in an extended sense, which is, however, fully justified by his very earliest treatment of this subject in the *Logical Investigations*.[4]

The appresentational structure of language involves

what in nonphenomenological philosophy are usually discussed as dimensions of *reference*. It will be convenient to discuss appresentation in these terms here, though it must be mentioned that the phenomenological notion of *appresentation* is both richer than the simple notion of *reference* and more involved than this abbreviated account would suggest at first glance. There is no other theory of the referentiality of linguistic expressions known to me which is as systematic and highly articulated as Husserl's.

In a general way we can distinguish four levels of appresentational reference in language, all of which are involved in viewing words as the *bearers* of meaning:

(1) First of all, as referring to the meaning-structure they primarily designate, words have two primitive and interrelated functions: (a) to designate or to point to experienced things, happenings, events, processes ("objects" in the widest sense), and (b) to signify or carry meanings. In their designating or pointing function, words enable the speaker to enlarge his life-space and life-time indefinitely. By means of words man can extend his perceptual field, he can manipulate (verbally) things not actually *given* in perception (though they may have been given previously and may be given again in the future). By means of words man can "live" in the past or the future; in short, by means of words man can manipulate "the absent." It is by the use of language that man *takes his distance* from the world of lived existence, distinguishes elements in the chaotic flux of experience, and thus experiences himself as transcending the objects of his experience. Words have a gestural function and some words can be simply replaced by facial or deictic gestures; but over and above this function and concomitantly with it, words enable us to organize experience and to communicate our version of it to others.

(2) Secondly, language is intrinsically referential in that it bears an intrinsic reference to its source, the intentional act of consciousness which is its correlate, man as expressive. Words are "historical" not only in the sense that each word has its own history, its own diachronic development in the linguistic evolution of a given culture. There was a time for each expression when it simply *was not*. Heidegger has said that it is the function of the thinker and the poet to "name"

new things, new aspects of experience, and thus to bring what was "unknown" and as yet hidden or lost in the chaotic flux of experience out into the open, into the realm of the "known"—into the public domain. Experiences which were *there* before they were "named" were as yet outside the realm of the "known" because they were not yet distinguished, they could not be used, they had no distinctive consistency, they had not yet become cultural objects about which men could think and discourse.

Just which regions of experience will be differentiated and disclosed by the linguistic process of naming them depends on many human and cultural factors, among which that of common "interest" and "attention" is perhaps the most central. Some regions of experience are more differentiated in some languages than in others. The Eskimos have many words for snow where we have only one; the Etruscans distinguished eleven kinds of thunder and lightning; the Bakairi Indians of Brazil have many names for parrots where we have only one; the Japanese have forty names for different kinds of rice but only one for what we call meat; the Arabs have several hundred words for camels where we have only a few; the illiterate peasant has an extremely rich vocabulary for animals and husbandry of which the literate city-dweller has never heard. But, once we are instructed as to what distinguishes these various types of things from one another, we also can learn to make distinctions in our experience by *attending* to differences of meaning which are normally below the level of our own cultural threshold. By *attending to* a given region of experience, we can lower the differential thresholds already sedimented in our language almost indefinitely and make what was implicit in our experience more and more explicit. This is one of the principal functions of linguistic expression and it clearly shows the referential character of language, not only as directed toward experienced things but also toward our *experience* itself.

(3) Thirdly, language as a means of intersubjective *communication* bears an intrinsic reference to the expressive-communicative context, which consists of both the "speaker" and the "others" *to whom* the expression is directed and *to whom* it is communicative. When an experi-

ence is "named" and when its name is communicated to others, a human social group is enabled to carry it in its collective consciousness, to return to it, to possess it and to use it as common property. The words of a given culture become its store of "sedimented meanings" which can be taught to others and handed down to posterity. Such sedimented meanings are the very basis of human culture and, taken together as a collective expression of experience, they constitute the world-view of a given linguistic community. Thanks to the sedimentation of meaning in words, man can "live in language," he can create the subuniverses of poetry, religion, history, philosophy, and science.[5] He can live on levels of meaning several times removed from the primary world of perception.

(4) Finally, given words carry the mark of the historical (sedimented) circumstances of their origin and use in ever new ways across history. When, for instance, in the history of philosophy we speak of "belief, in Hume's sense," of a "Kantian category" or an "Hegelian idea" we thereby designate, by a kind of historical shorthand, the distinctive meaning impressed on our general vocabulary by a great mind. To the extent that this element is important in our use of terms in philosophy, we can say that the appresentational structure of words involves a fourth dimension of reference: namely, reference to the philosopher or thinker who first defined (or redefined) a word in an original and systematic manner. As we shall see, this is particularly important for metaphorical words, which have a life of their own and remain an historical force even when their metaphorical character has been forgotten. Reference to their original meaning is *there* in the sedimented history of the words themselves.

3. MEANING AND EXPRESSION

MEANING CAN BE (phenomenologically) defined as the noematic correlate of experience. Meaning is *what* is experienced and consequently *what* we attempt to express in behavior, in gesture, in language. All experience is *experience of something*. Meaning arises only in the noetic-noematic contact with reality which we call *experience of.* . . . Words, thus, are not meanings; a word or a series of words may *point to* a meaning, but any number of words— including words yet to be invented—can be used to clarify and define a meaning by designating its various aspects and thus delineating its structure. A *meaning* is never exhaustively expressed in any *one word* or even in any combination of words; meaning always transcends any given attempt at its verbal expression.[6] Ordinarily, in using language we *attend* not to the words we are using but to the meaning which they appresent; we *see through* expressions to what they express, we live naturally on multiple levels of meaning, and it is only by a special effort that we can focus our attention on words as such. Words are only the *vehicles* of meaning.

In order to clarify our phenomenological approach to meaning and expression it may be helpful to distinguish it from purely abstract, logical analysis. The meanings we are speaking of here are not clear and distinct ideas, nor are they "concepts" of the kind isolated, analyzed, and defined through the logical analysis of language—which does not at all imply that we must relinquish the field of conceptual analysis to the logicians. The "concepts" with which logical analysis deals, which it tries to sort out and define as exhaustively as possible, can be called "closed" concepts, by which I mean clearly circumscribed, fully defined ideas. The goal of logical analysis is to render concepts as clear and distinct as the p's and q's of mathematical logic. But since all expression is appresentational in structure, since all language refers to experience, the meanings incarnate in verbal expression are hardly ever simple "closed" ideas. In short, we cannot analyze language without including reference (1) to what the person or community of persons using this language *mean* and (2) to the structure of the world-meaning thus perspectively appresented. There is a multiple relativity in all linguistic expression and therefore in all thought about experience.

For this reason phenomenology must define meaning as an "open" structure, as a nonfixed, morphological *eidos* which can be approached perspectively from an indefinite number of possible viewpoints but which can never be "possessed" wholly and completely under any one aspect. Any given meaning transcends all of its expressions; it is an eidetic structure (like a Kantian idea) which is the pole (noematic correlate) of an indefinite number of converging signifying acts but which will always escape exhaustive analysis. We can define world-meanings progressively and render them more and more explicit, but however far we carry our attempt to express them, there will always be more to say. The phenomenological clarification of experience is an infinite task, which, in principle, must be unending. Language is not composed of a number of discrete signs or symbols, each with its own clear, little, unequivocal signification; all of our signs and symbols together *allude to* a meaning which fixes our attention and *about which* we discourse but which is never totally or exhaustively expressed.

By means of expression (attending to experience) world-phenomena (meanings) can be more or less morphologically fixed through intersubjective constitution. But they remain possessed of an essential relativity. Though we all experience and express the same meanings (as we all live in *the* world), no two persons experience or *understand* the same thing concerning them in every respect. For this reason phenomenology is forced, by its fidelity to experience, to consider meaning as intrinsically ambiguous. By a special effort of abstraction it is possible, of course, to construct clear and distinct ("univocal") concepts for use in very restricted domains of language. But whenever these concepts are situated in relation to their experiential referents and viewed as expressions of experience, they reveal their intrinsic multiple relativity (their intrinsic "ambiguity").

4. METAPHORICAL EXPRESSIONS

WE HAVE SAID enough to indicate that the phenomenological elucidation of the expression of meaning and expression is not merely a problem of the "philosophy of mind." Man is not and has never been a pure consciousness. It is not sufficient to consider man as being or having a "mind" that refers, categorizes, thinks, and symbolizes clear and distinct interior ideas by means of external physical signs. Such a view is untenable in that it reduces man to only one of his functions and considers him as a disembodied "thinker." Man is not a pure consciousness; he *becomes conscious* little by little, with great effort, in the company of other men, across great lapses of historical time. Man's existence is spread out in time and space; he does not possess himself in pure immanent self-reflexive tranquility. Through the invention and use of language (and expression in general) man is enabled to orient himself in the confused world of lived experience. He is enabled to put order into his experience of the world, and, by so doing, to become gradually *human*. Thanks to the intersubjective constitution of meaning operated through language, man is enabled to become gradually *aware* of himself, of others, and of the world as the transcendent "horizon" of experience. All of this is to say that man *as a whole* is intentional of the world. His primary orientation is outward; he is first of all lost in the experience of things and it is through and in this intentional involvement with the world that he is able to become aware of his own transcendence as the "experiencer."

I would like here to illustrate this phenomenological theory of man as a world-intending organism from the point of view of his use of language in becoming aware of lived experience. More particularly, I will limit this discussion to what is ordinarily called metaphorical language, first to a brief discussion of metaphor in general and then to a consideration of a few fateful metaphors which have molded Western thought in the supposedly most detached realms of philosophical speculation.

Philosophers have traditionally adopted very superior attitudes with respect to metaphors. Metaphors, we have been told, belong to poetry, "emotive" literature, and anthropomorphic theology; philosophy does not need them and ought to avoid them. But the whole question is to know whether metaphors *can* be avoided and whether philosophers (or anyone else) should avoid their use. This much is certain: nearly the whole of extant, historical language consists of built up layers of metaphorical expression, and philosophers have been able to claim that they have escaped the hold of metaphorical language only because of their ignorance of the nature of language.[7] Since language is intrinsically appresentational of experience and therefore "anthropocentric," it is hardly surprising that it should be largely "anthropomorphic" as well. From the beginnings of language, men have invested objects of thought with the familiar aspects of the lived human body and its processes.

We effortlessly and constantly anthropomorphize the world of experienced objects. Visiting a floral display, we speak of a "witty pattern" of abstract colors. At the table we speak of our wines as "presumptuous," "robust," "generous," "impudent," "subtle," "seductive," "temperamental." The dentist tells us: "your children's teeth are in your hands." And David Hume tells us that when he discussed colors with the blind poet Blacklock the latter described scarlet as "the sound of a trumpet," the light of the sun as "the presence of a friend," green as "amiable sympathy."[8]

Animism is our first and primary attitude toward the world around us. To the prescientific mind it is evident that the forces of nature are "persons" with human characteristics. There are rainfalls of blood and rainfalls of javelins as well as rainfalls of gold and flowers. The gods—through their statues—weep and sweat; they also laugh and groan. Every anomaly in nature and history is the will of some spirit. There are the spirits of rain, the demons of the oceans, the sprites of the rivers and streams, and there are the high gods of thunder and lightning carried forward on the chariots of the clouds. Presocratic Greek science was conceived as the first "Western" attempt to deanthropomorphize the world of experience, to show that the cold wet "element" of water was the same "element" whether it was to be found in the mists of the clouds, thence to be condensed into rain, then collected in the reservoirs of the seas and rivers, and, when wintry conditions prevailed, to be finally frozen into ice as hard as rock. These were not *three different things,* ruled by different purposes, but just *the very same thing,* water, in three different states, gaseous, liquid, solid. Such a demythologization of natural phenomena which can show —by bringing together under one rule and one explanation —what had hitherto been experienced as bewilderingly complex and heterogeneous is very satisfying to the human mind: *it is the ability to see the many in the one.* This kind of impersonal, mechanical, third-person, deanthropomorphized explanation of reality, which we call "science" (*logos*), seems to promise to liberate us from metaphor (along with numerous other complex structures of prescientific experience).

But, on closer look, the deanthropomorphization of the world promised by this kind of "scientific" explanation is highly abstract and very incomplete. It must be extremely selective; it must "detotalize" the totality of the real and neglect all causalities of the first and second person. It is constrained to present us with a world in which the "I" and the "you" have nothing to do—the third-person world of the "it." Moreover—and this is the point we are primarily interested in here—it necessarily feeds on the more immediate and primitive metaphorical thematization of experience from which it draws its models.

We are, no doubt, sufficiently sophisticated in these matters today to see that neither Greek nor modern science has freed us from the processes of metaphor and analogy in our attempts to think the world. What Plato called "the most beautiful" form of reasoning (*Timaeus* 31C)—namely, reasoning through the analogical bond which ties things together—is still with us, and necessarily so. It is, after all, the distinguishing sign of the various degrees of intelligence, and one of the marks which distinguishes men from the apes, to be able to take something for something else, to be able to analogize. The models of contemporary science may be more sophisticated than the metaphors of animism or of ordinary speech, but they depend on the same fundamental ability. All intelligence tests are based on measuring this ability. And clearly if we were not, just as *homo sapiens*, possessed of a high degree of analogical ability, there would be no such things as languages.[9] Language, on all its levels, beginning with the discrimination of phonemes, relies on our ability to take something for something, and to refer to something by means of something else in purely arbitrary and conventional ways. Therefore, the ability to analogize is a sign of originality and intelligence; every scientific (or philosophical) theory begins with some very global, some very abstract form of analogizing. The comprehensible "category mistake," together with the counter-factual conditional, is the ultimate foundation of any progress in knowledge. Presocratic Greek science is certainly preferable to neolithic animism and our post-Newtonian and post-Einsteinian science preferable to that of the Greeks—at least for purposes of explanation—but they all exhibit the same fundamental structure.

It is this most fundamental structure of metaphor which concerns us. The relation of metaphor to ambiguity, to figurative language, to simile and parable, and even to symbol and myth, interesting and important as these questions are for a completed theory of metaphor, presuppose something more fundamental, namely, *the primordial attempt to articulate in language the structure and meaning of the perceptual life-world.*

If we attempt to resolve thought (in the form of words) into its *primitive elements,* we do not discover timeless, logical structures but experienced life-world events in terms of which historical men have oriented themselves in concrete existence. We are not talking here about the "painting with words" used in poetry and literature, nor with elaborate simile, parable, or other *recherché* forms of metaphorical thought used to evoke "mental pictures," "icons," or "images." We are not, then, concerned here with the *deliberate* literary, poetic, or scientific attempt to *invent* new symbols, models, images, or similes, but rather with the most fundamental, inescapable structures of linguistic expression in common language.

We are concerned here exclusively with the most fundamental metaphors which, consecrated by long use, have lost their power to evoke images and thus are no longer recognized as metaphorical. There are many categories of such hidden or *root* metaphors. Some of the most fundamental for language, and therefore for thought, are derived from the lived experience of bodily processes, from perceptual experience, from sensation, from lived-space and lived-time.[10] As a result the metaphorical use of such locutions as above-below, near-far, large-small, tall-short, pointed-blunt, sharp-flat, interior-exterior, open-closed, light-dark, before-after, right-left, front-behind, north-south[11] simply cannot be avoided even in the most purified meta-language. The metaphorical character of these expressions goes unrecognized because they have passed so completely into *common usage* on all levels that we do not advert to them any more.

Like the life-world, they are too close to us to be seen without special effort, they are too familiar. And this more than anything shows that the logical analysis of language is not sufficient of itself to clarify completely the expressive structure of language. We must go beneath the sedimented expressions of *common usage* to their experiential roots. In so doing we can come to a better understanding of what language is and why it presents *philosophical* problems.

But what *is* a metaphor? Again, we must begin with the life-world of perceptual experience. The impossibility of speaking on any level of meaning without using words denoting primary perceptual life-world phenomena is itself a demonstration of the primacy of perception and what phenomenologists call the "natural attitude" in our experience. That man must, first of all, speak in terms of his primary perceptual experience is an immediate result of the intentional structure of experience. There is a *prehensive* contact with the real (Whitehead) or a *compresence* with sensibly experienced things (Alexander), an existential "togetherness" with reality which precedes and underlies all thought about reality, all reflexive cognition. Perception precedes apperception.

We have already seen that the instrumentality of words derives from their being more flexible, more subtle forms of bodily gestures. And there seems to be little doubt that the most primitive words used to designate bodily processes, sensations, spatial and temporal relationships are primarily gestural.[12] Originally they serve only to distinguish and designate primary perceptions. But such words can then be used not merely to name things or to point out and distinguish perceptual experiences but also to enable us to bring within our ken and to com-prehend new, hitherto unnamed phenomena. A word which primarily designates a perceptual phenomenon—for example, the perception of light—once constituted, is available *for a new purpose* and can be used with a new intention—for example, to denote the process of intellectual understanding, and we speak of (mental) illumination. Once established, the metaphorical use of the original word is no longer noticed; its essential ambiguity tends to fall below the level of awareness from the moment that it is taken as designating another, now distinguishable, experience. With metaphors, as with all words, what fixes our attention is not primarily the verbal expression itself but *that of which* we are speaking *through* words. The metaphorical use of the word takes its place beside the primary sense of the word as the denotation of a distinct meaning. Moreover, metaphors of this kind are never "fixed pictures"; like all words, they point to distinctive human life-world experiences. They originate in the practical need to progress from "known" (already distinguished, already named) phenomena to what is as yet unknown and unnamed.

In principle, no experience, no aspect of experience is incapable of being named and thus made public. It is only because of his perceptual insertion in the world that man adopts a certain *metaphorical economy* in his language, using primary perceptual categories to designate experiences of a more complex and derivative nature. But any world-phenomenon, no matter how complex or derivative, once it has been named, becomes by that very fact suitable material for later figurative or metaphorical use. We build metaphors on metaphors as we progress from the "already-known" toward the "not-yet-known." The metaphorical use of words appears as the primary instrument of the discovery of "new" meaning.

5. GIAMBATTISTA VICO'S THEORY OF METAPHOR

THE FIRST modern philosopher of language, Giambattista Vico, developed a nonrationalistic theory of metaphor which, I believe, basically coincides with what I am saying here. Against Descartes and the rationalistic tradition which defined thought as the application of the laws of formally correct logical reasoning to fully discrete and perfectly clear and distinct "ideas," Vico argues in his treatise *On the Study Methods of Our Time* that these clear and distinct ideas are a rare and late accomplishment of only one of man's most rarefied (and intermittently exercised) faculties.

The abstract and "analytical" method of Descartes, says Vico, reduces thinking to only one of its *rare* functions, namely, the manipulation of perfectly defined categorial concepts in fully reflexive judgments. Thinking, as it is experienced in individual life and as it is traced in the history of the human race, is vastly more complex than this and follows laws of meaning-contexture and relevance which have a prelogical, affective, pragmatic morphology that is completely missed by rationalism. Rather than restrict his epistemology to a formal analytic, Vico requires that it also be a "wisdom" or a "prudence" which will descend to the historical life-world arena to study ideas as they emerge from the vague and amorphous meaning-structures of preverbal experience. We need not only an epistemology which does justice to the fully reflexive acts of intellectual judgment but one which recognizes and analyzes the role of prereflexive awareness in human thought. Ideas are not first of all and primarily "clear and distinct" mental definitions; they are tools and weapons, instruments through which man gradually comes to himself and achieves his humanity, little by little, through a vast and difficult historical process. What Descartes neglected completely and what Vico was the first to discover is the manner in which ideas are embodied in our total affective interest in the world, as the focus of our intentions and the stimulus to human action.

Descartes had no philosophy of language; according to Vico he produced only a philosophy of ideas. Against Descartes, Vico defined "philosophical ability" as the "capacity to perceive the analogies lying far apart and, apparently, most dissimilar. It is this capacity," he said, "which constitutes the source and principle of all ingenious, acute, and brilliant forms of expression."

> It should be emphasized that tenuity, subtlety, delicacy of thought, is not identical with acuity of ideas. . . . Metaphor, the greatest and brightest ornament of forceful, distinguished speech, undoubtedly plays the first role in acute . . . expression.[13]

Vico thus establishes his "new science" on the discovery that there are no "ideas" apart from natural languages and that men neither can nor do think except through a gestural and verbal extension of their perceptual and existential embodiment in a cultural world. Vico therefore turns to the "poetic characters" and "fantastic universals" of primitive thought to illustrate the growth of the human mind and its gradual acquisition of the *power to think* through its more primary experience of perceptual meaning.[14]

He writes:

> The rule and criterion of truth is to have made it. Hence the clear and distinct idea of the mind not only cannot be the criterion of other truths, but it cannot be the criterion of that of the mind itself; for while the mind apprehends itself, it does not make itself, and because it does not make itself it is ignorant of the form or mode by which it apprehends itself.[15]

Like British ordinary language philosophy and French structuralism, Vico places *homo loquens* at the pivotal center of his thought. He was concerned almost exclusively with "poetic wisdom" and with establishing a science of language founded on his early insight that poetic expression is both historically and eidetically prior to the logically ordered prose of syllogistic formulations.[16] Following his cardinal linguistic principle that "minds" are formed by language and not language by "minds," Vico gives a surprisingly lucid account of the origin of metaphorical language. "The human mind," he writes, "is naturally inclined by the senses *to see itself externally in the body,* and only with great difficulty does it come to understand itself by means of reflexion."[17]

He descends into what at first appears to be the chaos of primitive myth to establish the basis for a philosophical "etymology" and a philosophical "philology" which will enable us to assist once again at the primeval emergence of sense from non-sense, that is, the vast and primary realm of prelogical human experience which does "not yet" have sense because we have not yet learned to "name" its aspects and express its articulations. And he states his "universal principle of etymology in all languages" as follows: "words are carried over from bodies and from the properties of bodies to signify the institutions of the mind and the spirit. The order of ideas must follow the order of institutions."[18] Metaphorical language is a necessity of human expression and thought because man is naturally constrained to proceed from a few expressions that directly signify his most essential sensory life to the extension of this limited vocabulary to cover ever wider purposes of thought and communication.

The inescapability of metaphorical thought, says Vico, lies in the fact that (1) men are constrained in their attempt to "name" and thus understand the structures of the variegated chaos of preverbal experience by their deliberately associating (or "pairing") newly disclosed phenomena in experience with what has been previously discerned, and that (2) we naturally discover the factor of relevance which justifies such analogies in those aspects of the phenomena which most directly call forth perceptual experience, or human needs, interests, and instruments which have already been named.[19] "For the first language, spoken by the theological poets, was not a language in accord with the nature of the things it dealt with . . . but was a fantastic speech making use of physical substances endowed with life and most of them imagined to be divine."[20] Vico's theory of language is extremely valuable in thus showing that metaphors are not the enemies of serious thinking. *Metaphors are not accidental weaknesses of human thought which could be avoided if only we were more astute and tried a little harder.* It is distinctive of the "human condition" that the metaphorical use of words cannot be avoided. Our goal cannot be to escape metaphorical usage but only to understand its function.

We think primarily by "examples" and "likenesses,"[21] and only later are we able to examine the exact nature of the logical validity which justifies our using, for example, an agricultural vocabulary to designate the psychological processes of cognition. The results of Vico's investigations led him to recognize that "metaphor makes up the great body of the language among all nations"[22] and that, therefore, we cannot hope or plan to purify human language of metaphor but must rather attempt to understand its essential place in all the realms of human thought, from the most primitive to the most purified. The "privilege of reason" thus cannot consist in some superhuman possibility of thinking clear and distinct ideas divorced from the words of any natural language whatsoever, but rather in the power to analogize itself, that is, to take the primary perceptual and emotive processes themselves as the symbols of the cultural, religious, legal, and other institutions that they enable us to construct.

The "vulgar wisdom" which is the object of study in Vico's *New Science* is rooted in man's perspective-perceptual insertion in nature, man, as always, having a bodily *place* within being and among beings to whom he is related through common interests and projects. The works of this "wisdom" are the historical institutions which man adds to nature and which he attempts to understand by singing "the world according to man" in poetic gesticulation and ejaculation. It is not my claim that Vico has provided us with a complete or exhaustive theory of metaphor. He most clearly has not, nor has any other philosopher up to the present time. His importance lies rather in discerning one of the inescapable existential structures of human expression and thus in establishing a methodological principle which must be taken into account by any theory of language which would claim to give an adequate account of either the phenomenon of speech or the experience of meaning.

We certainly cannot simply adopt Vico's antirationalism without question, as we shall see below, nor can we content ourselves with observing that metaphor is the only mechanism of living thought and speech. But we must give this Vichian "truth" its due.

Once men have culturally organized their experience in a distinctive manner, and chosen their metaphors, they tend to think within the cultural-linguistic bounds that they have unwittingly set up for themselves. They no longer think as they *will* but as they *can*. For this reason it is a very fortunate thing for the human race that it does not speak one language only but has developed many different linguistic world-views. Different linguistic cultures (and even subcultures within a given linguistic community) organize their experience in distinctive ways. Thus through intercultural cross-fertilization (bilingualism, multilingualism), men are able with greater or lesser effort to break through the established linguistic sedimentations which constrict and limit their use of language. As a corollary it seems reasonable to suppose that linguistic analysis, at least insofar as it is directed toward the clarification of experienced meaning, can be successful only to the extent that it is based on the analysis of more than one and preferably several styles of linguistic expression. The empirical basis for serious linguistic analysis must be multilingualism.

6. METAPHORS IN PHILOSOPHY

IN ORDER TO illustrate the hold of metaphorical expression even on the level of fully reflexive categorial thought, let us turn briefly to the "sub-universe" of Western philosophy. One of the areas in which philosophers have tried, almost from the beginning, to think as clearly as possible is in the realm of what now goes under the title of epistemology. Since the life of the philosopher is a life of "thinking," of *theoria,* said the Greeks, nearly all philosophers have thought about thought and have attempted to come to grips with the subtle and elusive phenomena of thinking, knowing, understanding, comprehending, and so forth. In doing so they have relied on a number of fruitful metaphors invented at the dawn of Greek philosophy, which became quickly sedimented in the philosophical tradition and which have continued to guide Western epistemological investigations down to the present day.

In his extremely important work, *The Discovery of the Mind,* Bruno Snell illustrates the impossibility of speaking about the mind, the intellect, or consciousness itself without "falling back on metaphor." At least insofar as the Western intellectual tradition is concerned, it is clear from historical studies of language that the "mind" was not discovered until about the time of Homer or shortly afterwards. It was not that pre-Homeric man was incapable of what we now term "mental" or psychological experiences (emotion, imagination, reflexion, knowledge, etc.), but rather that he had not yet clearly distinguished processes of this kind within the great flux of worldly experience. We find, further, that when mental operations or processes were first named they were named by means of a metaphorical use of the terminology of sensation, particularly that of sight. A long preparation was necessary before it became possible to name even the primary sensory processes. Professor Snell cites a great number of early Greek terms used to designate the phenomenon of seeing and it is clear that these expressions are themselves primarily metaphorical, at least in the sense that they did not originally designate the experience of seeing in its specificity. Man is intentionally oriented toward the world, and only by being conscious of the world can he become conscious of his consciousness of the world. Thus he distinguishes aspects and qualities of sight before he is able to recognize sight as such. By way of example, let us take one of the early terms Professor Snell has analyzed:

> Derkesthai (δέρκεσθαι) means: to have a particular look in one's eyes. Drakon (δράκων), the snake, whose name is derived from derkesthai, owes this designation to the uncanny glint of his eye. He is called "the seeing one," not because he can see particularly well, not because his sight functions exceptionally well, but because his stare commands attention. By the same token Homer's derkesthai refers not so much to the function of the eye as to its gleam as noticed by someone else. . . . It denotes an "expressive signal" or "gesture" of the eyes.[23]

In the same way, we can say that the owl, as an animal, is anything but "wise." It is a creature of pure instinct and predatory force. But it can "look wise" because to men its large, blank, staring, Byzantine eyes come to signify the act of quiet contemplation.

It becomes extremely plausible, on the basis of such investigations as those made by Professor Snell and others, that nearly every word was originally a designation of a concrete world-phenomenon, that it called forth an extremely concrete image, that it was primarily a gesture. Words themselves are intramundane events; they are points d'appui for thought; on the basis of such lived image-gestures thought can go forward. This is what we mean when we say that if thought is analyzed into its primitive elements we will find not logical structures (which are in actuality highly derived and much later) but the experienced life-world itself as the apriori condition of any expression whatsoever.[24]

Let us continue with Professor Snell:

> The words which were later combined to form the principal parts of the verb "to see": horan (ὁρᾶν), idein (ἰδεῖν), opsesthai (ὄψεσθαι), show that to begin with there was no

one verb to refer to the function of sight as such, but that there were several verbs each designating a specific type of vision.[25]

Man acquired his power to designate even the primary sensory processes with great effort. Even the later and more technical term for sight, the one adopted by Plato and Aristotle for philosophical contemplation, *theorein* (θεωρεῖν), was not originally a verb but a noun, *theoros* (θεωρός), meaning "to be a spectator," from which it derived its later meaning of "looking at," ultimately "to contemplate." Here, clearly, the same word was used to designate in a confused way both seeing (the optical phenomenon) and intellectual comprehension, and this is even more clear with the term *noein* (νοεῖν), which in early Greek "stands for a type of seeing which involves not merely visual activity but the mental act which goes with the vision."[26] It was probably through the use of this word, *noein* (νοεῖν, νόος), that the Greeks were first enabled to distinguish clearly the experience of "thinking" as such. Then, through the process of analogy so important in the evolution of language, the classical word for sight, *idein*, also came to designate (especially in the form *eidenai*, εἰδέναι) the process of thinking, since the word for thought, *noein*, also meant, in its primary sense, "to see." Professor Snell has shown that in early Greek the eye served as the "model for the absorption of experiences,"[27] and we can add that the earliest epistemological vocabulary is therefore a vocabulary of *seeing*.[28]

This much is clear: at least in the development of the Greek language man is known to have proceeded in his noetic effort to name experiences from the recognition of what we call world-phenomena or meaning-structures in his primary life-world, to the naming of the particular acts or processes of experiencing by which he is revealed to himself as the experiencer, finally to the distinguishing and naming of various levels of this experiencing. This is, of course, a very rough and simplified schema; what we are interested in is the metaphorical use of words at each step of the process, the building of metaphors on metaphors which enabled man little by little to extend his ability to discover and *express* meaning.[29] Human comprehension involves metaphor at every step.[30]

On the basis of Professor Snell's studies we can conclude that one of the primary, if not *the* primary epistemological metaphor requires us to think of thinking as a *kind of seeing*. The metaphor of "intellectual sight" lies beneath a vast area of our Western epistemological vocabulary: *eidos, eidetic, idea, ideation, intuition, theory, theorize,* and the whole cluster of more directly "optical" expressions such as *reflect, speculate, focus, view, inspect, introspect, insight, outlook, perspective,* and so on. It no doubt also accounts for the frequency with which we use the metaphor of light or illumination (and words connected with these phenomena) to discuss the process of thought, since in order to *see* men must have light. It is extremely doubtful whether the metaphor of light or the conception of the intellect as a *lumen naturale* will ever be discarded.

The second most important sensory realm which has been studied up to now as a source of expressions for denoting mental operations and processes is that of touch (as gained through the use of the hands). Vico believed that the Latin vocabulary for knowledge was especially conditioned by the fact that when the Romans entered history they were a strictly agricultural people. When they needed words for the processes of understanding and thinking, they borrowed them, according to Vico, from an already established agricultural vocabulary, such as *intelligere* (to glean), *disserere* (to sow), to which we can add *recolligere* (to gather up), *observare* (to store away), and so on.[31] In any event, such words have in common the fact that they refer primarily to the use of the hands, the principal instruments of the sense of touch, and such locutions as *grasping, observing, apprehending, comprehending, recollecting,* and the like, have become commonplace in our epistemological vocabulary. In the full light of the eighteenth century David Hume was not better able to describe the difference between an idea that is "assented to" and a "fictitious" idea, and thus define his notion of *belief,* than by saying that the two *felt* different.

> It is evident [he writes] that belief consists not in the nature or order of our ideas, but in the manner of their conception, and in their feeling to the mind . . . in philosophy, we can

go no farther than assert that it [belief] is something *felt* by the mind. . . .[32]

Having established that at least some philosophers know how ideas "feel," we can proceed to some of the more complex metaphors that lie beneath our epistemological notions. It is not the purpose of this limited study to go through the whole "spectrum of the senses";[33] it is sufficient to show how some of the categories which belong primarily to the realm of sensory experience have been taken into technical philosophy.

Among the dialogues of Plato the *Theaetetus* and the *Sophist* have a privileged place in this regard. Not only did they mark a point of crisis, a turning point, in the development of Plato's own thought; they also scored a number of *firsts* in fixing philosophical terminology, which it would be unwise to say that Western philosophy, at least up to Heidegger, has ever broken through. Besides fixing for the first time a large number of technical philosophical terms and thus making mature philosophical thought *possible* for the first time, Plato, in his later dialogues, and particularly in the *Theaetetus* and the *Sophist*, gave us a series of epistemological metaphors in his statement of the problem of knowledge which have for twenty-three centuries supported the whole edifice of Western epistemological speculation. Without in any way attempting to be exhaustive, let us single out a few of these metaphors and sketch in a very preliminary way their historical influence.

The first of these, probably originated by Socrates, is the notion of thought as *conception*.[34] We find Plato's fullest account of the Socratic maieutic in the introduction to the *Theaetetus* (148e–151d). The young Theaetetus is discovered to be "suffering the pains of travail," about to give birth to an idea which he has within him but which he cannot get out until Socrates offers to serve as his "midwife." Socrates claims to be a midwife of the soul who can judge (1) whether a man's mind "has ever conceived at all" or "whether it is barren," (2) when it is "in labor with some thought it has conceived" and thus "about to give birth," and (3) whether the resultant concept is a "real child" or a mere "wind-egg," the result of a "miscarriage" or an "abortion." This is Socrates' "special art" and, thanks to his skillful practice in this case, Theaetetus says he is able "to give utterance to more than I had in me" (210b).

In the *Meno* the emphasis had been on "recollecting" (*anamnesis*), with great effort and by means of a dialectical interrogation, ideas which the soul already knew, had already *seen*. As we have seen, the word *idea* comes from the word for sight, whereas a *concept* is something produced by effort and requires the assistance of another, if not for its creation, at least for its production (its expression). In the later dialogues Plato is carried along by his own metaphor to say things which can be reconciled with his "metaphysical" theory of ideas only with difficulty. He maintains throughout that what he means by *ideas* (or forms, or kinds) are not mere mental events or psychic creations; ideas are the eternal, subsistent *objects* of thought. Yet, under the impetus of this metaphor of knowledge as conception, he is led more and more to focus his attention on the productive element in thinking, on the effort required to discover and formulate an idea, on the arduous interpersonal dialectic required to bring forth these *already seen* meanings. The conception metaphor requires a greater place for man the active "thinker" as the source not perhaps of the ideas but of all *knowledge* of the ideas.

Socrates, the midwife, claimed to be barren; in fact it was a necessity of the metaphor that the midwife (the dialectical interrogator) be beyond the age of "child-bearing." Hence, Socrates' continual refrain that he himself "knows nothing," and that his only ability is a certain gift he has for helping others bring forth what they already know but cannot say. Nevertheless, the sense of this metaphor as it is used in the *Theaetetus* (with reference to the dialectical begetting of knowledge) and in the *Symposium* and the *Phaedrus* (with reference to the begetting of virtue) clearly involves active intellectual intercourse and mutual impregnation. In the *Theaetetus* Socrates states that, as a good midwife, he is also a good "matchmaker." He can tell when the union of two souls will be mutually "advantageous for the good" and thus fruitful of ideas, and when it will be a barren union that can only result in miscarriages.

Many who have not been conscious of my assistance but have made light of me, thinking it was all their own doing, have left me sooner than they should . . . and thenceforward suffered miscarriage of their thoughts through falling into bad company; and they have lost the children of whom I had delivered them by bringing them up badly, caring more for false phantoms than for the true. . . . When they come back and beg for a renewal of our intercourse with extravagant protestations, sometimes the divine warning that comes to me forbids it; with others it is permitted, and these begin again to make progress. (150e–151a)[35]

The necessity of impregnation in order to conceive is even more stressed in the *Symposium* and the *Phaedrus*, though there the fruit of dialectical intercourse is "virtue" or "the good," or "spiritual beauty" (which of course are only other ways of saying "true knowledge" in Plato's sense). Here the "pregnancy of the soul" and "procreation in the beautiful" do not result from a mere *anamnesis* (remembering) but from the active intellectual intercourse of *thoroughbred* souls.[36]

In the *Theaetetus* and the *Sophist* the conception metaphor is given a still wider application in Plato's developing theory of knowledge.[37] Sensation according to Plato is the *intercourse* between the soul and the world of becoming. "We have intercourse with Becoming by means of the body through sense, whereas we have intercourse with Real being by means of the soul through reflection" (*Sophist*, 248a). The metaphor of sexual intercourse runs through Plato's analysis of sense perception as well as through his theory of the dialectical interrelations of ideas.[38]

This strong metaphor recommended itself to Aristotle, the biologist, and through him to the medieval Aristotelian tradition, and finally, through Oxford, to modern empiricism. According to Thomas Aquinas, for example, the *intentiones sensuum* (sense-data) flow into the soul (*"influunt nobis"*) and impregnate the passive intellect which then reacts and conceives a *conceptum* (*verbum mentis*).[39]

But the *Theaetetus* gives us yet a more important and more fateful metaphor.

Imagine then, says Socrates . . . that our minds contain a block of wax . . . and say that whenever we wish to remember something we see or hear or conceive in our own minds, we hold this wax under the perceptions or ideas and imprint them on it as we might stamp the impression of a signet-ring. Whatever is so imprinted we remember and know so long as the image remains.... (191c–d)[40]

The whole "empiricist" habit of speaking of knowledge in terms of *impressions* begins here. Aristotle took it up as an authentic description of the state of the mind before its awakening by sensation: the mind, he says, is like a (blank, wax) "writing-tablet on which as yet nothing actually stands written."[41] From Aristotle, through Aquinas and Ockham, to Locke and his disciples, this metaphor of the mind as a *tabula rasa in qua nihil est scriptum* is one of the constants of "empiricist" and "realist" epistemology. At the same time, because of his own interests and the "naturalistic" cast of his thought, Aristotle (and some of his followers) tended to "biologize" this rather mechanical metaphor. Thus the metaphor of the *assimilation* of reality by the mind (like the assimilation of food by the body) was conjoined to the *tabula rasa* metaphor in empiricist epistemology, and it has exercized a subtle influence on philosophers of all persuasions ever since. This "alimentary epistemology," as Sartre has termed it, cuts a wide swath in Western thought.[42]

To his wax-tablet image of consciousness Plato added another which, though it did not "catch on" in the same way, has been the more influential in that it does not so narrowly require an "empiricist" approach to knowledge for its adoption. Philosophers have not often spoken of the mind as an *aviary*, but they have never ceased speaking of it as *container* or *receptacle* in which more or less elusive ideas (whether innate or "captured" from without) are moving and associating with one another in unpredictable patterns (*Theaetetus*, 196d–199b). It is not here a question of whether or not it is possible or desirable to avoid such locutions as "the contents of consciousness" or "the contents of the mind." Heraclitus gave Western philosophy the notion of the soul as something "deep"; we still speak of "depth-psychology," of ideas and feelings as being "profound" or "superficial," and so on. The inner logic of such metaphors and the necessity of their use have still to be delineated. In fact, they have usually gone altogether unnoticed by philosophers. It is not my intention to suggest that we can express ourselves, even in philosophy, without the use of metaphors, but only to suggest that their analysis requires a method which will lead us back to the experience-meanings they appresent. There is a specificity of metaphorical expression which philosophers have too long neglected, and, since *nearly all language* is metaphorical, no philosophy of language can be complete until this problem is properly situated.

To conclude, let us examine very briefly two of our contemporary epistemological metaphors. The first concerns meaning only, since Wittgenstein, unlike Husserl, did not focus his attention primarily on consciousness or experience as the condition of meaning.[43] But he did focus on meaning and the complex, open, vague, and ambiguous interrelations which constitute the "family resemblances" of words. The philosophical analysis of meaning, according to Wittgenstein, consists in sorting out and tracing as best we can the many criss-crossing and interweaving threads that make up the strands of meaning in ordinary discourse. No single thread runs through the whole of a given strand, but the "continuous overlapping of fibers" leads us from one to another in a way that makes it possible for us to organize a "family" of interrelated meanings. In short, Wittgenstein views language as a complex, interlocking, tangled skein of meaning whose multiple and complex interrelations it is the job of philosophy to discover and distinguish.

It is noteworthy that this metaphor of *meaning as a fabric* is also an ancient one, though it was not much used between the time of Plato and Wittgenstein. Plato also conceived of his dialectical method as a study of the "texture of discourse." Plato's ideas or forms are the meanings referred to in all discourse and which are all "woven together" in a vast network.[44] This network or fabric of the forms (objective meanings) constitutes the real reality for Plato, and according to him the work of the philosophers is to trace the interrelationships of this articulate structure. Dialectic is the science of "knowing how to distinguish in what ways the several Kinds can or cannot combine."[45] The metaphor of *weaving* ("the art of combining," *synkritike,* συνκριτική) and of tracing or distinguishing already *woven* meanings ("the art of separating," *diakritike,* διακριτική) is frequent in Plato's later dialogues and serves to define the epistemological problem as it is posed in the *Sophist* and the *Statesman*.[46] While it probably always remained present in the metaphorical background of Western philosophical thought, it is Wittgensteinian linguistic philosophy which has given it a new force in contemporary epistemology.[47]

Bergson, in his radical criticism of traditional conceptualism (whether of empiricist or idealist inspiration), substituted for the reigning epistemological notions of his day a notion of consciousness as *action*, "less a kind of seeing than a contact,"[48] a dynamic, world-directed energy. Husserl, about the same time, elaborated a new phenomenology of consciousness with the aid of the ancient notion of "intention." As is usual in Husserl, he took the word in its primary etymological sense. *Intendere* in classical Latin meant primarily "a stretching out," "a straining towards," and is clearly related to such locutions as *attendere,* "to stretch towards," and *contendere,* "to stretch out vigorously, with effort."[49] By stressing consciousness in its active *Leistung* (doing), Husserl distinguishes his notion of *intentionality* from that which Brentano had borrowed from the Scholastics. In the Scholastics, and to a lesser degree in Brentano, the emphasis is on the *in-existence* of objectified, ideal entities *in* consciousness (in the mind).[50] But Husserl empties consciousness of all "objects" and defines it as *intentional of the world* in a completely de-substantialized and dynamic sense. *Intendere animum in* . . . , as the original Latin use of the term has it, signifies for Husserl *an effortful directing of consciousness towards the world.* Consciousness is *exertion.* Consciousness is no longer passive (as in empiricism); it is essentially an activity, a spontaneity, a movement. It is a *presence to* things in the sense of the presocratic *parousia* (παρουσία, presence to, directedness towards). Moreover, in virtue of this notion of intentionality, consciousness for Husserl is never a *thing,* nor does it contain anything; as Sartre writes, there is no "inside" in consciousness:

> Against the digestive philosophy of empirio-criticism, of neo-kantianism, against all "psychologism," Husserl never tires of repeating that we cannot dissolve things in con-

sciousness. . . . Husserl sees in consciousness an irreducible fact which cannot be rendered by any physical image, except, perhaps, the rapid and obscure image of bursting forth. To know, is "to burst out towards," to tear oneself away from the clammy gastric depths to slip outside of oneself over there, towards what is not oneself. . . . Now, consciousness is purified, it is as clear as a strong wind, there is nothing left in it, except a movement of escaping itself, a slipping outside of itself. If, by an impossible chance, you were to get "inside" a consciousness, you would be seized by a whirlwind and thrown back outside . . . for consciousness has no "inside."[51]

7. Theoretical Considerations

It is, therefore, clear that metaphorical usage is not some accidental weakness of human thought but that there are "necessary" metaphors which are inescapable as one moves from the level of unreflective speech to simile to myth to scientific thought. We *discover* our metaphors by a subsequent reflection; in the acts of creative usage in which metaphors are primarily used and understood there is no opposition to "literal" or "scientific" usage. The logical and scientific reflection which afterwards refines and restricts, which *explains* metaphors and limits their validity to their specific *tertium quid comparationis,* is itself made possible by prior metaphorical usage. It is clear that I agree with Bruno Snell that "verbal metaphors are indispensable for the description of all intellectual and spiritual phenomena," and that "the first principle by which [such] properties are ordered or understood is the behavior of our own sensuous perceptions."[52] The original sense of *phobos,* the Greek word for the psychological experience of "fear," was to designate "hair standing on end," then "hair-raiser," the demon which appears in Homer as "The Frightener" (*Phobos*). Only through this externalizing process could the Greeks come to name the mental experience of "fear."[53] The entire Greek vocabulary for mental processes (*psyche, thymos, nous, eidenai, gignoskein, synienai, epistasthai*) is developed by way of metaphor "by analogy with the physical organs and their functions."[54]

Some philosophers, after having discovered the pivotal

place of metaphor in language, namely, that the use of metaphor is not some treatable disease of speech but one of the
most fundamental—perhaps *the* most fundamental—structure of thought, proceed to extreme claims of the type: language is through and through metaphorical, all language is
metaphorical, and so on.[55]

This is not the position being defended here. Though I
hold that the uses of metaphorical thought are at the *creative center* of all linguistic innovations, it is equally clear to
me that not *all* of language is metaphorical, because there
are nonmetaphorical structures of *la langue* which are prior
necessary conditions for metaphorical speech.

Let us recall briefly the distinction made by structural
linguistics between *la langue* and *la parole. La langue* is
language under its aspect as a finite and closed system of
phonological, morphological, and syntactical rules which
govern the use of any given language and which are "im-
personally" and "objectively" available to any speaker who
knows the language and is able to speak grammatically
according to its rules (whether or not he can explicitly
formulate these rules in any given instance is irrelevant).
La parole, on the other hand, is a given speaker's *actual use*
of a given language as an already instituted and available
system of phonological, morphological, and syntactical rules
which (logically) preexist any present and actual use of the
language. But, *in the act of speaking*, he brings these rules
into play by producing ever new sentences and discovering
ever new ways of expressing meaning which he develops
according to the rules of *la langue* but which *la langue* itself,
as a "system," does not precontain.

Given this classical distinction, since all metaphors are
words, we begin by asking: what is the place of words in
la langue? In answer to this question we can say that, taken
in its formal structural function, *a word* is something which
is capable of being codified in the dictionary or lexicon of
some natural language in such wise that, if this codification
is to be complete, it must bear a definitive *syntactic marker*.
In other words, every word in a lexicon must be marked as
a "verb," or "noun," or "adjective," or "adverb," or "preposi-
tion," and so on, and further subdivisions must also be made,
such as "transitive" or "intransitive," "active" or "passive"

verbs, "proper," "plural," "singular," "animate," "inanimate" nouns, and so on. In short, it is a part of the essential polysemy of every word that, when we look it up in a dictionary to discover its various senses, it must be listed according to its possible grammatical usages. *Sentences, on the contrary, have no grammatical markers,* nor are there dictionaries of sentences. A grammatical marker is what every word must have in order to enter a sentence, to be given "syntactical form." Or rather, the grammatical markers given for a particular word in a particular lexicon of some natural language must include, if the lexicon is complete, all the possible syntactical "forms" of that word in that particular language.

Now, when a word occurs in a completed sentence—a sentence being the minimal *complete* unit of meaning possible in any language—it must always exercise just that place or that function which it *can* have in a sentence, just that place or function which is indicated in the dictionary by its grammatical marker, having received this "syntactical form" within the completed sentence. Words are the "substantive" elements of sentences and enable sentences to refer beyond themselves to the real world; syntactical form *refers to nothing beyond the sentence itself* but is the necessary articulation of the relationships among the words belonging to a given sentence and without which the words would be but juxtaposed bits of thought rather than meaningful wholes.

"Syntactical form" is, as we have argued earlier in this book, what thinking (in the strict sense) requires and what perceiving does not yet have. It is, one might say, what thinking adds to perceiving and to other forms of experience. There are intended objects in the perceptual world, in the world of imagination, in the world prior to thought, and these objects can be "appresented" by words in verbal experience; but acts of thinking in the strict sense generate "objects of thought" by giving objects (anything simply intended as such) a "syntactical form" and thus by fitting them together with other objects according to purely linguistic rules. Now, "syntactical form"—which is the most "universal" structure of language—has many interesting characteristics. Above all, it can be abstracted from the situation in which words are actually used in concrete speech-acts and is thus essentially independent of mere words as such.

Why is this? Words, over and above their syntactical markers found in the lexicon, have the characteristics of referentiality and contextuality in a way that syntax does not. Syntax does not refer to anything outside of the sentence and is, in this sense, context-independent. The facts of referentiality and contextuality, which are proper to words, take us away from merely syntactical considerations (the formal rules necessary to generate complete objects of thought) to *semantic considerations*. Syntax, in its abstract, formal purity, is utterly unaffected by semantics. Since it is free of both referentiality and contextuality, we are able on the level of syntax alone to discover strictly formal laws, strict synonymies, strict repeatabilities, strict idealities which words do not and cannot possess. Words have a form of ideality, namely, that of "ideal singulars." Syntactical forms, on the other hand, have the ideality of "ideal universals," and there is an essential difference between the two. The "finite," limited system of ideal syntactical forms which constitutes any given language is capable of absorbing any number of words in endless profusion. Syntax is *what words need* in order to make any complete or coherent sense at all but, by this very token, is independent of the words it uses.

My reason for emphasizing this aspect of the distinction between words and syntax at this juncture is to explain why there can be *no metaphorical use of language* on the level of syntax, or even on the more primitive levels of the purely formal grammatical structures of phonology and morphology. (Here the non-Vichian, "rationalistic" component of language comes to the fore.) If there were no such things as strict idealities and strict synonymies in natural languages, as some nominalists and empiricists seem to think, then it would be rigorously true that "*all* language is metaphorical." But this is not at all the case if one takes the *rules of the usage* of words into account and stops reducing "language" to "words" taken in isolation. It is true that all sentences are composed of nothing but words, but there is more to *sentences* than the words which make them up; there are the more abstract laws of phonology, morphology, and syntax, as a minimum. Phonology, morphology, and syntax all require the recognition of strict synonymies in language.

Even in turning to grammar it is not necessary to invoke the higher rules of syntax to show that strict linguistic synonymies are possible. If one takes the simple morpheme "s" that is used in the English language to form the plural [whether this be *pronounced* /s/ as in *spots,* or /z/ as in *horses*—because we happen to have two phonemes for this one morpheme in our language], this morpheme has *exactly the same meaning* every time it occurs. Synonymies are even more evident in phonology. The various phonemes which constitute the English phonological system occur *only once* in the language, as strictly ideal entities which *are not sounds* at all, are *never spoken,* are only *meant.* For instance, if one utters the sound "p" in the English language, one *uses* the phoneme /p/. This /p/ may be aspirated, as in *pin,* or unaspirated, as in *spin,* since, in English, we do not distinguish (as some other languages do) between these two (aspirated and unaspirated) sounds which are potentially separate phonemes.

One never does and one is never expected to produce on two separate occasions exactly the same phonetic sounds, the same raw phonetic material; this is neither necessary nor sufficient for understanding, and is, in any case, a physical impossibility. What *is* necessary and sufficient is that whatever is uttered, according to the syntagmatic and paradigmatic system of phonological opposables which are determined by the phonology of that language, *be meant and recognized as the same phoneme* which alone can hold that particular place in that particular phonological system. If someone, taken to be speaking the English language, systematically replaces the phoneme /p/ by the phoneme /b/, no matter how bad the accent, no matter how deformed the raw phonetic material, I will cease to have any difficulty at all in understanding this usage so long as I recognize the sound produced as *meaning* /p/. I have no difficulty at all in compensating for any number of various complex phonetic variations once I have grasped the abstract laws of this particular phonological system. Phonemes are not real sounds at all; they are, rather, the ideal elements which are opposable, according to rule, to all the other limited number of phonemes which constitute this language. On the level of phonemes there are no problems of metaphor.

Metaphor emerges only with *words*. After all, all the laws of phonology and morphology are at the service of our production of just those words which can be accepted into the lexicon of our natural language, but, with words we attain an entirely new and distinct level of meaning—a level of meaning that involves context and reference—and on that level we arrive at all the problems of semantics and a fortiori of metaphorical usage.

But we must now distinguish *words* as they occur in *la langue* and words as they are actually used in historical speech-acts, in *la parole*. In either case it is evident that the distinctive quality of linguistic meaning which we call polysemy and metaphor arises only on the level of words within sentences and texts.[56] Sentences are of special strategic importance because they constitute the minimal units of complete sense, being composed of words syntactically formed, and it is always within a sentence (and only within a sentence) that a word can take on a metaphorical sense.[57]

But if only words can become metaphors (a word being defined within *la langue* as the minimal linguistic element which *can* become a sentence and thus express a complete meaning), we must nevertheless recall that the metaphorical use of a word in a speech-act (an exercise of *la parole*) presupposes and requires that the metaphorically used word keep its original sense. Words are "ideal individuals" in themselves, without regard to the meaning or meanings they carry or appresent. Each word in the lexicon of a given natural language has its place as opposable to all the others of the same language. As an "ideal individual" within *la langue*, a word is unaffected by any particular usage of it. It remains always the *same* word, now uttered, now imagined, now mispronounced, now misspelled, now repeated in a different key or in a different context. It may be used frequently or rarely, but if it is to signify the meaning which a given lexicon of a given natural language assigns to it, it must be the *same* in every act of usage; in this sense a given word occurs *only once* in a given language—and it maintains its place and its function there for as long as it can be used in *its* sense. Even if the word is then used in a metaphorical, ironical, deformed, or changed sense, its own "original" sense must always also be "intended" in order for it to take on a new and added signification. Its place in *la langue* leaves it available for repetition; this *possibility of repetition*, whether realized or not in *actual acts* of repeating the word, is the linguistic "ideality" of the word as such, and while this structure of the word permits and is, indeed, an essential condition for metaphor, it is not—as a structure of *la langue*—itself metaphorical.

Therefore metaphor can arise only on the level of *la parole*. There are no metaphors in nature; there are no metaphors in perception. Metaphor can arise only when we try actually to put experience into words. And here we find the second condition for the possibility of metaphor. In actual acts of speaking a natural language no word is ever used in any given and particularized act of speech in exactly the same way and with just the same nuance of sense as it was used in any other speech-act. Human intentions enter in and we get a new sense of "usage"—not just the formal rules *according* to which we must speak and which *permit* speech, but, in addition, *the purposes for which* one speaks. At the same time all words in the lexicon of a natural language at any given synchronic point in history *do* always have a "literal" sense, namely the meaning which, by definition, enables each word to hold just *its own particular place* in the lexicon. Metaphor is possible only on the background of the ideality of words as they *can* occur in sentences; that is, a word can become a metaphor, take on a new sense, only because, and precisely because it can enable us *to take it as something else* without ceasing thereby to signify *its own original meaning*.[58] It is this experience of the word in actual usage which leads us away from the realm of syntax and grammar (or intralinguistic, syncategorematical meaning) on the one side to the realm of semantics, the realm of referentiality and contextuality, on the other. But just because the *real* situation in which any given word is uttered and the real purposes for which any speaker uses it are different in each historical occurrence of the word, we find in the structure of *la parole* the second necessary condition for metaphorical speech. In acts of speech, words enable us to break out of the "linguistic closure" of *la langue*—within which all words are held in place by all the others of the lexicon—to the extralinguistic reality to which words refer and thereby contextually denote.

Though "fully ideal" in their systematic linguistic aspect and in their intralinguistic function, words require—in their meaning—that they be employed in speech-acts, that they be *used*, and, for this reason, *words* (unlike syntax and grammar) transcend their own ideality, lead us to what is not *ideal*, to the usages of *la parole*.

8. NECESSARY METAPHORS

BUT JUST to situate metaphorical expressions within language by describing these two necessary conditions is clearly insufficient. For *not all speech-acts are metaphorical* and, though it is true to say that in every actual *use* of a given word the meaning-contexture of that word subtly changes, this sense of polysemy provides us with nothing more than the general framework within which metaphor *in its specificity* emerges.[59] A word is not a metaphor just because it is *used*, though this is a necessary condition; a word becomes a metaphor when it is used to refer with a new purpose, *with a new intention,* to a previously disclosed aspect of experience in order to reveal a hitherto unnamed and indistinct experience of a different kind. The metaphorical use of words thus brings about a reorganization, a refocusing of experience, which continues to grow in complexity with each further use of the word in a distinctively new sense, with each new *purpose*. As a number of theorists have said, metaphorical usage is a form of *seeing as,* or "aspect seeing," by which we detach ourselves from, tear ourselves out of, our ordinary way of perceiving things to see and express a new viewpoint, which, if it is somewhat systematic, provides us with a new "model" and perhaps even a new "theory" of some experienced thing or some realm of experience.

But this, too, is still too general and too vague. The number of theories of metaphor which have attempted to deal with metaphorical expression in its specificity are, as we all know, uncountable. I certainly will save my readers from the rehearsal of yet another taxonomy of theories of metaphor,[60] mainly because, like theories in aesthetics, they are so abstract, each one so one-sided, so boring in their pretensions, and so unfruitful in their consequences that any one of us would gladly sacrifice them all for one good piece of art, for one good poem, for an epigram, for a metaphor. Even the authors of these theories cannot remember them when they are actually standing before or immersed in a work of art, and it is extremely doubtful whether anyone's actual appreciation of a work of art, plastic or literary, has ever been influenced in the least by any one of these theories—not even the one the viewer or reader himself may have held at the time.

Nevertheless *theory is necessary* to explain to ourselves, after the fact, what has happened, what we have been doing, what we have experienced. It is the work of reflective consciousness—and it is what we are about as philosophers —but it should be kept as close as possible to the experience with which it deals, it should be restricted to a minimum, and it should make as few "unbelievable" generalizations as possible.

I therefore propose a wholly "ideal" division based on the most fundamental opposition which runs through contemporary theories of metaphor and which allows us to divide them into two groups—without naming names. I emphasize that these are two *ideal types*, since if one were to descend into the nuanced details, second thoughts, ad hoc qualifications, the reversals and ambiguities of each single theory, it would be utterly impossible to come to any clear problematic at all. It is interesting and important that the plethora of theories of metaphor which at first glance look so different from one another—because of their distinctive and uncoordinated vocabularies and choices of examples, because of their different and frequently opposed philosophical biases, because of their diverse audiences and the varied polemical occasions of their being written—nevertheless really do illustrate, when taken globally, this ideal division. In any case let us try to proceed in this eidetic, "impersonal" manner.

The touchstone for the division we wish to make is the question of whether or not a given theory of metaphor recognizes the kind of distinction which Roman Jakobson developed by distinguishing *metonomy* from *metaphor* or the kind of distinction which Philip Wheelwright introduced between *epiphor* and *diaphor*, and, *if it recognizes such a distinction*, what it does with it.[61] We are, as we said, proceeding "eidetically." There are, no doubt, important differences between Jakobson and Wheelwright, and we do not intend to endorse the details of either theory or even to claim that their authors would grant that we have done justice to the distinctions they were making, but this distinction comes down to a fundamental discrimination between two types of metaphorical discourse. In the *first* (metonomy, epiphor) the mind proceeds by a process of comparison of experienced objects which can be substituted for one another in endlessly fascinating ways; it *sees similarities in differences*. It creates similes, verbal images, verbal icons, parables and myths. Philip Wheelwright defines *epiphor* as "the outreach and extension of meaning through comparison."[62] This species of metaphor, as Ricoeur says,[63] proceeds along the axis of the concatenation and juxtaposition of experiences to reveal unexpected but immediately recognizable truths. "Philosophy is a disease." "Solzhenitsyn is a great bear of a man with an ursine temper." "Richard is lion-hearted." "Edmund is thighed and hipped like Achilles." "Cordelia is whiter than an egg." "Genevieve is sweeter than honey." Such examples come immediately to mind, and this kind of metaphorical thinking, in increasing degrees of complexity, especially in poetry, makes up the great body of metaphorical usage.

The *second* species of metaphor is what Wheelwright calls *diaphor* and defines as "the creation of new meaning by juxtaposition [through] synthesis."[64] Here the emphasis has to be on *synthesis* and the manner in which some metaphorical usages not only bring together and juxtapose different images or experienced objects but also make us see what has not before been seen and force on us a new perspective. Here we proceed along the axis of the subordination of one way of seeing to another, we filter one field of experience through another, and thus create new realms of meaning and thereby enable ourselves to see what before could not be seen. These are the more fundamental, root, and "necessary" metaphors which are frequently not recognized as metaphors at all because of their absolutely fundamental function of organizing experience; some of the best examples of such metaphors are given above in section six of this chapter.

If we *were* to do a taxonomy of theories of metaphor, we would find that all the theories which depend on mental images, or verbal icons as their central structure, as all the theories which explain metaphor as a form of "seeing as" or a "taking *as if*," all theories based centrally on such notions as "sort-crossings," "category mistakes," "verbal oppositions," and so on, tend to emphasize and explain the first kind of metaphor. They may not deny the second kind, and they may frequently—somewhere in the footnotes—speak of metaphors as "creative," as least for producing a novel sense of words, but such theories do not make the above distinction central and thus do not pose the question of "necessary" metaphors.

Apart from Wheelwright and Jakobson, mentioned above, Paul Ricoeur[65] and Max Black[66] seem to be the philosophers who most emphasize the kind of metaphorical usage which *creates* and *brings similarities to be* rather than merely formulating them, the kind of usage which genuinely extends meanings rather than merely introducing new uses of old terms.

But we have said that we would eschew a taxonomy of theories, and we certainly do not want to hand out prizes or punishments. Let us return to our eidetic standpoint. What we want to know—the central question—is whether everything which can be said metaphorically can be restated literally without any important loss of meaning, or, in other words, whether or not there are any "necessary" metaphors —because only *this* is of any philosophical importance.

As Bruno Snell writes:

> . . . metaphors which are based on a sensory impression of similarity are . . . relatively unimportant. Designating a piece of paper a "leaf," or using the same term to describe a part of a table, because both are thin, long, and wide: this kind of metaphor may be appropriate, it may be striking, and even witty, but it lacks the element of necessity which would make it philosophically profitable.[67]

Philosophers—just as philosophers—instinctively feel that everything which can be said metaphorically can also be said literally. Among recent theorists of metaphor, however (except for such courageous souls as Urban[68] and Herschberger[69]), this question is usually left ambiguously unposed and unanswered, as if such theorists—knowing what they should say—are embarrassed to say what they really *think*. So we turn to the Ancients. As we all know, the three "giants" of ancient philosophy, Plato, Aristotle, and Aquinas, were not at all hesitant about their stand; they took the "philosophical" position that all metaphors could be explained according to a theory of analogical proportionality which in any comparison would give us the *tertium quid comparationis* and in any proper proportion of the form $A:B::C:D$ would enable us to understand the *explicandum*.

In the *Gorgias* Plato constructs the proportion: Rhetoric is to philosophy as cooking is to medicine. What he wants to "explain," of course, is *philosophy* (the unknown x), and this is to be done by metaphorical comparisons, but by metaphorical comparisons raised by the means of analogical reasoning to the level of logical understanding. Philosophy and medicine are both "sciences" and give us "real," epistemic knowledge, as contrasted with rhetoric and cooking, which give us only "apparent" or "seeming" knowledge and have no "scientific" or "demonstrative" power. At the same time, in opposition, rhetoric is *like philosophy* in that it also affects the soul, whereas medicine and cooking can affect only the material, transient body. The proportion is thus perfectly symmetrical, an exhaustive, self-contained system of opposables such that if any three are known, the fourth will then be understood as well.[70]

Aristotle and Aquinas develop this doctrine of reasoning by analogy much farther, but what is here more important to see is its ultimate theoretical foundation in the view, articulated by Aristotle,[71] that metaphors are, in fact, nothing other than elliptical *similes*, that is, comparisons which can be fully clarified if only we can discover their *tertium quid*, that resemblance which makes them look "like" or appear "as" one another. Homer says, alternatively, that "Ajax is a lion" or that "Ajax is an ass"—which Aristotle must interpret as the alternatives that Ajax is *like* a lion and is *seen as* a donkey. We can, therefore, answer that everything which can be said metaphorically can also be rendered literally whenever we can find a clear *tertium quid comparationis*—and this seems always to be the case in the first species of metaphor ("epiphor") which we distinguished above, but clearly seems *not* to be the case in the second species, that of *diaphoric* expression.

Therefore, it is possible to completely demetaphoricize metaphors *to the extent that metaphors are similes*. But this is precisely the point at issue. Bruno Snell argues, on the contrary, that far from metaphor being a form of simile, *simile itself originates from metaphor.*[72] Aristotle, like a good logician, wanted to "rationalize" metaphor and bring it fully within the limits of completely clarified and univocal philosophical discourse. But the question is to know whether the perception of two events, qualities, functions, or aspects of things and their verbalization in metaphor presupposes the prior existence of a "concept" which we can then thematize, or whether, on the contrary, this experience itself generates something which we can *in later reflection* call a "concept," or at least try to explain conceptually, but which is always logically prior to and which always overflows any "concept." Insofar as the metaphorical verbalization of experience itself *creates resemblances* which could not be seen up to that time and, in that sense, were *not there* before, it would seem that there are "necessary" metaphors. Professor Snell believes that the ancient language of Homer and of the first Greek philosophers shows us the meaning of the "necessary" metaphor.

> We realize that the reality which [the "necessary" metaphor] expresses lies far below the level of human or animal activity, that it is one with the very roots of our existence. This is the life which cannot be grasped intellectually, by the principle of the excluded middle.[73]

The examples of metaphors which we developed above in section six of this chapter are meant to help establish this conclusion. It is impossible to understand the human mind or human behavior except by making a metaphorical detour, not only through the human body, but through the objects in the world which first polarize human bodily activity and enable the self to experience itself as distinct from the world, by reciprocally endowing the world with human characteristics and itself with the characteristics of experienced objects in order, then, to rediscover these characteristics as its own. These are not the only examples of necessary metaphors which could be given, but they are the most philosophically persuasive which have been discovered up to now.

Notes

I: The Ideality of Language

1. Edmund Husserl, *Formal and Transcendental Logic*, tr. Dorion Cairns (The Hague, 1969), p. 41. Hereafter cited as *FTL*.

2. Ibid., p. 25.

3. Ibid.

4. Ibid., p. 313.

5. *Logische Untersuchungen* (Tübingen, 1913), Vol. 1, chap. 11. Cf. Marvin Farber, *The Foundation of Phenomenology*, 2nd ed. (New York, 1962), p. xlv.

6. Jean-Paul Sartre, *Being and Nothingness*, tr. Hazel Barnes (New York, 1965), p. xlv.

7. *Ideas*, tr. W. R. Boyce Gibson (New York, 1931), pp. 67–68.

8. *FTL*, pp. 113–114. Cf. Gaston Berger, *Le cogito dans la philosophie de Husserl*, chap. 3, p. 54, cited by Gurwitsch, *Field of Consciousness*, p. 167: "Ce qui s'opère, dans la reduction phénoménologique, c'est moins le passage de l'objet au sujet, que la prise de conscience du monde en tant qu'objet, en tant que phénomène—*qua cogitatum*—il *y a une catégorie plus profonde* que celle d'être ou de non-être, c'est celle d'objet pensé." Cf. also: Aron Gurwitsch, "Towards a Theory of Intentionality," *Philosophy and Phenomenological Research*, Vol. XXX, March 1970, pp. 364ff.

9. The only difference between Frege and Husserl in their analysis of the distinction between sense and reference is terminological. Whereas Frege uses the term "*Sinn*" for *meaning*, as distinct from "*Bedeutung*," which he uses as *reference*, Husserl uses "*Sinn*" and "*Bedeutung*" more or less interchangeably as close synonyms for *meaning* (on the basis that this is

closer to ordinary German usage) and generally uses the term
"*Gegenstand*" for the *object of reference* in the real world. Cf.
Husserl, *Logical Investigations*, tr. J. N. Findlay (New York,
1970), Vol. I, *First Investigation*, para. 15, p. 292: " 'Meaning'
(*Bedeutung*) is . . . used by us as synonymous with sense (*gilt
als gleichbedeutend mit Sinn*). It is agreeable to have parallel,
interchangeable terms in the case of this concept, particularly
since the sense of the term 'meaning' is itself to be investigated.
A further consideration is our ingrained tendency to use the two
words as synonymous, a circumstance which makes it seem
rather a dubious step if their 'meanings' are differentiated, and if
(as G. Frege has proposed) we use one for meaning in our sense,
and the other for the objects expressed." Cf. Gottlob Frege, "Sinn
und Bedeutung," in *Translations from the Philosophical Works
of Gottlob Frege*, tr. Peter Geach and Max Black, 2nd ed. (Oxford: Blackwell, 1960), p. 59. Cf. also Hubert L. Dreyfus, "Husserl's Phenomenology of Perception: From Transcendental to
Existential Phenomenology," unpublished dissertation, Harvard
University, pp. 4ff.

10. *Ideas*, p. 67.

11. Ibid., pp. 77–78.

12. Ibid., p. 51.

13. *The Crisis of the European Sciences and Transcendental Phenomenology*, tr. David Carr (Evanston: Northwestern
University Press, 1970), section 51, p. 173.

14. Cf. Martin Heidegger, *The Essence of Reasons* (*Vom
Wesen des Grundes*), tr. Terrence Malick (Evanston: Northwestern University Press, 1969), pp. 49ff.

15. Husserl, *Ideas*, p. 51. I may be forcing Husserl here to
say more than he means, since he is here speaking of the natural
attitude, but this thesis is later incorporated into transcendental
phenomenology without any change of meaning insofar as the
primacy of perceptual consciousness is concerned.

16. Apart from Gurwitsch, I have in mind above all Sartre's
contributions to the phenomenology of the imagination in the
Psychology of the Imagination (New York, 1949), and in *Being
and Nothingness*.

17. Aron Gurwitsch, *The Field of Consciousness* (Pittsburgh: Duquesne University Press, 1964), p. 388.

18. Ibid., p. 389.

19. Ibid., p. 391.

20. Ibid., p. 404.

21. J. N. Mohanty, *The Concept of Intentionality* (Saint
Louis: Warren H. Green, 1972), pp. 33–35, 123–127, 158–159.

See also my review of this book in the *Southwestern Journal of Philosophy*, Spring 1974, pp. 205–218.

22. From the Third Meditation, *The Philosophical Works of Descartes,* tr. Elizabeth S. Haldane and G. R. T. Ross (New York: Dover, 1955), Volume I, p. 157. See also a parallel passage in the Second Meditation, ibid., p. 153.

23. *FTL,* p. 19.

24. See Chapter II below.

25. See for example "The Modes of Meaning," Chapter III of *An Analysis of Knowledge and Valuation,* by C. I. Lewis (La Salle, Illinois: Open Court, 1946), pp. 35–70. In reading these parts of Lewis one is continually struck by the similarity of his approach to that of Husserl in making these distinctions, even down to and including the kinds of examples he produces in evidence. C. I. Lewis was the "Husserl" of American philosophy.

26. See my article "Necessary Truth and Perception: William James on the Structure of Experience," in *New Essays in Phenomenology* (Chicago: Quadrangle Books, 1969), pp. 254ff.

27. "Each attempt to transform the being of what is ideal (*das Sein des Idealen*) into the possible being of what is real, must obviously suffer shipwreck on the fact that possibilities themselves are ideal objects. Possibilities can as little be found in the real world, as can numbers in general, or triangles in general." Edmund Husserl, *Logical Investigations,* tr. J. N. Findlay (New York, 1970), Volume I, p. 345.

28. Ibid., p. 193.

29. R. H. Robins, *General Linguistics* (London, 1964), p. 143.

30. Ibid., pp. 125–126.

31. Charles F. Hockett, *A Course in Modern Linguistics* (New York, 1958), pp. 116–118.

32. Ibid., p. 25. See also p. 134 on the abstract or ideal character of morphemes.

33. These observations and distinctions call forth numerous matters which require further elaboration. Some of them have already received consideration in an unjustly ignored article by Dorion Cairns, "The Ideality of Verbal Expressions," *Philosophy and Phenomenological Research,* 1941, pp. 453–462.

34. *FTL,* p. 20.

35. Ibid., p. 21. "The uttered word, the actually spoken locution, taken as a sensuous, specifically an acoustic, phenomenon, is something that we distinguish from the word itself or the declarative sentence itself, or the sentence-sequence itself

that makes up a more extensive locution. Not without reason—in cases where we have not been understood and we reiterate —do we speak precisely of a reiteration of the *same* words and sentences. . . . The word itself, the sentence itself, is an ideal unity, which is not multiplied by its thousandfold reproductions." *FTL*, pp. 19–21. See also, *Logical Investigations*, Vol. I, pp. 278ff., and Jacques Derrida, *La voix et le phénomène* (Paris: Gallimard, 1967), pp. 58ff.

36. Richard Rorty, *The Linguistic Turn* (Chicago: University of Chicago Press, 1967), p. 11.

37. See the excellent study of Husserl's criticism of Hume by C. V. Salmon, "The Central Problem of David Hume's Philosophy," in *Jahrbuch für Philosophie und phänomenologische Forschung*, ed. Edmund Husserl (Halle: Niemeyer, 1929), pp. 299–449. This treatise, which appeared in the same number of the *Jahrbuch* as Husserl's first edition of *Formal and Transcendental Logic*, deserves to be rescued from the obscurity of this defunct journal and published in its own right.

38. *Logical Investigations*, p. 345.

39. Ibid., p. 350.

40. Ibid., pp. 367–368.

41. Nelson Goodman, *The Languages of Art* (New York: Bobbs-Merrill, 1968), pp. 113–122, 195–198.

42. Of course there are the borderline cases of founding and stamping (if we take the bronzes, terra cottas, and coins of antiquity as works of art) as well as woodcuts, engravings, and etchings (whose techniques date from the Middle Ages), not to mention printing (which we have had since the Renaissance) as well as lithography and photography (which entered the scene in the nineteenth century). Particularly with photography (even leaving films as artforms aside since there may be a way of establishing some "grammar" for films so as to make them analogous to music and literature) one wonders whether or not any work of art, and any part of a work of art, is not infinitely reproducible. How many copies of the *Mona Lisa* had conditioned the Japanese for the hysteria which broke out when the "real thing" was transported from the walls of the Louvre to Tokyo? Having seen so many copies, is it still possible to see *the real autograph* itself? It would be better to say, therefore, with Walter Benjamin, that what is not "reproducible" in an autographic work of art, such as an architectural monument, a painting, a work of sculpture, is its *authenticity*. "Even the most perfect reproduction of a work of art is lacking in one element: its presence in time and space, its unique existence at the place

where it happens to be. . . . The presence of the original is the prerequisite to the concept of authenticity." Walter Benjamin, "The Work of Art in the Age of Mechanical Reproduction," in *Illuminations* (New York: Schocken, 1969), pp. 217ff.

43. I have treated of this at greater length, without reference to Goodman, in my article on "The Problem of Enactment," *The Journal of Aesthetics and Art Criticism*, 1971, pp. 307ff.

44. Paul Ziff, "Goodman's Languages of Art," in *The Philosophical Review*, 1971, p. 515. Ziff's "nominalism" is even more evident and crushing in his major work, *Semantic Analysis* (Ithaca: Cornell University Press, 1960). Even if we leave completely to one side the cumbersome methodological and linguistic proposals Ziff uses for the investigation of the meanings of words (Cf. Jerrold J. Katz, *Review of Semantic Analysis, Language*, Vol. 38, 1962, pp. 52–69), from a purely philosophical point of view what is most disconcerting is not Ziff's laborious but jejune conclusion but rather his strange conception of his task. As for his conclusion, after painstakingly setting up one hundred and sixty "non-deviant" or "non-odd" linguistic "environments" (i.e., typical sentences) in which the word "good" can properly occur, he concludes that the *meaning* of the word "good" in the English language is "answering to certain interests" (p. 247). Clearly such an unspecific and vague definition is useless since there are very many other words in English (and other) languages which would fall under it; the category of "interest" words is most capacious. But it is Ziff's conception of his task which is the root of his problem. In writing a book to illustrate his method for looking for the meaning of words he limits his goal to asking what the *English* word "good," or rather the sound specified in some international phonetic alphabet as [gʊd], can mean (p. 102). This, he assures us, is not a question which Aristotle or Heraclitus could have asked. It is a question which could not have been asked prior to 400 A.D., apparently the birthdate of the English language. Meaning, on such an account, cannot in any way transcend the empirically given regularities of speech-sounds (do we know, by the way, whether "good" has always been pronounced [gʊd] from 400 A.D. to the present?) and cannot in any way be divorced from the melodic contours of any one particular natural language. The absurdity of such a point of departure for the analysis of meaning simply boggles the mind—however entertaining and witty the details of Ziff's analysis may be.

45. Cf. Ludwig Wittgenstein, *Notebooks 1914–1916*, ed.

G. H. von Wright and G. E. M. Anscombe (Oxford: Blackwell's, 1961), p. 40.

46. Derrida first develops this theme and thus founds his "grammatological" version of Structuralism in his commentary on Husserl's *The Origin of Geometry*, which he translated and edited in the French version: Edmund Husserl, *L'Origine de la géometrie*, tr. Jacques Derrida (Paris: Gallimard, 1962). See in particular pp. 83ff. of his translator's introduction. From this flow in remarkably systematic, if egregiously manneristic form, his later works, such as: *De la grammatologie* (Paris: Minuit, 1967), *La voix et le phénomène* (Paris: Gallimard, 1967), *L'écriture et la différence* (Paris: Seuil, 1967), *Marges de la philosophie* (Paris: Minuit, 1972), and many others.

47. *The Crisis of the European Sciences*, p. 361.

48. Cf. Etienne Gilson, *Linguistique et philosophie* (Paris: Vrin, 1969), pp. 233ff. and *passim*. See also my review of this book in *Journal of the History of Philosophy*, Vol. IX, 1971, pp. 116–125.

49. William P. Alston, *Philosophy of Language* (Englewood Cliffs: Prentice-Hall, 1964), p. 33n.

50. "Ich nenne alle Erkenntnis *transzendental,* die sich nicht sowohl mit Gegenständen, sondern mit unserer Erkenntnisart von Gegenständen, sofern diese a priori möglich sein soll, überhaupt beschäftigt. . . ." Kant, *Kritik der reinen Vernunft,* 2nd ed., p. 25. Cf. Husserl's first chapter of *Ideas*, "Facts and Essence," trans. W. R. B. Gibson (New York: Macmillan, 1931), pp. 51ff., and Aron Gurwitsch, *The Field of Consciousness*, pp. 196–197. It is, no doubt, unnecessary to remark that we are here using the term "object" in its Husserlian sense, namely, as "object of consciousness" which refers to a possible *Gegenstand* but which has a "meaning-structure" or "essence" independent of any actual experience. As we turn correlatively from "fact" to "essence," the word "object" can signify an *object-as-experienced* or its *meaning*. It is within the experience of "objects," phenomenologically elucidated, that we find the basis for the distinction between meaning and reference.

51. Cf. Newton Garver, "Analyticity and Grammar," in *The Monist*, Vol. 51, 1967, pp. 397–425.

52. "Although many philosophers influenced by Wittgenstein have made use of this idea in discussing the meaning of particular expressions, virtually nothing has been done by way of going beyond Wittgenstein's cryptic remarks to an explicit analysis of semantic concepts." William P. Alston, *Philosophy of Language,* p. 33.

53. I want to leave in suspense here the question of whether language is essentially a question of communication. Certainly we use language for other purposes, as in philosophical writing for instance, to clarify and bring to consciousness the articulations of experience. Merleau-Ponty and others argue that, although communication is an essential possibility of language, language as such is not primarily "to communicate." The least we can say is that, if communication is essential to language, this is a "formal" condition of its essence, i.e., language essentially involves the possibility of its being understood by others and is thus intersubjective and "public" by its (logical) nature.

54. Alston, *Philosophy of Language,* p. 39. For the present, I am using this notion uncritically. There is a difficulty with the notion of an "illocutionary act" in that it does not involve a clear distinction between the psychological act (*noesis*) itself and its content (*noema*). It is not clear that Alston would accept such a distinction.

55. Ibid., p. 36.

56. Husserl treats of this in detail in the *First* and the *Fifth Investigations.* Cf. Marvin Farber, *Foundation of Phenomenology,* pp. 221ff., 333ff.

57. Alston, *Philosophy of Language,* p. 36.

58. Ibid., pp. 28–32.

59. Ibid., pp. 40–41. We must limit ourselves to instancing only one of the several interesting examples Alston uses to make his point, but, although we perforce lose the richness of variation and detail of his analysis in such an abridgement, we do not, I think, lose his central point.

60. This latter distinction is much less clear in Alston's examples than the former, perhaps because of the behavioristic framework of his general theory; his theory requires that he "touch" on this distinction but somehow prevents him from making it explicitly. To this extent the analysis falls short of our expectations.

61. We cannot here go into the theories of *hermeneutics* developed by Heidegger, Gadamer, Ricoeur, and others which this observation permits, but it is worthwhile to note that they have an essential place in any completed phenomenology of language and the expression of meaning.

62. In this respect Alston's own account suffers from psychologism and, insofar forth, is unsatisfactory. He wants to account for the necessity of meaning-conditions of this kind in terms of the "responsibility" a person takes for his sentences, in much the same sense, he says, in which "an administrator is

responsible for the efficient functioning of the department in his charge" (p. 41). Our interpretation, therefore, imposes a heavier weight on Alston's analysis than his own psychologistic language permits. This reproach of "psychologism" is, unfortunately, one which must be addressed to most of the "methodological nominalists" of contemporary philosophy. Alston wants to account for meaning-conditions in terms of "moral responsibility." Paul Ziff wants to define "good" as "answering to certain interests" as if the word "good" simply means "I like it" or "I want it." Quine wants to define "stimulus analyticity" in terms of dispositions of certain persons to assent to certain judgments (*Word and Object* [Cambridge, Mass.: M.I.T. Press, 1960], p. 55). Others try to account for the rules of language in terms of "permissions" to engage in such and such behavior, and so on. All these psychologisms are bound to fail when tested against the ideal objectivity of meaning; what a word or a sentence means is utterly independent of whether or not I like it, whether I am disposed or not to assent to it (with or without force), whether or not permissions or promises are given, etc. The depsychologization of the ideal is the greatest task of the contemporary philosophy of language.

63. When Bertrand Russell rendered Meinong's rather harmless German term *bestehen* as "to subsist" rather than, as he could have, as "to be the case," he apparently inoculated a whole generation of British and American philosophers with behavioristic tendencies against all talk of "ideal objectivities" and other "ghosts" and "queer entities" (Cf. Herbert Spiegelberg, *The Phenomenological Movement*, The Hague: Nijhoff, 1960, I, 96ff.). In writers like Alston we see a behavioristic theory of meaning, which puts the speaker at the center of interest and discovers his "acts" of meaning on the verge of giving a sophisticated behavioristic sense to the kinds of experience with which Meinong and Husserl began.

64. John R. Searle, *Speech Acts, An Essay in the Philosophy of Language* (Cambridge: Cambridge University Press, 1969), p. 7.

65. Ibid., pp. 11–12.

66. *Logical Investigations*, p. 343.

II. Husserl's Conception of *The Grammatical* and Contemporary Linguistics

1. Edmund Husserl, *Logische Untersuchungen* (Tübingen: Niemeyer, 1968), II. (Cited hereafter as *LU*. All references are to Volume II.) I will also add references to the English transla-

tion (referred to as *ET*) of J. N. Findlay (New York: Humanities Press, 1970), though I will keep my own translation from the German original in the text. The reference here is to *LU* p. 342, and *ET*, p. 529.

2. Edmund Husserl, *Formal and Transcendental Logic*, tr. Dorion Cairns (The Hague, 1969), p. 49. (Cited hereafter as *FTL*.)

3. The word "pure" in Husserl's terminology seems to be a synonym for "formal." In the first edition of *Logische Untersuchungen* he spoke simply of "pure grammar"; but since he later recognizes that there are other aprioris than the logical ones he is concerned with, which govern the study of grammar, in the second edition he speaks of "pure logical grammar" (*LU*, p. 340, *ET*, p. 527).

4. One of the few studies of Husserl's notion of a pure logical grammar published up to now suffers, it seems to me, from some serious confusions and an inordinate amount of Carnapian bluster. Yehoshua Bar-Hillel ("Husserl's Conception of a Purely Logical Grammar," *Philosophy and Phenomenological Research*, XVII [1957], 362–369) states a number of points "somewhat dogmatically" (p. 365) because they had previously been argued in his doctoral dissertation on the *Theory of Syntactical Categories* (Jerusalem, 1947), in Hebrew. I am not competent to read Hebrew and thus do not know if Bar-Hillel there took account of Husserl's more developed conception of pure logical grammar as it is found in *Formal and Transcendental Logic;* but in this article he seems to be mesmerized by Husserl's somewhat naive vocabulary (his talk of "parts of speech" etc., as if these were properly refined grammatical categories) and by the material examples given in the *Fourth Investigation*. He also believes, like others, that Husserl was misled in taking the surface structures of Indo-European languages as ultimate grammatical categories; and, of course, his mind boggles at notions like "apodictic evidence," Husserl's conception of the apriori, and presumably "eidetic intuition," though he does not mention this last. We cannot discuss this confused article in detail and must limit ourselves to making a few corrective remarks. We concede that Husserl's vocabulary is linguistically unsophisticated at some points in the *Fourth Investigation*. As Suzanne Bachelard has pointed out (*A Study of Husserl's "Formal and Transcendental Logic,"* tr. Lester E. Embree [Evanston: Northwestern University Press, 1968], pp. 6–7), Husserl's choice of examples in the *Fourth Investigation* can easily mislead the unwary because they are of material (or

synthetic) countersense and have not been properly formal-ized; it is only in *Formal and Transcendental Logic* that he more completely formalized his expressions. This is because the "investigations" were introductory and directed to his contem-poraries; they were meant to "stimulate thinking" and were not meant to be definitive; by using examples which were easier to understand, we are told, Husserl hoped to initiate his readers to certain distinctions, and he feared to impose on his readers a completely abstract form of exposition, a fear nowhere pres-ent in *Formal and Transcendental Logic.* Bar-Hillel is thus able to argue that, since the form *S is p* can be rendered materially not only by "This tree is green" but also by "This tree is a plant," Husserl's "intuition" that only "adjectives" could take the place of *p* in the *Urform* is shown to be unsound. But Husserl's point properly concerns *predicates* (whatever their "nonsyntactical form" may be) and not just the "adjective" as a "part of speech" in ordinary German grammar. Even in ordinary school grammar we do distinguish between predicate nouns and predicate adjectives; but the important point is that only *predicates,* syntactically formed as such, can be predicated of a substantive, and this is a question not of the surface grammar of Indo-European languages but of categories of signification or meaning. Since Bar-Hillel apparently thinks the move from grammatical categories to meaning-categories is illegitimate, he can, on that basis, effortlessly make nonsense of most of what Husserl says: but this seems to me to miss the real point Husserl is making. Another critical victory is claimed by show-ing that "the full stop belongs essentially to the word sequence" (Bar-Hillel, p. 366) because such a sequence as "is a round or" is perfectly well formed if it is taken as a part of a sen-tence like "This is a round or elliptical table." But this is merely to throw sand into the eyes of the reader, at least of the reader who takes Bar-Hillel's account of Husserl's theory, even as that theory appears in the *Fourth Investigation,* as a faithful ac-count. The "full stop" does not belong essentially to just any word sequence but only to sentences; and "is a round or" may be a "piece" of the sentence given for it, but it is not a "mem-ber" of such (or any other) sentence. Husserl has clearly met Bar-Hillel's "full-stop" requirement for sentences because a sentence is an independent unit of meaning. The word sequence "is a round or" is *unsinnig* precisely because it is not a unit of meaning and is not a well-formed expression, it is not an inde-pendent unit of meaning, and it is not even a dependent "mem-ber" of the complete sentence which Bar-Hillel constructs for it. It is neither a dependent nor an independent unit of meaning, though in a unified sentence, such as "This is a round or elliptical table," elements in this string help constitute the dependent syntactical categories that function properly within the sentence. I believe that Bar-Hillel's hypercritical and unsympathetic reading of Husserl comes from his Carnapian enthusiasm exclusively. In an earlier article ("Logical Syntax and Semantics," *Language*, XXX [1954], 230–237), Bar-Hillel credits Carnap with both distinguishing and then fusing together grammar and logic, "with grammar treating approximately the formational part of syntax and logic its transformational part." "The relation of *commutability* may be sufficient," he writes, "for formational analysis, but other relations, such as that of formal consequence, must be added for transformational analysis" (pp. 236–237). But this is surely part of the point Husserl was making in the *Fourth Investigation*, and Bar-Hillel grudgingly admits this in his 1957 article (pp. 366ff.). These two articles by Bar-Hillel should, in my opinion, not be read except in conjunction with the reply to the 1954 article by Noam Chomsky ("Logical Syntax and Semantics, Their Linguistic Relevance," *Language*, XXXI [1955], 36–45) and Bar-Hillel's own uncharacteristically temperate remarks in "Remarks on Carnap's Logical Syntax of Language" in *The Philosophy of Rudolf Carnap*, ed. P. A. Schilpp (La Salle, Ill.: Open Court, 1963), pp. 519–543. For a different kind of "rejoinder" to Bar-Hillel's attack on Husserl, see J. N. Mohanty, *Edmund Husserl's Theory of Meaning* (The Hague: Nijhoff, 1964), pp. 104–115.

5. As Bar-Hillel has shown with filial devotion, Husserl's work can be read as a flawed precursor of Carnap's, but we should keep in mind the essential difference that, from the beginning to the end, Husserl was concerned, not with artificially constructed "ideal" languages or the use of algorithms to define some independent mathematical system which could, in some extended sense, be called "language," but with *natural language itself*.

6. *LU*, p. 338, *ET*, p. 525.

7. *LU*, p. 339, *ET*, p. 526.

8. *LU*, p. 337, *ET*, p. 524. Cf. Bachelard, *A Study of Husserl's "Formal and Transcendental Logic,"* pp. 10–11.

9. See André de Muralt, *L'Idée de la phénoménologie* (Paris: Gallimard, 1958), pp. 115ff., and Bachelard, *A Study*, pp. 18ff., 33ff.

10. "We should never forget that meanings, essences, are

directly expressed in language. *Language is the true locus of essences, of the ideal existence of meanings*, because language, taken in itself, abstracts from the factual existence of objects, and grasps only significations. This is the meaning of the excellent formulation by Merleau-Ponty: 'separated essences are those of language' [*Phenomenology of Perception*, tr. Colin Smith (New York: Humanities Press, 1962), p. xv]. In other words, a thought which moves solely on the level of language moves necessarily within the phenomenological reduction; it is on a level with the eidetic realm of pure, experienced meanings. This is why the *Logical Investigations* which begins with an extremely careful analysis of language and its functions develops a logic which makes no reference at all to the phenomenological reduction but which nevertheless possesses an authentically phenomenological spirit ... this is necessary because, *from the moment that one considers language in itself, one has implicitly operated the phenomenological reduction.*" De Muralt, *L'Idée de la Phènoménologie*, pp. 124–25.

11. *LU*, *Prolegomena*, Chapter Eleven, the *Fourth Investigation;* and Bachelard, *A Study*, p. 3.

12. *FTL*, p. 70.

13. *LU*, p. 341, *ET*, p. 528. There is also an important discussion of this distinction in Aron Gurwitsch, *The Field of Consciousness* (Pittsburgh: Duquesne University Press, 1964), pp. 331ff., on "Philosophical Problems of Logic."

14. *LU*, p. 342, *ET*, p. 528.

15. *LU*, pp. 327–328, *ET*, p. 518.

16. *LU*, p. 330, *ET*, pp. 521–523.

17. *Meno*, 75B.

18. *LU*, pp. 252–253, *ET*, pp. 440–441.

19. See the excellent article by Robert Sokolowski, "The Logic of Parts and Wholes in Husserl's *Investigations*," *Philosophy and Phenomenological Research*, XXVIII (1968), 537–553, esp. pp. 538ff., and 542ff., 548ff. Note also that I must neglect many fundamental aspects and applications of Husserl's general theory in this brief reference to it. Sokolowski gives a good outline of the various other applications of this general theory in Husserl's later phenomenology. See also Gurwitsch, *The Field of Consciousness*, pp. 194–197.

20. "The proposition as a whole has forms appertaining to wholeness; and, by their means, it has a unitary relation to the meant as a whole, to what is categorially formed thus and so . . . ; each member is *formed* as entering into the whole" (*FTL*, pp. 298–299).

21. *FTL*, p. 50.

22. *LU*, p. 336, *ET*, p. 523. Husserl here gives his own list of the tasks of pure logical grammar.

23. Husserl, of course, does not use the current term "marker" (*LU*, p. 317, *ET*, p. 502). See Marvin Farber, *The Foundation of Phenomenology* (New York, 1962), p. 317.

24. *FTL*, p. 305.

25. The "copular unity-form" is a specification of more general "conjunctive" forms (*FTL*, pp. 300, 308).

26. *FTL*, p. 298.

27. *FTL*, pp. 308–309.

28. *FTL*, p. 303.

29. *FTL*, pp. 52–53. Cf. *LU*, pp. 328ff.

30. *FTL*, p. 311. Cf. *LU*, pp. 324–325, *ET*, pp. 515–516.

31. *FTL*, p. 310. Let us note in passing that derivations of this kind involve us in the essential distinction between "naming" and "judging." A *proper* judgment, that is, an original, experienced, and asserted judgment, consists of material terms through which things in the world (a "state of affairs") are *named* and then *determined* (*S is p*); it is through its material terms that the judgment, thanks to the categorial form given these terms in the judgment, refers to the world and asserts something about it. When a proposition (*S is p*) is then taken as a unit and "nominalized" (as in *Sp is q*), the original proposition is no longer asserted; but the state of affairs to which it referred is only named, and something further is asserted of it as a new determination. The logical functions of naming and of judging are, according to Husserl, not only eidetically distinct, but the logical function of "naming" is prior to predicative thought as such. J. N. Mohanty, *Edmund Husserl's Theory of Meaning* (The Hague: Nijhoff, 1964), pp. 99–101, gives a discussion of this distinction with reference to recent logical literature on this subject.

32. *Ideen I* (*Husserliana* III [The Hague: Nijhoff]), p. 327; *FTL*, p. 52.

33. "When we penetrate more deeply, it becomes apparent that syntactical forms are separated according to levels: *Certain forms*—for example: those of the subject and the predicate —make their appearance *at all levels* of compositeness. Thus a whole proposition can function as a subject just as well as a simple substantive can. *Other forms*, however, such as those of the hypothetical antecedent and consequent, *demand stuffs that are already syntactically articulated in themselves*" (*FTL*, p. 307); cf. J. N. Mohanty, *Edmund Husserl's Theory of Mean-*

ing, pp. 106ff. Mohanty gives an account of Husserl's conception of pure logical grammar which differs in some respects from mine.

34. André de Muralt, *L'Idée de la phénoménologie,* p. 142. Cf. *LU,* p. 333, *ET,* p. 526.

35. *LU,* pp. 336–337, *ET,* pp. 524–525.

36. *LU,* pp. 337ff., *ET,* pp. 525ff. Cf. Bachelard, *A Study,* p. 10.

37. In *FTL,* p. 30, Husserl recognizes that what Plato and Descartes envisaged in terms of "innate ideas" involved an insight which "tended blindly in the same direction" as his own investigations into the formal apriori structures of thought (and therefore of judgment, and therefore of language). Husserl, however, takes the apriori in a sense which is closer to Kant than to Descartes, namely, as those conditions necessary and sufficient for a given structure of experience to be formally determinable as such. Reason is capable of accomplishing a complete investigation of *its own sense,* not only as a *de facto* ability, but in its essentially necessary structural forms; and it is in the elaboration of these necessary structural forms that it discovers the ultimate "formal apriori in the most fundamental sense" (*FTL,* p. 30), namely, the formal apriori of reason itself. The means for the elaboration of the ultimate structures of reason are found noematically in the structures of judgment and, thus, of language. But there is here no investigation into some transempirical *source* of experience or *ability* conceived as being temporally prior to experience; it is rather the present, logical explication of what this experience essentially means. For Husserl's relation to Kant in this regard see Gurwitsch, *The Field of Consciousness,* p. 197. See also Bachelard, *A Study,* pp. lvii–lix. In short, rather than take "apriori" to mean, as Chomsky supposes, some physiological or psychological (he has called it both "biological" and "mentalistic") mechanism hidden deep in the human organism, it may be possible to give the aprioris of language a "transcendental" explanation. That Chomsky himself would not accept this transformation of the "innate" into the "transcendental" is unimportant so long as it can be theoretically justified. And that is what we believe to be not only possible but necessary.

38. Noam Chomsky, *Language and Mind,* enlarged edition (New York, 1972), pp. 175, 180 and *passim.*

39. Cf. Husserl's discussions of Spencer and "species relativism" in chapter five of the *Prolegomena* to the *Logical Investi-*

gations as well as in chapter one, paragraph five, of the *First Investigation*.

40. Noam Chomsky, *Aspects of the Theory of Syntax* (Cambridge, Mass., 1965), pp. 16–17.

41. Noam Chomsky, *Current Issues in Linguistic Theory* (The Hague, 1967), p. 9, and *Language and Mind* (New York, 1972), p. 37.

42. "The inability of surface structure to indicate semantically significant grammatical relations (i.e., to serve as a deep structure) is one fundamental fact that motivated the development of transformational generative grammar, in both its classical and modern varieties" (Noam Chomsky, "Topics in the Theory of Generative Grammar," in *Current Trends in Linguistics*, ed. Thomas A. Sebeok [The Hague, 1966], III, 8). Bertrand Russell has of course distinguished logical form from grammatical form within "philosophical grammar" ("The Philosophy of Logical Atomism," in *Logic and Knowledge, Essays 1901–1950*, ed. R. Marsh [London, 1956], pp. 175–282), and Wittgenstein distinguished "deep grammar" from "surface grammar" (*Philosophical Investigations* [Oxford, 1953], p. 168) as structures of natural language—not, therefore, in the sense of Carnap. Whether these can be properly related to the sense in which Husserl and Chomsky make this distinction requires much more thorough study.

43. Noam Chomsky, *Cartesian Linguistics* (New York, 1966), pp. 59–60.

44. Chomsky, *Aspects of the Theory of Syntax*, p. 30.

45. Ibid., p. 117.

46. Ibid., p. 18.

47. Ibid., p. 33.

48. Ibid., pp. 58–59.

49. *Ideen I*, chapter one.

50. Cf. Maurice Merleau-Ponty, "Phenomenology and the Sciences of Man," in *The Primacy of Perception and Other Essays*, ed. James M. Edie (Evanston, 1964), pp. 51ff., 56ff., and 66–73. This seems to me to be one of the best and most suggestive discussions of the method of eidetic intuition and its relation to "inductive procedures" which has yet been written. Merleau-Ponty points out that even in the empirical sciences, insofar as they formulate general laws, one instance is frequently sufficient to demonstrate the law. See also Gurwitsch, *The Field of Consciousness*, pp. 194–197.

51. Chomsky, *Aspects of the Theory of Syntax*, p. 209.

52. Chomsky, *Cartesian Linguistics*, pp. 59–60.

53. *FTL*, p. 52.

54. *FTL*, p. 79, and Bachelard, *A Study*, pp. 34 and 77.

55. *FTL*, p. 53.

56. We here touch a point of great importance for Husserl's phenomenology as a whole: it is through the intermediary of the operation of nominalization that we can establish the interrelation between apophantics (which studies the categories of signification) and formal ontology (which studies the categories of objects), or, we might say, between "logic" and "metaphysics." See Bachelard, *A Study*, p. 34. In *Ideen I*, p. 249, Husserl writes: "Thought of as determined exclusively by the pure forms, the concepts that have originated from 'nominalization' are formal categorial variants of the idea of any objectivity whatever and furnish the fundamental conceptual material of formal ontology. . . . This . . . is decisively important for the understanding of the relationship between formal logic, as a logic of the apophansis, and the all-embracing formal ontology" (*FTL*, p. 79).

57. *FTL*, p. 310.

58. See de Muralt, *L'Idée*, p. 136, and Mohanty, *Edmund Husserl's Theory of Meaning*, pp. 112–113.

59. Chomsky, *Cartesian Linguistics*, pp. 33–35. See also *Language and Mind*, pp. 29ff., where Chomsky discusses the same structures, giving them a more formal presentation.

60. G. Benjamin Oliver, "The Ontological Structure of Linguistic Theory," *The Monist*, LIII (1969), 270. The principal reference to Chomsky is *Aspects of the Theory of Syntax*, pp. 106ff. I would also like to express here my indebtedness to Oliver's unpublished dissertation, "The Relevance of Linguistic Theory to Philosophy: A Study of Transformational Theory," Northwestern University, 1967, pp. 24ff.

61. One might well qualify this sentence by saying: "perhaps even too explicit." Professor Oliver has developed some serious criticisms of this aspect of transformational theory based on the "ontological" claims which it apparently makes and which, he argues, cannot be properly substantiated. I limit myself here to calling attention to the *kind* of conditions on sentences which transformational grammar might be able to justify; I certainly do not mean to endorse, at this stage of contemporary linguistic theory, any of the details of that theory. The general point I am making would remain valid if it can be shown that there is necessarily *some* categorial relativity of verb phrases to noun phrases, whatever the precise rules of cate-

gorization and subcategorization which govern this relationship may turn out to be.

62. Maurice Merleau-Ponty, "On the Phenomenology of Language," *Signs*, tr. Richard C. McCleary (Evanston, 1964), pp. 83ff. Merleau-Ponty's criticism of the notion of pure logical grammar goes far beyond reflections on the diachronic development of language, and this is only a small part of his own theory; I intend to deal with Merleau-Ponty's criticism of Husserl in greater detail in the next chapter.

63. Charles F. Hockett, *The State of the Art* (The Hague, 1968), pp. 60ff. As for Merleau-Ponty against Husserl, this argument against Chomsky on the part of Hockett is only a part of a much broader discussion. For almost ten years the structural linguists have been more or less silent in the face of Chomsky's onslaught; they will again be able to take heart behind Hockett's well-articulated counterattack, and it is to be hoped that the debate which is now opening within linguistics will be of great interest and instruction to philosophers concerned with the nature and structure of language.

64. One excellent example of this kind of argument is provided by Johannes Lohmann, "M. Heidegger's 'Ontologische Differenz' und die Sprache," *Lexis*, I (1948), 49–106. Needless to say, we do not at all agree to the validity of such an approach but we cite it to show how many of the phenomenologists, particularly those with "existentialist" leanings, would side with the empiricists and nominalists against the eidetic apriorism of a Husserl.

65. *LU*, pp. 319–320, *ET*, pp. 493–494. Cf. André de Muralt, *L'Idée*, p. 138.

III. Merleau-Ponty's Structuralism

1. Merleau-Ponty made four major attempts to explain Husserl's conception of "rational grammar," and to show that Husserl abandoned, in his later writings, his early proposal for an eidetics of grammar: namely, in (1) the section on "linguistics" in "Les sciences de l'homme et la phénoménologie" (Cours de Sorbonne) (Paris: Centre de Documentation Universitaire, 1951), English translation, "Phenomenology and the Sciences of Man," in *The Primacy of Perception and Other Essays*, ed. by James M. Edie (Evanston: Northwestern University Press, 1964), 78–85, (2) "Sur la phénoménologie du langage," in *Problèmes actuels de la phénoménologie* (Paris, 1952), English translation, "On the Phenomenology of Language," by Richard C. McCleary, in *Signs* (Evanston: Northwestern University

Press, 1964), 84–97, (3) "Le philosophe et la sociologie," *Cahiers internationaux de sociologie* (1951), English translation, "The Philosopher and Sociology," in *Signs*, 98–113, and (4) *La prose du monde* (Paris: Gallimard, 1969), 37ff. I consider this attempt on the part of Merleau-Ponty to "push Husserl further than he wanted to go himself" (Cf. *The Primacy of Perception*, p. 72, for a similar admission) to be not only historically unsound, given the fact that there is no evidence whatever that Husserl ever abandoned his early views on logical and universal grammatical invariants, but also phenomenologically misguided. It is interesting to note, moreover, that even devotees of Husserl's logical works, and particularly of *Formal and Transcendental Logic*, such as Suzanne Bachelard, who translated this work into French and wrote a commentary on it, regard Husserl's attempt to "revive the debate over the possibility of a general and reasoned grammar" as highly dubious. Cf. Suzanne Bachelard, *A Study of Husserl's Formal and Transcendental Logic* (Evanston: Northwestern University Press, 1969), p. 6. It can thus hardly be claimed that it is Merleau-Ponty's "existentialism" alone that is the explanation of his opposition to Husserl in this regard since no philosopher is less tainted by existentialism than Miss Bachelard.

2. Note that Wittgenstein was also quite innocent of scientific linguistics, though in his discovery of the algorithmic structure of the kind of linguistic rules that always "permit us to go on" and thus give language its structured and yet open-ended and innovative potentialities he employed ideas that are fundamental to structuralism insofar as these apply to language.

3. A number of "phenomenologists" have taken up their cudgels, such as Sartre in a special issue of *L'Arc* (Paris, 1966), 87ff. (where he argues that structuralism misunderstands the ontological dependence of *la langue* on *la parole* and ignores the historicity of language), and Mikel Dufrenne in *Pour l'homme* (Paris, 1968), which is a critical analysis of each of the several versions of structuralism currently in vogue in France. Paul Ricoeur has also criticized structuralism in the manner one would expect from a phenomenologist and a philosopher of the *cogito*, first in a special issue of *Esprit* dedicated to this debate, "Structure et hermeneutique," *Esprit* (1963), 593–653, and then in a more definitive article, "La structure, le mot, l'événement," *Esprit* (1967), 801–821; but in his most recent work he has attempted, more and more, to accommodate himself to the Structuralists and particularly to Claude Lévi-Strauss.

4. This is particularly true of Lacan and Lévi-Strauss, but is also true of Derrida and others.

5. *Phénoménologie de la perception* (Paris: Gallimard, 1945), English translation, *Phenomenology of Perception*, by Colin Smith (New York and London: Humanities Press, 1962), p. 188. I will note here for the record that though my quotations from Merleau-Ponty are taken from the English translations as a matter of principle, I have occasionally slightly corrected these translations when this was found necessary to give the exact nuance of the original French.

6. Ibid., 183, 186, 193–194.

7. Ferdinand de Saussure, *Cours de linguistique générale* (Paris: Payot, 1969), p. 145.

8. Maurice Merleau-Ponty, *Phenomenology of Perception*, tr. Colin Smith (New York: Humanities Press, 1962), pp. 178–179.

9. Ibid., pp. 187–188. Lest one be tempted to think that Merleau-Ponty may perhaps have disowned or mitigated his ideas on this score in his later writings, it is useful to cite a passage from his last work, *La prose du monde*, p. 161. "Nous avons plusieurs fois contesté que le langage ne fut lié à ce qu'il signifie que par l'habitude et la convention; il en est beaucoup plus proche et beaucoup plus éloigné. En un sens il tourne le dos à la signification, il ne s'en soucie pas. . . . Les phonologues ont admirablement vu cette vie sublinguistique dont toute l'industrie est de différencier et de mettre en système des signes, et cela n'est pas vrai seulement des phonèmes avant les mots, c'est vrai aussi des mots et de toute la langue, qui n'est pas d'abord signe de certains significations, mais pouvoir reglé de différencier la chaine verbale selon des dimensions caractéristiques de chaque langue. En un sens, le langage n'a jamais affaire qu'à lui-même: dans le monologue intérieur comme dans le dialogue il n'y a pas de 'pensées': ce sont des paroles que les paroles suscitent et, dans la mesure même ou nous 'pensons' plus pleinement, les paroles remplissent si exactement notre esprit qu'elles n'y laissent pas un coin vide pour des pensées pures et pour des significations qui ne soient pas langagières."

10. Alphonse De Waelhens, *Une philosophie de l'ambiguité: L'existentialisme de Maurice Merleau-Ponty* (Louvain, Publications de l'Université de Louvain, 1951), p. 159.

11. *Phenomenology of Perception*, p. 189.

12. *Phenomenology . . .*, p. 179.

13. *Phenomenology*, p. 179.

14. *La prose du monde*, ed. Claude Lefort (Paris: Gal-

limard, 1969), pp. 45, 161. English translation, *The Prose of the World*, tr. John O'Neill (Evanston: Northwestern University Press, 1973), pp. 31, 115. Please note that in citing this work we will refer to the English translation (*ET*) in our references but will generally keep our own translation from the original French.

15. "La Conscience et l'acquisition du langage," *Bulletin de Psychologie*, Paris, November 1964, pp. 226–259. English translation, *Consciousness and the Acquisition of Language*, tr. Hugh J. Silverman (Evanston: Northwestern University Press, 1973). Please note that here also, in citing this work, we will refer to the English translation (*ET*) in our references but will generally keep our own translation from the original French.

16. See for example the summary of recent empirical research in Ronald W. Langacker, *Language and Its Structure* (New York: Harcourt, Brace and World, 1968), p. 14 and *passim*.

17. Noam Chomsky, *Language and Mind*, enlarged edition (New York: Harcourt, 1972), p. 10. "Language is a species-specific human possession, and even at low levels of intelligence, at pathological levels, we find a command of language that is totally unattainable by an ape that may, in other respects, surpass a human imbecile in problem-solving ability and other adaptive behavior."

18. See Langacker, *Language and Its Structure*, p. 142: "The fact that we vocalize in a highly systematic and coordinated manner, while they [the higher primates] do not, must therefore be attributed to neurological factors rather than to gross anatomical differences." This conclusion may be in need of refinement. I am indebted to Noam Chomsky for pointing out to me in a private communication that recent research (by Kelemen and Lieberman) indicates that the evolution of the peripheral physiological structures used in human speech may have taken place quite late and thus could be specific to man and his unique language capacity.

19. "La Conscience," pp. 226–259. This is the single most important study, but one finds parallel passages in the chapter on "The Body as Expression, and Speech" in *Phenomenology of Perception*, pp. 174–199; in the chapter "On the Phenomenology of Language" in *Signs*, pp. 84–97; and in the section on "Linguistics" in *The Primacy of Perception*, pp. 78–85.

20. "La Conscience," p. 255, *ET*, p. 90. Cf. *Phenomenology of Perception*, p. 185: "I do not understand the gestures of others by some act of intellectual interpretation; communication be-

tween consciousnesses is not based on the common meaning of their respective experiences, for it is equally the basis of that meaning. The act by which I lend myself to the spectacle must be recognized as irreducible to anything else. I join it in a kind of *blind recognition* which precedes the intellectual working out and clarification of the meaning" (italics added).

21. "La Conscience," pp. 230ff., *ET*, pp. 15ff. Merleau-Ponty suggests that certain aspects of interior monologues in adults, the nonformulated thoughts that precede and surround speech, are a continuation of this original babbling. William James has an interesting section on a similar phenomenon in his *Principles of Psychology:* "We think it odd that young children should listen with such rapt attention to the reading of stories expressed in words half of which they do not understand, and of none of which they ask the meaning. But their thinking is in form just what ours is when it is rapid. Both of us make flying leaps over large portions of sentences uttered and we give attention only to substantive starting points, turning points, and conclusions here and there. All the rest, 'substantive' and separately intelligible as it may *potentially* be, actually serves only as so much transitive material. It is *internodal* consciousness, giving us a sense of continuity, but having no significance apart from its mere gap-filling function. The children probably feel no gap when through a lot of unintelligible words they are swiftly carried to a familiar and intelligible terminus" (I, 264–265).

22. Merleau-Ponty, *Signs,* p. 88. See also the essay on "The Child's Relations with Others," in *The Primacy of Perception,* esp. p. 99.

23. Merleau-Ponty, *Phenomenology of Perception:* "Spoken or written words carry a . . . coating of meaning which sticks to them and which presents the thought as a style, an affective value, a piece of existential mimicry, rather than as a conceptual statement. We find here, beneath the conceptual meaning of words, an existential meaning which is not only rendered by them, but which inhabits them, and is inseparable from them" (p. 182). "The link between the word and its living meaning is not an external link of association, the meaning inhabits the word. . . . We are therefore led to recognize a gestural or existential significance in speech. . . . The human body is defined in terms of its property of appropriating, in an indefinite series of discontinuous acts, significant cores which transcend and transfigure its natural powers" (p. 193).

24. The most important of these essays are the following:

(1) *Langage et communication* [1948], Cours de l'Université de Lyon, unpublished. Cf. also the unpublished lectures on Saussure at the Ecole Normale Supérieure in 1948–49, mentioned in the "Translator's Preface" to *Consciousness and the Acquisition of Language,* by Hugh J. Silverman, p. xxxvi. One of the principal values of this "Preface" is its discussion of all of Merleau-Ponty's unpublished courses. (2) "Consciousness and the Acquisition of Language" [1949], see above, chapter three, note 15. (3) "Phenomenology and the Sciences of Man" [1951], English translation in *The Primacy of Perception and Other Essays,* ed. James M. Edie (Evanston: Northwestern University Press, 1964) pp. 43–95. (4) "On the Phenomenology of Language" [1951], English translation in *Signs,* pp. 84–97. (5) "The Philosopher and Sociology" [1951], English translation in *Signs,* pp. 98–113. (6) "Indirect Language and the Voices of Silence" [1952], English translation in *Signs,* pp. 39–83. (7) "An Unpublished Text by Maurice Merleau-Ponty: A Prospectus of His Work" [1953], English translation in *Primacy of Perception,* pp. 3–11. This is the prospectus of his work which Merleau-Ponty presented to the Collège de France as a candidate for a professorship of philosophy there; it gives an historical outline of the development of his thought and shows how he himself interpreted his growing interest in language and the place of his philosophy of language in his work as a whole (8) *In Praise of Philosophy* [1953]. His inaugural address at the Collège de France. (9) "The Sensible World and the World of Expression" [1953], his first course at the Collège de France, English translation in *Themes from the Lectures at the Collège de France, 1952–1960,* tr. John O'Neill (Evanston: Northwestern University Press, 1970), pp. 3–11. (10) "Studies in the Literary Use of Language" [1953], English tr. in *Themes,* pp. 12–18. (11) "The Problem of Speech" [1954], English tr. in *Themes,* pp. 19–26. (12) "From Mauss to Claude Lévi-Strauss" [1959], English tr. in *Signs,* pp. 114–125.

25. These are the first lines of Merleau-Ponty's famous article "On the Phenomenology of Language," which is included in *Signs,* tr. Richard C. McCleary (Evanston: Northwestern University Press, 1964), p. 84. This is, however, my own translation of Merleau-Ponty's words; emphasis mine.

26. Maurice Merleau-Ponty, *In Praise of Philosophy,* tr. James M. Edie and John Wild (Evanston: Northwestern University Press, 1963), pp. 54–55. These statements in Merleau-Ponty's inaugural address of 1953 are in striking contrast with his earlier statements in *Humanism and Terror* (tr. John

O'Neill, Boston: Beacon Press, 1969) in an essay written in 1946, "The Yogi and the Proletarian," that Marxism is not just one philosophy of history but is *the* philosophy of history. Cf. *Humanism and Terror*, p. 153. Merleau-Ponty's development toward structuralism in the period between this essay (1946) and his course on "Consciousness and the Acquisition of Language" (1949) brought a profound development and reinterpretation of his early work, a reinterpretation which has not been sufficiently noted by his commentators. This is a theme to which he frequently returns in his later writings, such as in *La prose du monde* (Paris, 1969), pp. 33ff.: "Saussure a l'immense mérite d'accomplir la démarche qui libère l'histoire de l'historicisme et rend possible une nouvelle conception de la raison. Si chaque mot, chaque forme d'une langue, pris separément, reçoive au cours de son histoire une série de significations discordantes, il n'y a pas d'équivoque dans la langue totale considerée en chacun de ses moments. Les mutations de chaque appareil signifiant, si inattendues qu'elles paraissent à le considerer tout seul, sont solidaires de celles de tous les autres et cela fait que l'ensemble reste moyen d'une communication." Whether Saussure really *deserves* (or would himself have accepted) the role Merleau-Ponty assigns him is, of course, another matter. At least one commentator, in an article criticizing Merleau-Ponty's over-optimistic interpretation of Saussure, doubts this. Cf. Maurice Lagueux, "Merleau-Ponty et la linguistique de Saussure," *Dialogue* (1965), 351–364.

27. In the essay entitled "The Primacy of Perception and its Philosophical Consequences," which was a presentation of the central argument of the *Phenomenology of Perception* to the Société française de philosophie on November 23, 1946. See *The Primacy of Perception*, ed. James M. Edie (Evanston: Northwestern University Press, 1964), pp. 12ff.

28. From "An Unpublished Text by Maurice Merleau-Ponty: A Prospectus of His Work," in *The Primacy of Perception*, p. 11. This is the English translation of the program which Merleau-Ponty submitted to the professors of the Collège de France in presenting his candidacy for his chair of philosophy in 1952.

29. See the "Avertissement" by Claude Lefort to Maurice Merleau-Ponty, *La prose du monde* (Paris, 1969), pp. i, ix–xi, *ET*, pp. xi, xvii–xxi.

30. *The Primacy of Perception*, p. 20.

31. Ibid., p. 19.

32. Ibid., p. 20.

33. Ibid., p. 22.

34. Ibid., p. 17.

35. *Phenomenology of Perception*, tr. Colin Smith (New York: Humanities Press, 1962), pp. 414–439.

36. *The Primacy of Perception*, p. 25.

37. *Phenemonology of Perception*, p. 394, italics mine.

38. From "An Unpublished Text . . . ," *The Primacy of Perception*, p. 6.

39. *The Primacy of Perception*, p. 17.

40. From "An Unpublished Text . . . ," *The Primacy of Perception*, p. 6.

41. Ibid., p. 10.

42. Ibid., italics mine.

43. *La prose du monde*, p. 56, *ET*, pp. 39–40.

44. F. P. Ramsey, *The Foundations of Mathematics*, pp. 115–116, as quoted by Renford Bambrough in "Universals and Family Resemblances," in *Wittgenstein*, ed. George Pitcher (New York: Doubleday, 1966), p. 198. I am indebted to Margaret Urban Coyne for first pointing out and explaining Ramsey's maxim to me.

45. *The Primacy of Perception*, p. 20; *Phenomenology of Perception*, p. 386.

46. *Phenomenology of Perception*, p. 396.

47. Ibid., p. 385. I am indebted to the graduate students who took my Merleau-Ponty seminar in 1972 for several important insights into the problems being discussed here, in particular Margaret Urban Coyne and Harrison Hall.

48. Ibid., pp. 386, 388, italics mine.

49. I am using this term in a very vague sense and am not taking sides for or against Kant, who would say that the apriori is what consciousness has put into things, or a philosopher of language like Garver, who would say that the apriori is a "grammatical" matter (See Newton Garver, "Analyticity and Grammar," *The Monist*, 51, 1967, pp. 397ff). I am very sympathetic to the latter approach so long as by "grammar" one understands the whole of linguistic usage, and with the proviso that the relation of thinking to using language be understood in the manner in which Husserl understands it in *Formal and Transcendental Logic*. This is obviously not the place to go into these difficult problems. I am using "linguistic" in this context as a synonym for "thought."

50. See chapter three, note 26 above.

51. Particularly in "On the Phenomenology of Language" (1951) in *Signs*, tr. Richard C. McCleary (Evanston: Northwestern University Press, 1964), pp. 84–97, "Indirect Lan-

guage and the Voices of Silence" (1951), in *Signs,* pp. 39–83, in the completed sections of *La prose du monde,* and in several of his courses at the Collège de France (the outlines of which are published in *Themes from the Lectures at the Collège de France* 1952–1960, tr. John O'Neill [Evanston: Northwestern University Press, 1970]).

52. *Phenomenology of Perception,* pp. 184, 189.

53. These are the "final pages" *we* have; they were not the end he himself planned for this uncompleted book.

54. *The Visible and the Invisible,* tr. Alphonso Lingis (Evanston: Northwestern University Press, 1968), pp. 131–133, italics mine.

55. In an interesting article we mentioned in note 26, Maurice Lagueux accuses Merleau-Ponty of misrepresenting Saussure on at least two points, namely by claiming falsely that Saussure gave the primacy to *la parole* over *la langue* in his study of language and, further, by stating in his article "On the Phenomenology of Language" that Saussure distinguished "a synchronic linguistics of speech" from "a diachronic linguistics of language" (see *Signs,* 86). The fact is, as Lagueux shows, that both *synchrony* and *diachrony* are aspects of *la langue,* whereas the study of *la parole* falls completely outside a scientific study of language. While it is difficult not to accept Lagueux's verdict, it is nevertheless true that many of Saussure's own texts are ambiguous and the account Merleau-Ponty gives in *La prose du monde* (pp. 33ff), for instance, would meet most if not all of Lagueux's criticisms and would give us solid ground for holding that even though Merleau-Ponty sometimes, even frequently, quotes Saussure very freely, he does not seriously misunderstand his intent. The essential point is that one must distinguish a science of the given state of a linguistic system (*la langue*), which Saussure calls "synchronic linguistics," from the historical science of the linguistic changes that any given language has undergone, which Saussure calls "diachronic linguistics." Now clearly the object with which diachronic linguistics deals is something that can *only* be studied "objectively" and in which present, ongoing human experience can play no essential role. But, conversely, the object of synchronic linguistics, though it is the "form" or "system" of the present state of a given language and not the speech-act itself, is nevertheless nothing other than the presently given, incubating and changing structure of the sum total of all presently recognized acts of speaking that take place within a given community, and it is nothing but the description of the structure of these acts. Moreover, since

each historical state that can be distinguished in the diachronic study of a given language was at one time a living, future-directed, synchronic system, we can see the sense in which "a synchronic linguistics of speech" envelops and takes precedence over "a diachronic linguistics of language." Once one fully understands why Merleau-Ponty speaks this way and what he means by the terms one will see that he is not opposed to Saussure in any essential respect.

56. Ferdinand de Saussure, *Cours de linguistique générale* (Paris: Payot, 1922), pp. 30, 36–39. It is interesting to note that, until most recently, the analytical philosophy of language, as it developed from Moore to Russell, through Wittgenstein, and as it has lately culminated in "Oxford philosophy," takes just the opposite approach. There, it is the "speech-act" that is central focus of attention and very few of the important philosophers in this group have shown any special interest in linguistic structuralism or, indeed, in scientific linguistics at all until very recently. Merleau-Ponty is apparently the first philosopher of any great influence to have attempted an assessment of the importance of linguistics for the philosophy of language, but it is noteworthy that he also gives the primacy to *la parole,* or the speech-act.

57. *Signs,* 117.

58. *Signs,* 39.

59. *Themes from the Lectures at the Collège de France,* 19–20. The thesis that the "meaning" of words is as much in the interstices between them, in what is *not said,* in the silence that surrounds speech, is one that Merleau-Ponty develops primarily in his later writings and above all in *The Visible and the Invisible.* This is particularly important for a theory of literature.

60. Saussure, *Cours,* p. 99. Lagueux states, on p. 356 of the article cited in note 26, that Merleau-Ponty sometimes writes as if Saussure himself had questioned the arbitrary and conventional character of the relationship between the "acoustic image" (*signifiant*) and its associated "concept" (*signifié*), and it is therefore necessary to point out that it is not Saussure but Merleau-Ponty who gives this interpretation to his notion of the "sign." Nevertheless, it seems clear that Saussure did indeed think of the "sign" as containing, indissolubly, the two aspects of sound *and* meaning.

61. Saussure, *Cours,* p. 116.

62. Cf. "La conscience et l'acquisition du langage," *Bulletin de Psychologie,* 226–259, esp. 255ff.; *Signs,* 91; *Themes from*

the *Lectures at the Collège de France*, 13–15; *The Visible and the Invisible*, pp. 124–125; *La prose du monde*, pp. 13–15.

63. Cf. Alphonse De Waelhens, "La philosophie du langage selon M. Merleau-Ponty," in *Existence et Signification* (Louvain, 1958), 135.

64. "Each word *has* a meaning only insofar as it is sustained in this meaning-function by all the others. . . . For a word to keep its sense it has to be held in place by all the others." ("La conscience et l'acquisition du langage," 256). *ET*, p. 92.

65. Noam Chomsky, *Language and Mind*, p. 20.

66. *La prose du monde*, pp. 37ff., 166ff., *ET*, pp. 25ff., 118ff.

67. *Signs*, p. 87.

68. Ibid.

69. *Phenomenology of Perception*, p. 188.

70. *Signs*, p. 119.

71. *Phenomenology of Perception*, p. 189.

72. *Signs*, p. 87.

73. *La prose du monde*, p. 56, *ET*, p. 39.

74. *La prose du monde*, p. 56, *ET*, pp. 39–40.

75. *Signs*, pp. 118–120, emphasis mine.

76. *The Visible and the Invisible*, p. 116.

77. *Signs*, p. 119.

78. *The Visible and the Invisible*, p. 116. Cf. *The Primacy of Perception and Other Essays*, p. 68.

79. *The Primacy of Perception*, p. 70.

80. *Signs*, pp. 105, 107, 109–111, emphasis mine.

81. *The Primacy. . . ,* p. 53. It would be interesting to compare the phenomenological method of eidetic intuition (*Wesenschau*), which falls somewhere between an aprioristic method of deduction and a pure empiricism of induction, with C. S. Peirce's theory of *abduction*. Peirce also saw clearly that creative scientific thinking is not a matter of pure induction but involves some kind of rational intuition into the facts that is provided not by the facts themselves but by the "guessing instinct" of the subject, which enables him "to put a limit on admissible hypotheses" and to construct a general law that will cover all the facts of a certain category on the basis of a very small number of instances, and even frequently on the basis of a single instance. See C. S. Peirce, "The Logic of Abduction," in *Peirce's Essays in the Philosophy of Science*, ed. by Vincent Tomas (New York, 1957). It is interesting that Noam Chomsky (*Language and Mind*, pp. 78ff.), who is unacquainted with

phenomenology in any of its forms but who feels the need to discover the method by which a child, for instance, learns a language on the basis of a "knowledge" that extends, from the beginning stages, enormously beyond his actual experience and even enables him to recognize much of the data of his actual experience as defective and deviant, suggests that a theory of abduction might serve this purpose.

IV. The Levels of Meaning in Language

1. The principal defect of structural linguistics is its denigration of syntax and universal grammatical structures independent of the various phonological systems of natural languages and its ignorance of "deep structures" even when these apply to phonology itself; in Merleau-Ponty this becomes blindness to the significance of Husserl's contributions to "pure logical grammar" and his unconscionable attempt to interpret the later Husserl as having abandoned this program.

2. Merleau-Ponty, *Signs*, p. 91. See also *Phenomenology of Perception*, p. 194: "We must therefore recognize as an ultimate fact this open and indefinite power of giving significance . . . by which man transcends himself towards a new form of behavior, or towards other people, or towards his own thought, through his body and his speech." See also Chomsky, *Language and Mind*, p. 18, with reference to the romanticist definition of language as that which makes infinite use of finite means (Humboldt), and the following citation from the Port-Royal *Grammar*, which calls language "that marvellous invention by which we construct from twenty-five or thirty sounds an infinity of expressions, which, having no resemblance in themselves to what takes place in our minds, still enable us to let others know the secret of what we conceive and of all the various mental activities that we carry out."

3. I do not mean, of course, that this is the only, or even the primary, way in which the categorematic/syncategorematic distinction is to be understood, but that this gives a first idea of the "immanent" functions of words within language itself. See note 33 below.

4. Cf. Ronald W. Langacker, *Language and Its Structure* (New York, 1967), pp. 71ff., my example.

5. Cf. Noam Chomsky, *Cartesian Linguistics* (New York, 1966), p. 41.

6. Langacker, *Language and Its Structures, loc. cit.*

7. Maurice Merleau-Ponty, "La conscience et l'acquisition du langage," *Bulletin de Psychologie*, November 1965, p. 256,

ET, p. 92. I am certainly not suggesting, as Gilbert Ryle has, that *all* words are *only* syncategorematic expressions ("Meaning and Necessity," *Philosophy*, 1949, p. 71), but only that something of the "immanent" meaning—a holding within the system—which is an exclusive characteristic of syncategorematic words, is to be found in a less exclusive way in all words.

8. I believe that Merleau-Ponty is mistaken in this, and that the existence of phonological meaning does not in any way inhibit natural languages from realizing within themselves universal grammatical structures of the kind spoken of by Husserl and now the object of investigation by transformational grammarians. Chomsky argues, it seems to me on sound bases, that even the more general and abstract rules of phonetics lead one to suppose that there may be universal structures common to all languages even here. Cf. Noam Chomsky, *Language and Mind* (New York, 1968), pp. 40ff.

9. Ordinary language "is never composed of absolutely univocal meanings which can be made completely explicit beneath the gaze of transparent constituting consciousness. It will be a question not of a system of forms of signification clearly articulated in terms of one another—not a structure of linguistic ideas built according to a strict plan—but of a cohesive whole of convergent linguistic gestures, each of which will *be defined less by a signification than a use value* (*valeur d'emploi*)." Maurice Merleau-Ponty, *Signs*, p. 87, italics mine.

10. Merleau-Ponty, "La conscience. . . ," pp. 229ff., *ET*, pp. 13ff.

11. Cf. Norman O. Brown, *Life Against Death* (New York, 1959), p. 72, and Merleau-Ponty, "La conscience. . . . ," p. 252: "The original form of language would thus be a kind of chant. Men would have sung their feelings before communicating their thoughts. Just as writing was originally painting, language was first a chant which, through later analysis, became a linguistic sign; it was through this original singing that men discovered their power of expression." *ET*, p. 81.

12. Merleau-Ponty, *Phenomenology of Perception*, p. 193. Cf. chapter three, note 23, above.

13. Merleau-Ponty, *Phenomenology of Perception*, p. 179.

14. Merleau-Ponty, *Signs*, p. 88, my italics.

15. Merleau-Ponty, *Phenomenology of Perception*, p. 182. Merleau-Ponty's emphasis on the "gestural" content of meaning even within verbal expressions, with its musical ability to transmit meaning directly and beneath the level of either the conceptual content which words enable us to think or the things

in the world to which they refer, is a precursor not only of
present-day proponents of body language and the "rhetoric" of
sit-ins, lie-ins, love-ins, marches, etc., but also of such the-
oreticians of the theater as Jerzy Grotowski and Antonin Artaud.
No other philosopher could so well justify the attitude toward
language in contemporary experimental theater in which many
plays do without sentences at all, though they use sounds,
words, and other acoustic effects to transmit meaning directly
and for the most part nonlinguistically even though they may
be using words (but not sentences) of some known language.
Cf. Antonin Artaud, *The Theater and its Double* (New York:
Grove, 1958), pp. 71, 75, and *passim*. Note also the phenomenon that domesticated animals, particularly dogs, are able to
respond to whatever language may be addressed to them; this
is not because they are polyglot but because they respond to the
expressive values of intonation rather than to the meant content
of the words and sentences we speak to them. I get exactly the
same results in speaking in English to "French" or "German"
dogs that I do speaking to "American" or "British" dogs.

16. Merleau-Ponty, "La conscience . . . ," p. 253, *ET*, p. 86.

17. Ibid., p. 242, *ET*, p. 50.

18. Husserl treats of the distinction between sense and reference especially in the First, Fifth, and Sixth Investigations of
the *Logische Untersuchungen;* for Frege see, principally, "On
Sense and Reference," in *Translations from the Philosophical
Writings of Gottlob Frege*, eds. Peter Geach and Max Black
(Oxford: Blackwell, 1960), pp. 56ff. Frege referred to "meaning" as *Sinn* and its "reference" as *Bedeutung*. Since the words
Sinn and *Bedeutung* have the same meaning in ordinary German, Husserl took them as synonymous and uses them to express "meaning"; he used terms like *Gegenstand, Objekt*, and
Erfüllung to express "reference." Cf. chapter one, note 9 above.

19. Paul Ricoeur, "La structure, le mot, l'événement," first
published in *Esprit*, May 1967, was republished in *Man and
World*, February 1968, pp. 10–30, and *Philosophy Today*, Sum-
mer 1968, pp. 114–129.

20. Cf. Merleau-Ponty, "La Conscience. . . ," pp. 230ff., *ET*,
p. 16.

21. "As a matter of fact, it has not been sufficiently observed
that a work of the mind is by nature *allusive*. Even if the author's aim is to give the fullest possible representation of his
object, there is never any question as to whether he is telling
everything. He knows far more than he tells. This is so because
language is elliptical. If I want to let my neighbor know that a

wasp has gotten in by the window, there is no need for a long speech. 'Watch out!' or 'Hey'—a word is enough, a gesture. . . ." Jean-Paul Sartre, *What is Literature?* tr. Bernard Frechtman (New York: Harper, 1965), p. 62.

22. "Dans le dictionnaire, il y a seulement la ronde sans fin des termes qui se définissent en cercle, qui tournoient dans la clôture du lexique. Mais, voici: quelqu'un parle, quelqu'un dit quelque chose; le mot sort du dictionnaire; il devient mot au moment où l'homme devient parole, où la parole devient discours et le discours phrase." Ricoeur, "La structure," p. 25.

23. ". . . it often happens that we find ourselves knowing something which we have learnt by means of words without being able to remember a single one of the words which conveyed it to us." Jean-Paul Sartre, *What is Literature?* p. 14 [but I have used the superior translation found in Anthony Manser, *Sartre, A Philosophic Study* (New York: Oxford University Press, 1966), p. 106]. And: ". . . the important thing about a train of thought is its conclusion. That is the meaning, or, as we say, the topic of the thought. That is what abides when all its other members have faded from memory. Usually this conclusion is a word or phrase. . . . The parts of the stream that precede these substantive conclusions are but the means of the latter's attainment. . . . The relative unimportance of the means appears from the fact that when the conclusion is there, we have always forgotten most of the steps preceding its attainment. When we have uttered a proposition, we are rarely able a moment afterwards to recall our exact words, though we can express it in different words easily enough. The practical upshot of a book we read remains with us, though we may not recall one of its sentences." William James, *The Principles of Psychology* (New York: Dover, 1950), I, 260. Just as "the absence of a sign is a sign" on the morphological level (see Merleau-Ponty, "La conscience . . . ," p. 253, *ET*, p. 85), so too with words: the absence of a word can be felt as a meaningful gap in our thought. "Suppose we try to recall a forgotten name. The state of our consciousness is peculiar. There is a gap therein; but no mere gap. It is a gap that is intensely active. . . . If wrong names are proposed to us, this singularly definite gap acts immediately so as to negate them. . . . And the gap of one word does not feel like the gap of another . . . the feeling of an absence is *toto caelo* other than the absence of a feeling. . . . The rhythm of a lost word may be there without a sound to clothe it. . . ." William James, *Principles of Psychology*, pp. 251–252.

24. Erich Fromm, *Zen Buddhism and Psychoanalysis* (New

York: Harper, 1960), pp. 100ff. For the importance of syntax in translation and for illustration of how the syntactical forms of various languages may find equivalents in others—even though their morphologies may be very different—see: Roman Jakobson, "On Linguistic Aspects of Translation," in *On Translation*, ed. Reuben A. Brower (Cambridge: Harvard University Press, 1959), pp. 232–239. However, even on the level of mere words, one should not too easily grant "untranslatibility," since any human experience ought, at least in principle, be made intelligible to any other member of the human species no matter how foreign his language. It is certainly a surprising phenomenon that there are *so many* languages and that so many variants and incubating changes are constantly producing more; but the work of translating one linguistic mode of expression into another can greatly enrich one's understanding even of his own mother tongue. John Hollander gives the example of German students preferring to read Norman Kemp Smith's translation of Kant's *Critique of Pure Reason* because this helped them as native speakers of German "neutralize certain stylistic elements of the original that they felt insignificant with respect to their philosophical concerns." John Hollander, "Versions, Interpretations and Performance" in *On Translation*, p. 214. And Walter Benjamin, in his introduction to the German translation of Baudelaire's *Tableaux Parisiens*, argued that the true problem of the translator was not to put Baudelaire into German but to put the German language into Baudelaire—and he believed that, at the limit, this goal could be achieved. Walter Benjamin, *Illuminations* (New York: Schocken, 1969), pp. 69–82.

25. Jean-Paul Sartre, *Being and Nothingness*, tr. Hazel Barnes (New York: The Philosophical Library, 1956), pp. 514–517.

26. Merleau-Ponty, *Signs*, p. 91.

27. Ricoeur skillfully uses the structural analysis of personal pronouns by Émile Benveniste to make this point. The important thing about the pronoun *I* is not that its reference each time it is used is unique but that language is so organized that it permits each speaker to appropriate it as a whole by designating himself as "I" when he speaks. The whole impersonal mass becomes his personal thought. By speaking in the first person I incorporate the whole system for my own purposes and make it say something from my point of view. Ricoeur, "La Structure," pp. 19–20. At this point Ricoeur was a good deal closer to Merleau-Ponty's theory of the speech-act than

he is in his most recent "structuralist" publications. Merleau-Ponty, in interpreting Saussure for his own purposes, argued (in his essay "On the Phenomenology of Language" and elsewhere) that the "diachronic linguistics of language" can be absorbed in a "synchronic linguistics of speech" and that it is the latter which generates the former in such a way that there seems to be a total ontological dependence of *la langue* on *la parole*. Paul Ricoeur, in his more recent writings, has become critical of this position inasmuch as this way of approaching the ideal linguistic structure formalized by the scientific linguist makes any sustained dialogue between Merleau-Ponty (or his followers) and contemporary linguistics impossible. (Cf. Ricoeur, *Le conflit des interpretations* [Paris: Seuil, 1969], pp. 244ff.) By claiming that the ideal system (*la langue*) is only an accident or by-product of the subjectively experienced acts of speakers, Ricoeur argues, Merleau-Ponty does not take the formal, algorithmic aspect of language, which he otherwise recognizes to exist, with sufficient seriousness. Merleau-Ponty's followers, on the other hand, could answer that he would be the last to exclude "structure" from experience since his very first book was on the "Structure of Behavior" and he made it his life's work to show the relationship between the impersonal structures of the "objective body" and the subjective, conscious structures of the "lived body"—which are not two different "bodies" but the very same body from two different perspectives, correlative, each given together, but one "actual" and the other the "virtual," "habitual," or "inert." It is clear, of course, that Merleau-Ponty accords ontological priority to the speech-act over the linguistic system itself. In this he is closer to the ordinary language philosophers than to scientific linguistics.

28. Noam Chomsky, *Current Issues in Linguistic Theory* (The Hague: Mouton, 1967), pp. 7–8.

29. As we should expect, since structural linguistics considers syntax a rather trivial matter, it made very little contribution to the study of syntactical structures. Cf. Noam Chomsky, *Language and Mind*, p. 20.

30. Cf. Noam Chomsky, *Aspects of the Theory of Syntax* (Cambridge, Mass.: M. I. T. Press, 1965), p. 163, where, at the end of the section on "The Boundaries of Syntax and Semantics," he concludes: "To conclude this highly inconclusive discussion, I shall simply point out that the syntactic and semantic structure of natural languages evidently offers many mysteries, both of fact and of principle, and that any attempt to delimit the boundaries of these domains must certainly be quite tentative."

31. Husserl discusses this primarily in the *Fourth Investigation* and in *Formal and Transcendental Logic,* section 13, and throughout. Cf. also Marvin Farber, *The Foundation of Phenomenology,* 2nd ed. (New York: Paine-Whitman, 1962), pp. 311ff., and Suzanne Bachelard, *A Study of Husserl's Logic,* tr. Lester Embree, (Evanston, Ill., 1968), pp. 3ff. and 131ff. The best introduction to Husserl's thought on this (and many other) subjects for the uninitiated is: Aron Gurwitsch, *The Field of Consciousness* (Pittsburgh, Duquesne University Press, 1964), pp. 195ff., 331ff.

32. It is for this reason that grammar and the rules of syntax are utterly unaffected by what we use them to say; grammar is essentially untouched by our actual use of words. We can invent new words and give old words new meanings, we can create meanings, without altering our syntax in the least. The number of new sentences we are capable of formulating is practically infinite, but the rules of grammar remain finite and invariant through long periods of historical time (cf. Chomsky, *Language and Mind,* p. 79). Since the move from the grammatical to the semantic is a *metabasis eis allo genos,* "transformational generative grammar" can provide an explanation of the conditions of necessity for the emergence of sense but no more than structural linguistics can it give a complete account of the experience of meaning.

33. This distinction, then, enables us to understand better than hitherto how certain words, like syncategorematic words, can have *only* syntactical meaning and remain unaffected by roles of context that material terms require when they are put within the formal grammatical structure provided by syntactical forms. At least as a hypothesis we could say that syncategorematic words are related in their meanings to categoremetic words as syntax is related to semantics; they have meaning only within the formal system and not by pointing beyond it to meanings transcendent to the system or to things. At the same time there is no doubt that they do have one level of *meaning,* limited to a function within the linguistic system, and that there is such a thing as a "concept" of *and,* of *but,* of *if,* of *etc.,* etc.

34. Let me point out an historical development which is altogether missed by most contemporary philosophers of language and that is that "methodologically" both phenomenologists and ordinary language philosophers are primarily concerned with the "speech-act" in the same highly idealized methodological fashion. They both presuppose the "ideal speaker." I have in mind, in particular, the most insightful and synthetic discus-

sion of what the "linguistic turn" may mean for the future of philosophy in Richard Rorty's "Introduction" to *The Linguistic Turn* (Chicago: University of Chicago Press, 1967). "One hears," he writes, "less and less in the current literature about 'dissolving problems' or 'giving analyses.' Instead, one finds claims to have discovered necessary truths about various sorts of entities (intentions, actions, sensation, thoughts, etc.), without any suggestion that these truths are deduced from analyses of statements about such entities . . ." (p. 30). But even when the analysis is devoted primarily to "statements about such entities," linguistic philosophy proceeds, like phenomenology, by the way of *example* rather than demonstration or deduction. It relies on observations that we say such and such but we do not say such and such, we ask whether . . . but we do not ask whether . . ., we usually say . . . but it would be odd to say . . ., and then proceeds to explicate the necessary implications of meaning behind the given use of words. This method, when one thinks of it, is not clearly different from the method of "free variation in imagination" proposed by Husserl in *Ideas* and in *Formal and Transcendental Logic* and employed explicitly from the *Logical Investigations* onward, a method which Husserl called the *Wesenschau* ("intuition of the essential"). Some authors seem to feel that one of the differences between analytical techniques and those of phenomenology is that the former *argues* but the latter, relying on intuition, only *shows*. But, when one examines the structure of "argument" in linguistic philosophy, one finds that it consists of varying a given expression in imagination, by looking for a limited number of well-chosen paradigm cases, which, when enumerated, show a logical or necessary truth about the given use of words. There is no *exhaustive* enumeration or *complete* demonstration. That would be otiose and unnecessary, precisely because one is looking for an "essential" truth about a given usage; when it is seen, through a finite number of examples—and, as in the verification of a scientific hypothesis, *one instance* is sometimes sufficient to establish the case—that the meaning of such and such is what it is and cannot be otherwise, the further multiplication of instances becomes redundant. Certainly the essential truth on the basis of the paradigms chosen does not become "more true" the more exhaustive the enumeration of instances; there comes a point when it is simply "seen" by any normal user of the language that this is what such and such an expression *means*, and that it cannot mean otherwise, that no appeal to future experience will affect it, and that, if one does not see this, he simply does not know the meaning of the phrase yet. The method of "free variation" used by Husserl to determine, for instance, the *essence* of a physical object in the phenomenology of perception is not different, except that, in this case, it is directed toward an object of experience rather than to a category of meaning. (Cf. Rorty, p. 21, with reference to Stanley Cavell's "Must We Mean What We Say?")

35. Émile Benveniste, *Problèmes de linguistique générale* (Paris: Gallimard, 1966), pp. 119ff.

36. See the extremely interesting article by Robert Franck, "Langue, discours et significations," *Revue philosophique de Louvain*, Vol. 67, 1969, pp. 306–321, which goes far beyond this brief analysis and criticism of Benveniste's chapter on "Les niveaux de l'analyse linguistique" in *Problèmes de linguistique générale*.

37. Jean-Paul Sartre, *What is Literature?* (New York: Harper & Row, 1965), p. 14. Cf. Anthony Manser, *Sartre: A Philosophic Study* (New York: Oxford University Press, 1967), p. 107.

38. Merleau-Ponty, *Phenomenology of Perception,* p. 186 (corrected).

39. Merleau-Ponty, *Primacy of Perception*, p. 30; *Phenomenology of Perception*, p. 104; *Signs*, p. 95.

40. See Merleau-Ponty's commentary on Husserl (*Formal and Transcendental Logic* and *Der Ursprung der Geometrie*) in *Signs*, pp. 84ff. William James has a very interesting discussion of the "intention to speak" in *Principles of Psychology* (New York: Dover Publications, 1950), I, 241ff. and esp. 253. Cf. Jean-Paul Sartre, *Being and Nothingness*, pp. 514ff.:

> For a long time psychologists have observed that the word is not the concrete element of speech—not even the word of the dialect or the word of the family with its particular variation; the elementary structure of speech is the sentence. It is within the sentence, in fact, that the word can receive a real function as a designation; outside of the sentence the word is just a propositional function—when it is not a pure and simple rubric designed to group absolutely disparate meanings. Only when it appears in discourse, does it assume a "holophrastic" character, as has often been pointed out. This does not mean that the word can be limited by itself to a precise meaning but that it is integrated in a context as a secondary form in a primary form. The word therefore has only a purely virtual existence outside of complex and active organizations which integrate it. It can not exist "in" a consciousness or an unconscious *before* the use which is made of it: the sentence is not made out of words.

But we need not be content with this. Paulhan has shown in *Fleurs de Tarbes* that entire sentences, "commonplaces," do not, any more than words, pre-exist the use which is made of them. They are mere commonplaces if they are looked at from the outside by a reader who recomposes the paragraph by passing from one sentence to the next, but they lose their banal and conventional character if they are placed within the point of view of the author who saw the thing to be expressed and who attended to the most pressing things first by producing an act of designation or re-creation without slowing down to consider the very elements of this act. If this is true, then neither the words nor the syntax, nor the "ready-made sentences" pre-exist the use which is made of them. Since the verbal unity is the meaningful sentence, the latter is a constructive act which is conceived only by a transcendence which surpasses and nihilates the given toward an end. To understand the word in the light of the sentence is very exactly to understand any given whatso-ever in terms of the situation and to understand the situation in the light of the original ends.

To understand a sentence spoken by my companion is, in fact, to understand what he "means"—that is, to espouse his movement of transcendence, to throw myself with him toward possibles, toward ends, and to return again to the ensemble of organized means so as to understand them by their function and their end. The spoken language, moreover, is always inter-preted in terms of the situation. . . .

But if the sentence pre-exists the word, then we are referred to the speaker as the concrete foundation of his speech. A word can indeed seem to have a "life" of its own if one comes upon it in sentences of various epochs. This borrowed life resembles that of an object in a film fantasy; for example, a knife by itself starts slicing a pear. It is effected by the juxtaposition of instanta-neities; it is cinematographic and is constituted in universal time. But if words appear to live when one projects a semantic or morphological film, they are not going to constitute whole sentences; they are only the tracks of the passage of sentences as highways are only the tracks of the passage of pilgrims or caravans. The sentence is a project which can be interpreted only in terms of the nihilation of a given (the very one which one wishes to designate) in terms of a posited end (its designa-tion which itself supposes other ends in relation to which it is only a means). If the given can not determine the sentence any more than the word can, if on the contrary the sentence is nec-essary to illuminate the given and to make the word understand-able, then the sentence is a moment of the free choice of myself and it is as such that it is understood by my companion. . . .

If on the other hand, it is by speaking that we cause words to exist, we do not thereby suppress the necessary technical connections or the connections in *fact* which are articulated inside the sentence. Better yet, we found this necessity. But in order for it to appear, in order for words to enter into relations with one another, in order for them to latch on to one another or repulse one another, it is necessary that they be united in a synthesis which does not come from them. Suppress this synthetic unity and the block which is called 'speech' disintegrates; each word returns to its solitude and at the same time loses its unity, being parcelled out among various incommunicable meanings. Thus it is within the free project of the sentence that the laws of speech are organized; it is by speaking that I make grammar. Freedom is the only possible foundation of the laws of language.

Furthermore, for whom do the laws of language exist? Paulhan has given the essential answer: they are not for the one who speaks, they are for the one who listens. . . . In fact, there can be no laws of speaking before one speaks. And each utterance is a free project of designation issuing from the choice of a personal for-itself and destined to be interpreted in terms of the global situation of this for-itself. What is primary is the situation in terms of which I understand the *meaning* of the sentence; this meaning is not in itself to be considered as a given but rather as an end chosen in a free surpassing of means.

41. Merleau-Ponty, *Phenomenology of Perception*, p. 194.

42. See: Etienne Gilson, *Linguistique et philosophie* (Paris: Vrin, 1969), pp. 15–19, 117, 121–128, 165–169, 175–176, 206, and *passim*, as well as my review of this book in the *Journal of the History of Philosophy*, Volume IX, 1971, pp. 116–125.

v. On Metaphorical Expressions

1. We might find it hard to incorporate the Husserl of the *Cartesian Meditations* into this particular statement, but the Husserl of *Ideen II* fully agrees with us and, as we have already indicated, we accept Husserlian philosophy only with the necessary and indispensable corrections which have been made particularly by Merleau-Ponty and Paul Ricoeur and which are sufficiently well known not to need to be repeated here. See chapter one above and my article, "The Concept of Intentionality," in *The Southwestern Journal of Philosophy*, Spring 1974, pp. 205–217.

2. See Joe K. Adams, "Expressive Aspects of Scientific Language," *On Expressive Language,* ed. Heinz Werner (Worcester, Mass.: Clark University Press, 1955), pp. 47–52. Adams concludes that "no strict line can be drawn between expressive language and scientific language" (p. 52).

3. Maurice Merleau-Ponty, *Signs*, tr. Richard M. McCleary (Evanston: Northwestern University Press, 1964), p. 90. This is my own translation from *Signes* (Paris: Gallimard, 1960), p. 113.

4. Husserl first took up this question in *Investigation VI*, sections 14–15, 26 (*Logical Investigations*, tr. J. N. Findlay, Volume II [New York: Humanities Press, 1970], pp. 710–718, 740–742), and then developed it in *Ideas*, tr. W. R. Boyce Gibson (New York: Macmillan, 1931), section 43, pp. 135ff., in *Cartesian Meditations*, tr. Dorion Cairns (The Hague: Nijhoff, 1960), sections 49–54, pp. 106–120, and as Appendix II to *Formal and Transcendental Logic*, tr. Dorion Cairns (The Hague: Nijhoff, 1969), pp. 313–329.

5. The expression "sub-universes" in this sense was coined by William James, *Principles of Psychology* (New York: Dover, 1950), Vol. II, chap. 21; cf. also Alfred Schutz, "On Multiple Realities" in *Philosophy and Phenomenological Research*, 1945, pp. 533–557.

6. It is clear that not all syntactic elements distinguished in a given language carry meaning *of themselves* when isolated from their linguistic "environment." Moreover, cultures have divided their words in many very diverse ways. Some languages are highly inflexional, like Latin, Greek, and Russian for instance, and it may normally require twice as many *words* to render (roughly) the same meaning in an "analytical" language like English as Latin requires. Highly analytical languages, like English and Chinese, have large numbers of *words* which have little or no semantic value when isolated from their complements. Other languages, like those of the Eskimos, some American Indians, and some Siberian tribes, are "polysynthetic" and they may express whole sentences of an Indo-European tongue in *one word*. Still others, like German and Turkish, are highly agglutinative and are able to string together words to form complexes which we can translate only by elaborate circumlocutions. Thus it is clear that *one word* does not mean *one meaning*, and because people think and speak in terms of meanings rather than words, they normally think and speak in complex phrases and sentences, not simple words. The *meanings* of words are much larger and more inclusive than any series of given words used to express them. For this reason it is impossible to restrict the analysis of meaning narrowly to the analysis of sedimented verbal expressions. No one word can be understood except in terms of the whole linguistic horizon of which it is a part.

7. There is an amusing statement by Aquinas in this connection in his commentary on the *De Anima* of Aristotle, I. 8: "Plato habuit malum modum docendi. Omnia enim figurate dicit, et per symbola docet: *intendens aliud per verba, quam sonent ipsa verba;* sicut quod dixit animum esse circulum. Et ideo ne aliquis propter ipsa verba incidat in errorem, Aristoteles disputat contra eum quantum ad id quod verba eius sonant" (italics mine). We can almost hear Bertrand Russell comparing Frege to Bergson.

8. E. C. Mossner, *Life of David Hume* (Oxford: Clarendon Press, 1954), pp. 379–380. There is a closely related phenomenon which has not, so far as I know, been studied, namely, our tendency to see events, institutions, things, and other persons through the conceptual typology we have formed of our friends, acquaintances, and any other persons who have influenced us. This provides us with a use of proper names which is not at all exhausted by its referential function. We use phrases like "to pull a Wilson," "to pull a Kissinger," "to pull a Jobert," in much the same ways that we speak of friends ("it's not at all like John to do that") or of colleagues and deans ("just like old Jonesy"). Edward Gibbon said once that "mankind is governed by names." The name "Caesar," a family name, became the title of the king of the Romans, of the Greeks, of the Franks, and then of the Germans, because Augustus would not assume the title "king"— which had occasioned the murder of Julius Caesar—but assumed the name "Caesar" itself instead. On January 8, 1963, Senator Barry Goldwater referred to President Johnson's State of the Union message in the terms: "He out-Roosevelted Roosevelt, out-Kennedyed Kennedy and even made Harry Truman look like a piker!" And then there was the wag who remarked after one of Heidegger's more obscure lectures in the late 1950s: "Das Nicht nichtet, die Welt weltet, und der Heidegger heideggert." These usages (which could be multiplied at will) show two things, namely (1) that, though these words for the most part will never appear in dictionaries, we *do* have universalizable "concepts" of individuals designated by proper names, that we *do* see our friends, acquaintances, and other persons known to us as "types"—even in their individual idiosyncrasies—and (2) that we make social and historical experience intelligible to ourselves by investing other beings with the characteristics of the individuals thus typified. This latter is certainly a species of metaphorical transfer which needs to be studied.

9. Let me cite E. B. de Condillac: "L'analogie: voilà donc à quoi se reduit tout l'art de raisonner, comme tout l'art de parler;

et dans ce seul mot, nous voyons comment nous pouvons nous instruire des decouverts des autres, et comment nous en pouvons faire nous-mêmes. Les enfants n'apprennent la langue de leurs pères, que parce qu'ils en sentent de bonne heure l'analogie: ils se conduisent naturellement d'après cette methode, qui est bien plus à leur portée que toutes les autres. Faisons comme eux, instruisons-nous d'après l'analogie, et toutes les sciences nous deviendront aussi faciles qu'elles peuvent l'être. Car enfin, l'homme qui parait le moins propre aux sciences, est au moins capable d'apprendre des langues. Or une science bien traitée n'est qu'une langue bien faite." From "La langue des calculs," *Oeuvres*, ed. G. Le Roy (Paris: Presses Universitaires de France, 1948), Vol. II, p. 420.

10. This is a difficult and important linguistic question which we can only allude to here. The eight original cases of nouns in Indo-European languages (nominative, genitive, dative, accusative, vocative, instrumental, locative, and ablative) seem to indicate primarily spatial or directional relationships for which, in English, we now rely mainly on "prepositions" like *at, of, to, towards, by, with, in, from,* etc. Whether a language uses inflexions, prepositions, or postpositions it seems that some means of designating primordial spatial relationships such as these are among the most primitive elements around which words are built up.

11. Excellent studies have been done on the phenomenology of time and on the phenomenology of space. Nevertheless there are a number of the most fundamental spatial metaphors which fully merit, but which have not yet received, attention. Take, for example, the manner in which we use the geographical locutions "north-south" and "east-west." We invest these locutions with temperamental, psychological, moral qualities. There is North America and South America, but also "The North" and "The South" within the United States, not to mention Northern and Southern California or Eastern and Western Texas. There is North Dakota and South Dakota, but just within North Dakota there is a perceived difference between those farmers who live north, near Canada, and those who live south, near South Dakota, which, in its turn, has *its* north and south, each with distinctive characteristics. Canada is "to the north," but it is not *all* "northern" since the inhabitants of Toronto (who are conscious of living farther "south" than Chicago) distinguish themselves temperamentally from the rude "northerners" of Edmonton. When one goes overnight from Paris to Nice one *perceives* a change in the temperamental and moral qualities of the coun-

try and its inhabitants even greater than those which separate New York from New Orleans. The trip from Milan to Palermo is no less disturbing, but the *whole* of Italy—for the one who lives there—is certainly far more "northern" than Tunisia or Morocco, yet completely "southern" when compared with Sweden. There are certainly many grounds for these distinctions, in terms of language, dialect, economics, the perception of time and space, climate, hours of sunlight per year, and all the rest, but, over and above this, there are the subtle metaphorical transfers associated with the qualities of these geographical locutions. In my own small, midwestern hometown of less than thirty thousand inhabitants there is a very different quality of life perceived by the people living on the "south side" from those living on the "north side"—not to mention the unspeakable "east side" (in *this* town there is *no* "west side," though there is certainly room for one geographically). From a purely formal (grammatical) and geographical point of view, "north," "south," "east," and "west" are necessarily correlatively opposable elements always co-present in the possible description of any physical region. But in lived experience these categories take on ever-changing anthropomorphical-metaphorical qualities which greatly transcend their literal meanings and use in any given instance. One might think that because we are so used to looking at maps these geographical locutions might be related to such words as up-down, left-right, but they are not. In going north to Maine we are going "down East," and in England one goes "up" to London but "down" to Edinburgh. The study of the fundamental vocabulary of such deeply engrained metaphorical ways of looking at and evaluating the world might be highly instructive.

12. Cf. N. H. Tur-Sinai, "The Origin of Language," *Language: An Enquiry into its Meaning and Function*, ed. R. N. Anshen (New York: Harper, 1957), pp. 41–79. According to Tur-Sinai's theory, "Prior to names and to any concrete term, language . . . had short demonstrative words serving to point out and refer to the simplest relations: here and there, above and below, flat, pointed, and the like," which were neither singular nor plural, masculine nor feminine, nouns nor verbs, etc. They were rather primitive "adverbs" which gradually turned into nouns, then into verbs, then were divided into singular and plural forms, etc. (pp. 50ff.). Whatever the merits of his theory, Tur-Sinai has carefully illustrated the gestural origin of words.

13. Giambattista Vico, *On the Study Methods of Our Time*, tr. Elio Gianturco (Indianapolis: Bobbs-Merrill, 1965), p. 24.

14. See Antonino Pagliaro, "La dottrina linguistica di G. B. Vico," in *Atti della Accademia Nazionale dei Lincei,* 1959, Serie Ottava, Memorie, Vol. 8, pp. 457–458.

15. Giambattista Vico, *De antiquissima Italiorum sapientia,* in *Opere,* vol. I, ed. G. Gentile and F. Nicolini (Bari, 1914), p. 136, as given in the English translation of Vico's *Autobiography* (Ithaca, New York: Cornell University Press, 1944), p. 38.

16. Giambattista Vico, *The New Science,* tr. Thomas G. Bergen and Max H. Fisch, revised edition (New York: Doubleday, 1961), par. 34: "We find that the principle of these origins both of languages and of letters lies in the fact that the early gentile peoples, by a demonstrated necessity of nature, were poets who spoke in poetic characters. This discovery, which is the master key of this Science, has cost us the persistent research of almost all our literary life, because with our civilized natures we [moderns] cannot at all imagine and can understand only by great toil the poetic nature of these first men."

17. Ibid., par. 236, italics mine.

18. Ibid., pars. 237–238.

19. W. K. Wimsatt, Jr., in *Philosophic Words* (New Haven: Yale University Press, 1948), pp. 13–14 and *passim* argues, on the basis of formidable documentation that in the historical development of English vocabulary "we drew out of our own bodies and from such human activities as cutting, stretching, and pulling the sensory concepts of force and pressure and the like; that we then externalized these concepts in tools and machines and turned them into abstract laws of mechanics; and that finally we proceeded to re-apply the laws to the familiar objects (our bodies) from which we had abstracted them, and to our minds, and so turned our previous notions inside out." Other observations made as Wimsatt develops and defends this reading of the historical formation of a vocabulary with which to speak of higher mental processes seem consonant both with Vico and with the work done by Bruno Snell to which we will turn presently. This is not merely a question of the etymological derivation of terms like "pressure", "tension," "exacerbation," "intensity," "volatile," and the like, which originally designated observable physical processes before becoming attributes of the body and then the mind, but, more fundamentally (though I am interpreting Wimsatt here), a question of how we are forced to discover and interpret the concepts we use to name mental activities through prior, more directly world-directed physical and bodily activities.

20. *The New Science,* par. 401. The theory of the origins

and nature of metaphorical usage developed by Percy Bysshe Shelley was very similar to this. See "A Defense of Poetry," in *The Selected Poetry and Prose of Shelley*, ed. H. Bloom (New York: New American Library, 1966), pp. 418ff.

21. *The New Science*, par. 424.

22. Ibid., par. 444.

23. Bruno Snell, *The Discovery of the Mind*, tr. T. G. Rosenmeyer (New York: Harper, 1960), p. 2.

24. The word "primitive" in this connection does not refer to history. It should not be necessary to remark that the search for the metaphors lying beneath the surface of words is not merely a question of historical etymology. The etymology of words may occasionally guide research but a word may be influenced by historical metaphors or carry a metaphorical sense which has nothing whatever to do with its etymology.

25. Snell, *The Discovery of the Mind*, p. 4.

26. Ibid., p. 13.

27. Ibid., p. 18.

28. It would be highly desirable to be able to complete this account with an investigation of the vocabulary of sound and hearing as well as of all the other sense modalities. We would like to take up the "alternative" tradition of the mysticism of sound in the Pythagoreans, in the "preachers of the Gospel," and in the Christian (and other) mystics. But our research here must be more modest—limited to suggesting an avenue of approach and proceeding a significant way along it but without any claim to being exhaustive. All the modalities of sense experience provide us with root metaphors to which we hardly ever advert and, given our ignorance of these structures, which we can hardly understand.

29. It is not necessary to go through the entire prephilosophical vocabulary of knowledge to make this point. To take a last example, the family of words related to the Greek *gignoskein* (γιγνώσκειν), such as *cognoscere* in Latin, *connaître* in French, *recognize* in English, originally signified "to be with" and then "to recognize" in the sense of "seeing or meeting the same person again." It designated the ability to identify other persons—as one recognizes one's friends, acquaintances, one's comrades in battle, etc. We have in the distinctive use of this word (i.e., for persons rather than for things) a primitive awareness of the distinction between "knowing" an aspect of the environment in an impersonal way and "knowing" a person (cf. the German *wissen* and *kennen*). For that reason the term *gignoskein* (and its cognates) is a much richer, while remaining a much vaguer,

term than *noein* or *idein*. It seems to have been used originally for any knowledge of another person and frequently designated sexual knowledge of another. In most ancient languages we find a word for *knowing* (cf. *know* in English) which is also used for the most intimate personal relationships. In knowledge we are "together with" what we know.

30. Snell, *The Discovery of the Mind,* p. 201.

31. Cf. R. G. Collingwood, *The Idea of History* (Oxford: Oxford University Press, 1946), p. 70.

32. David Hume, *A Treatise of Human Nature,* Everyman edition, p. 100.

33. This usage is from Erwin Straus, "Aesthesiology and Hallucinations," in *Existence,* ed. May, Angel, and Ellenberger (New York: Basic Books, 1958), p. 157.

34. Again, note that this is a question not of etymology but of *metaphor.* The only primarily "sexual" term to receive a place in Plato's technical philosophical vocabulary was *koinonia* (κοινωνία), "intercourse," used by Plato both for the "intercourse" of the soul with its objects of knowledge (whether through sensation or intellectual intuition) and for the "participation" or "combining of ideas among themselves" (cf. Francis M. Cornford, *Plato's Theory of Knowledge* [New York, 1957], pp. 47, 239, 255–256). The actual word for conception, *kyein* (κύειν), though used in the relevant passages where this metaphor is developed, never became in Greek, as it did in Latin and in our language, a technical philosophical term. The metaphor of knowledge as conception was simply attached to the already existing epistemological vocabulary (of sight). The metaphors behind words thus cannot be simply deduced from their etymologies. Cf. Snell, *The Discovery of the Mind,* p. 193. See also: Jacques Derrida, "La mythologie blanche," in *Marges* (Paris: Minuit, 1972), pp. 304ff. where he argues against "l'etymologisme."

35. In quoting from the *Theaetetus* and the *Sophist* I am using Cornford's translation, with one or two minor alterations, since I judge it to be far superior to all the others available. In quoting from the *Symposium* I have relied mainly on Lamb's translation in the Loeb Classical Library edition, though it has been necessary to retranslate certain words.

36. Cf. *Republic* 490a; *Symposium,* 206c–207b, 208e–209c, 212a; *Phaedrus,* 246b ff., 251a–252e. This is no exhaustive list of the passages in which this metaphor occurs, but in the event that the reader may feel I am exaggerating Plato's reliance on the image of physical intercourse, or has been misled

by Victorian translations from the Greek, an examination of the terminology of these passages should be sufficient. In the *Republic*, Plato applies the metaphor to the knowledge of reality: the soul is moved by "passion" (ἔρως) for being; it "approaches and marries" being (πλησιάσας καὶ μιγεὶς); through this union it "begets" (γεννήσας) knowledge and is finally freed from the pains of "travail" (ὠδῖνος). In the *Symposium* all men are declared to be "pregnant" (κυοῦσι, 206c), overflowing with desire "to beget and bring forth" (τίκτει καὶ γεννᾷ 206d); they approach "the beautiful one" in order "to engender and beget in the beautiful" (τῆς γεννήσεως καὶ τοῦ τόκου ἐν τῷ καλῷ, 206e). The soul is "set on fire" (ἁπτόμενος, 209c) and "consorts" (ὁμιλῶν) with the fair one in order to "conceive" (ἐκύει), "bear" (τίκτει), and "give birth" (γεννᾷ, 209c). Such words as ἰέναι, "to encounter," συνεῖναι, "to come together," and κοινωνία, "intercourse" also occur frequently in this sense. Thus there is a "pregnancy of the soul" (ἐν ταῖς ψυχαῖς κυοῦσιν, 209a), which results from the marriage of the soul with truth (beauty, goodness) and whose fruit it virtue and knowledge (212a). Cf. also A. E. Taylor, *Plato* (London: Methuen, 1926), pp. 227ff. As concerns the *Theaetetus* and the *Sophist*, I refer the reader to Cornford's excellent translation of the passages cited and to his commentary, *Plato's Theory of Knowledge*, especially pp. 27f., 47, 239, 246–247, 255–257.

37. Cf. Cornford, *Plato's Theory* . . . , p. 246.

38. Ibid., pp. 255–256.

39. Thomas Aquinas, *Summa Theologiae*, I, 78, 4, and ibid., 79, 2. See also *Quaestio Disputata de Anima*, 13, and the commentary on the *De Anima*, II, 24, and ibid., III, 4–13, passim.

40. Cf. also Plato's "ontological" use of this metaphor in *Timaeus*, 50d–51a, in reference to his doctrine of the "receptacle" (ἡ ὑποδοχή) of the forms which Aristotle took up as an image of the mind (νοῦς), *De Anima*, II, 12; III, 4.

41. Aristotle, *De Anima*, III, 4. Aquinas in his commentary calls this the "conveniens exemplum de sigillo et cera" and develops it at length (II, 24).

42. J.-P. Sartre, *Situations* I (Paris: Gallimard, 1947), p. 31.

43. I do not know of any specifically Wittgensteinian metaphor for consciousness unless it is that of the fly in the fly-bottle, entrapped by the web of meanings it cannot get through: "Was ist dein Ziel in der Philosophie?—Der Fliege den Ausweg aus dem Fliegenglas zeigen." *Philosophical Investigations* (Oxford: Blackwell, 1958), p. 103.

44. "All discourse," says Plato, "consists of the weaving together (συμπλοκή) of Forms," *Sophist*, 259e.

45. *Sophist*, 253c. Cornford gives the whole Platonic vocabulary for the "combination" and "separation" of forms, *Plato's Theory* . . . , pp. 239 and 255–256. See also pp. 183, 186, 261–264.

46. Cornford, *Plato's Theory* . . . , pp. 182–183.

47. We are not at all claiming to have done justice in these few remarks to the inexhaustible variety and burgeoning complexity of Wittgenstein's fervid imagination which has given us such suggestive metaphors as "logical space," "logical geography," "idling [mental] engines," language "holidays," and all the other pregnant thoughts which drove him in desperation from his philosophy classes to the cinema in hope of relief. No philosopher was more tormented by his inability to think the (as yet) unthinkable than Wittgenstein. A thorough study of his metaphors would be most instructive.

48. Henri Bergson, *La pensée et le mouvant* (Paris: P.U.F., 1934), p. 141.

49. In discussing consciousness Husserl liked to use words indicating effort. Thus even when using the word *Schauen* (which implies the "viewing" metaphor), Husserl intensified it by inventing the neologism *Er-schauen* (viewing or intuition achieved through effort). Herbert Spiegelberg, *The Phenomenological Movement* (The Hague: Nijhoff, 1960), vol. I, p. 119.

50. For Franz Brentano see *Psychologie vom empirischen Standpunkt* (Leipzig, 1874), vol. I, pp. 124–125. For the Scholastic notion of intentionality see Thomas Aquinas' commentary on the *De Anima* II, 24, apparently Brentano's chief source. However Aquinas' commentary on the *Metaphysics*, IV, 4, no. 574, is more explicit on the in-existence of "intelligible intentions" in the soul, and the passage noted earlier from the *Summa Theologiae*, I, 78, 4, is clearer on the in-existence of the "intentions of the senses."

51. J.-P. Sartre, *Situations* I, pp. 32–33.

52. Bruno Snell, *The Discovery of the Mind*, pp. 195, 198.

53. Ibid., pp. 230, 320.

54. Ibid., pp. 198ff. Snell shows (p. 318) that even the word "to be" has a similar metaphorical origin. (In this connection see the less developed but parallel and independent discussion in: Julian Marias, "Philosophic Truth and the Metaphoric System," in *Interpretation: The Poetry of Meaning*, ed. S. R. Hopper and D. L. Miller [New York: Harcourt].) It is necessary to

242 / NOTES FOR PAGES 182 TO 186

point out here that Snell's analyses serve a wider purpose than that which interests us here. His purpose is to show how logical thinking arose from myth (after simile, and then how "extended simile," or "myth," has arisen from metaphor) and thus to trace *the great Greek invention of scientific explanation*. The study of this Greek experience has a privileged place both in the history of philosophy and in the study of the philosophy of language for the following reason: "Greek is the only language which allows us to trace the true relation between speech and the rise of science; for in no other tongue did the concepts of science grow straight from the body of the language. In Greece, and only in Greece, did theoretic thought emerge without outside influence, and nowhere else was there an autochthonous formation of scientific terms. All other languages are derivative; they have borrowed or translated or got their terms by some other devious route from the Greeks. And it was only with the help of the unique achievement of the Greeks that the other societies were able to progress beyond their own pace of conceptual development" (Snell, p. 227). It is because we fully agree with Professor Snell that we have paid primary attention to the metaphorical vocabulary of the first Greek philosophers.

55. Both Vico and Snell get very close to this position, as does Percy Bysshe Shelley in "A Defense of Poetry," but the most extreme version known to me occurs in Jacques Derrida's "La mythologie blanche," *Marges* (Paris: Minuit, 1972), pp. 247–324, in which he reduces the whole history of Western philosophy to sequences of systems of dead metaphors. In this connection see also Charles Mauron, *Des metaphores obsedantes* (Paris, 1962), in which the author—with the richest examples from French literature—argues in great detail that we do not *use* metaphors at will but, rather, the fundamental metaphors *use us*.

56. Historically speaking, the study of the "multiple senses" of *texts* preceded the more minute turn to sentences and words we are concerned with here. The work of "hermeneutics" was first and foremost a study of the allegoric function of language (its ability to say something else while stating its literal message), particularly in the Scriptures. For a discussion of the polysemy of texts by which we have been influenced but with which we are not dealing in this book, see: Paul Ricoeur, "Le problème du double-sens comme problème hérméneutique et comme problème sémantique," *Le conflit des interpretations* (Paris: Seuil), pp. 64–79.

57. The author with whom I am most in agreement here is Paul Ricoeur. In his paper "La structure, le mot, l'événement," *Man and World*, Vol. I, 1968, p. 26, Ricoeur argues that "metaphor is the pivot of semantics" because it is in the historical acts of usage of *la parole* that the semiological system which we call *la langue* can come into play. In his paper "Le problème du double sens," p. 71, he repeats this position and, on p. 78, states that metaphor (polysemy, equivocity) occurs only "dans le discours."

58. Ricoeur, "Le problème du double-sens," p. 65. This is the very definition of "allegory": while signifying one thing, at the same time to signify something else, while continuing to signify the first.

59. This is true of "ambiguity" as well. Metaphors are like ambiguities in that they have to be "disambiguated," but the experience of ambiguity is far more general than that of metaphor. See the excellent study of the relations between ambiguity and metaphor by C. W. Dwiggins, "The Phenomenon of Ambiguity," *Man and World*, Vol. 4, 1971, pp. 262–275.

60. Two of the best recent taxonomies of theories of metaphor are (1) Monroe Beardsley's article on "Metaphor" for *The Encyclopedia of Philosophy*, ed. Paul Edwards (New York: Macmillan, 1967), pp. 284–289, and George E. Yoos, "A Phenomenological Look at Metaphor," *Philosophy and Phenomenological Research*, 1971, pp. 78–88. I came across Yoos' article only after this chapter was written, and take a number of his conclusions as confirmation of my own orientation. He seems to me to be absolutely correct in pointing out that "when we use or apprehend a metaphor" we are not *interpreting* it; we are just *using* it. In any usage of words we rarely attend to the words we are using, but rather to that about which we are speaking. Any apprehension of a verbal opposition or a conflict between the literal and metaphorical senses of the words we are using at any given moment can arise only in later reflection. It is the actual thinking in metaphors which is primary and which gives rise, in later, critical reflection, to the problems which theories of metaphor try to solve. But metaphors themselves occur in acts of usage, without such awareness of problems, and it is these "acts" which most theories of metaphor neglect. As Yoos shows, most theorists read back into their description of the experience itself the theory of metaphor they happen to hold. As James would say, they commit "The Psychologist's Fallacy."

61. Roman Jakobson, *Essais de linguistique générale*

(Paris: Editions de Minuit, 1963), Chapter II, esp. pp. 61ff. Philip Wheelwright, *Metaphor and Reality* (Bloomington: Indiana University Press, 1962).

62. Wheelwright, *Metaphor and Reality*, p. 72.

63. Paul Ricoeur, "Le problème du double sens," p. 72.

64. Wheelwright, *Metaphor . . .*, p. 72. We slightly interpret Wheelwright's definition to bring out what he really means.

65. Paul Ricoeur, *Le conflit des interpretations, passim*, and in his most recent lectures on metaphor, soon to be published by the University of Toronto Press.

66. Max Black, *Models and Metaphors* (Ithaca: Cornell University Press, 1962), p. 37, and *The Importance of Language* (Englewood Cliffs: Prentice Hall, 1962), p. 236. Most of those who hold "tension" or "interaction" theories of metaphor seem to agree that metaphors *create* the similarities.

67. Bruno Snell, *The Discovery of the Mind*, p. 198. Cf. also Charles M. Myers, "Inexplicable Analogies," *Philosophy and Phenomenological Research*, 1962, pp. 326–333. What, indeed, could be the *tertium quid comparationis* in speaking of a family, as William James did, that they had "blotting-paper" voices? Myers gives many interesting examples, but they all seem to fall within the first species of metaphor (epiphor) we have distinguished even though they are certainly very difficult to explicate the way Aristotle would want us to.

68. W. M. Urban, *Language and Reality* (New York: Macmillan, 1939), Chapters 9–10.

69. R. Herschberger, "The Structure of Metaphor," *Kenyon Review*, Volume 5, 1943, pp. 433–443.

70. Cf. Snell, *The Discovery of the Mind*, pp. 221–222.

71. Aristotle, *Rhetoric*, III. iv., 1–3; x.

72. Snell, *The Discovery of the Mind*, p. 205.

73. Ibid., p. 220. See also: W. K. Wimsatt, *The Verbal Icon* (Lexington: The University of Kentucky Press, 1954), p. 127, where Wimsatt gives examples of metaphors which lead him to state that in order to understand metaphor we must consider not how A explains B but what *new* meanings are generated when A and B are brought together.

Selected Bibliography

Allemann, Beda. "Metaphor and Antimetaphor," in *Interpretation: The Poetry of Meaning*, Stanley R. Hopper and David L. Miller, eds. New York: Harcourt, Brace & World, 1967, pp. 105–122.

Alston, William P. *Philosophy of Language*. Englewood Cliffs, N.J.: Prentice-Hall, 1964.

Anshen, R. N. (ed.). *Language, An Enquiry into its Meaning and Function*. New York: Harper, 1957.

Aristotle. *Poetics*. Cambridge: Cambridge University Press, 1968.

———. *Rhetoric*. Cambridge, Mass.: Harvard University Press, 1967.

Arnold, Matthew. "On Translating Homer," *Essays Literary and Critical*. New York: Dutton Everyman's Library, No. 115, 1933, pp. 175–210.

Arrowsmith, William, and Roger Shattuck, eds. *The Craft and Context of Translation*. Austin: University of Texas Press, 1961.

Austin, J. L. *How to Do Things With Words*. Oxford: Clarendon Press, 1962.

Auzias, Jean Marie. *Clefs pour le structuralisme*. Paris: Seghers, 1967.

Bach, E. *An Introduction to Transformational Grammars*. New York: Rinehart & Winston, 1964.

Bach, Emmon, and Robert Harms. *Universals in Linguistic Theory*. New York: Holt, Rinehart and Winston, 1968.

Bachelard, Suzanne. *A Study of Husserl's Logic*, tr. Embree. Evanston, Ill.: Northwestern University Press, 1968.

Baensch, Otto. "Art and Feeling," in *Reflections on Art,* S. K. Langer, ed. Baltimore: Johns Hopkins Press, 1959.

Baldinger, Kurt. "Sémantique et structure conceptuelle." *Cahiers de Lexicologie,* VIII–1, 1966, pp. 3–46.

Bally, Charles. "Langue et parole." *Journal de psychologie,* 1926, pp. 693–702.

———. *Linguistique générale et linguistique française.* Berne: Franke, 1932; 2nd Edition, 1944.

———. "Notions grammaticales d'absolu et de relatif." *Journal de psychologie,* 1933, pp. 341–355.

———. *Traité de stylistique française.* 2nd Edition. Heidelberg-Paris, 1934.

Barbut, Marc. "Le sense du mot 'structure' en mathématiques." *Les Temps Modernes,* 1966, pp. 791–814.

Barfield, Owen. *Poetic Diction, A Study in Meaning.* London: Faber and Faber, 1967.

Bar-Hillel, Yehoshua. *A Report on the State of Machine Translation in the United States and Great Britain.* Jerusalem: Naval Information Systems Branch. Technical Report No. 1, 1959, pp. 1–12.

———. "Can Translation Be Mechanized?" *American Scientist,* 42, 1954, pp. 248–260.

———. "Husserl's Conception of a Purely Logical Grammar." *Philosophy and Phenomenological Research,* XVII, 1957, pp. 362–369.

———. "Idioms," in *Machine Translation of Languages,* W. N. Locke, and A. D. Booth, eds. New York and London, 1955, pp. 183–193.

———. "Linguistic Problems Connected with Machine Translation." *British Journal for the Philosophy of Science,* 20, No. 3, 1953, pp. 117–155.

———. "Logical Syntax and Semantics." *Language,* XXX, 1954, 230–237.

Barthes, Roland. "Éléments de sémiologie." *Communications,* 4, 1964, pp. 91–135.

———. *Essais critiques.* Paris: Seuil, 1964.

———. *Système de la Mode.* Paris: Seuil, 1967.

Bastide, Roger. *Sens et usages du terme 'structure.'* The Hague: Mouton, 1962.

Bazell, C. E. "La Semantique structurale." *Dialogues,* III, 1953, pp. 120–132.

Beardsley, Monroe. *Aesthetics.* New York: Harcourt, 1958, Chapter 3.

———. "Metaphor." *Encyclopedia of Philosophy,* ed. Paul Edwards, Vol. V. New York: Macmillan and The Free Press, 1967.

———. "The Metaphorical Twist." *Philosophy and Phenomenological Research*, 22, March 1962, pp. 293–307.

Benjamin, Walter. "The Task of the Translator, An Introduction to the Translation of Baudelaire's *Tableaux Parisiens*," from *Illuminations*. New York: Schocken, 1969, pp. 69–82.

———. "The Work of Art in the Age of Mechanical Reproduction," from *Illuminations*. New York: Schocken, 1969, pp. 217–251.

Benveniste, Émile. *Problèmes de linguistique générale*. Paris: Gallimard, 1966.

Berggren, Douglas. "The Use and Abuse of Metaphor." *Review of Metaphysics*, XVI, 1962–63, pp. 237–258, 450–472.

Bergson, Henri. *Introduction to Metaphysics*, tr. T. A. Hulme. Indianapolis: Bobbs-Merrill, 1955.

Birdwhistell, Ray L. *Kinesics and Context*. Philadelphia: University of Pennsylvania Press, 1970.

Birren, F. *Color Psychology and Color Therapy*. New Hyde Park, N.Y.: University Books, 1961.

Black, Max. *Language and Philosophy*. Ithaca, N.Y.: Cornell University Press, 1949.

———. *Models and Metaphors*. Ithaca, N.Y.: Cornell University Press, 1962.

———. *The Importance of Language*. Englewood Cliffs, N.J.: Prentice-Hall, 1962.

———. *The Labyrinth of Language*. New York: Mentor, 1969.

Blair, Hugh. *Lessons on Rhetoric and Belles Lettres*. Philadelphia: R. Aiken, 1784.

Bloch, Bernard, and George L. Trager. *Outline of Linguistic Analysis*. Baltimore: Linguistic Society of America, 1942.

Bloomfield, Leonard. "A Set of Postulates for the Study of Language." *Language*, II, 1926, pp. 153–164.

———. *Introduction to the Study of Language*. New York: Holt, 1914.

———. *Language*. New York: Holt, 1933.

———. "Meaning." *Monatshefte für deutschen Unterricht*, 35, 1943, pp. 101–106.

———. "Philosophical Aspects of Language," in *Studies in the History of Culture: Essays in Honor of Waldo Leland*. Menasha, 1942, pp. 173–177.

Boas, Franz. "Introduction," in *Handbook of North American Indian Languages*, Part 1. Bureau of American Ethnology Bulletin 40, 1911.

Boller, M., and Kurt Goldstein. "A Study of the Impairment of 'Abstract Behavior' in Schizophrenic Patients." *Psychiatric Quarterly,* 1938.

Boudon, Raymond. *A quoi la notion de "structure"?* Paris: Gallimard, 1968.

Bouwsma, O. K. "The Expression Theory of Art," in *Aesthetics and Language,* W. E. Elton, ed. Oxford: Basil Blackwell, 1967, pp. 73–99.

Bréal, M. J. A. *Semantics: Studies in the Science of Meaning,* tr. Mrs. H. Cust. London and New York, 1900.

Brøndal, Viggo. *Essais de linguistique générale.* Copenhagen, 1943.

Bronowski, J., and Ursula Bellugi. "Language, Name, and Concept." *Science,* May 8, 1970, pp. 669– .

Brough, J. "Some Ancient Indian Theories of Meaning." *Transactions of the Philological Society.* London, 1953, pp. 161–176.

Brower, R., ed. *On Translation.* Cambridge, Mass.: Harvard University Press, 1959.

Brown, Roger. *Words and Things.* New York: The Free Press, 1958.

———, and Ursula Bellugi, eds. *The Acquisition of Language. Child Research Monographs,* Serial #92, 29, 1, 1964.

———, and Ursula Bellugi. "Three processes in the child's acquisition of syntax." *Harvard Educational Review,* 34, no. 2, Spring 1964, pp. 133–151.

Bullough, Edward. *Aesthetics.* London: Bowes and Bowes, 1957.

Buyssens, E. "La conception fonctionnelle des faits linguistiques." *Journal de psychologie,* No. 1, 1950, pp. 37–54.

———. *Les langages et le discours.* Brussels, 1943.

Cairns, Dorion. "Review: Edmund Husserl, *Die Frage nach dem Ursprung der Geometrie als intentional-historisches Problem.*" *Philosophy and Phenomenological Research,* I, 1940, pp. 98–109.

———. "The Ideality of Verbal Expressions." *Philosophy and Phenomenological Research,* 1941, pp. 453–462.

Carnap, Rudolf. *Meaning and Necessity.* Chicago: University of Chicago Press, 1947.

Carroll, John. *Language and Thought.* Englewood Cliffs, N.J.: Prentice-Hall, 1964.

———. *The Study of Language: A Survey of Linguistics and*

Related Disciplines in America. Cambridge, Mass.: Harvard University Press, 1953.

————. "Words, meanings and concepts." *Harvard Educational Review,* 34, no. 2, Spring 1964, pp. 178–202.

Cassirer, Ernst. *An Essay on Man.* New Haven: Yale University Press, 1942.

————. *Language and Myth,* tr. Suzanne Langer. New York and London: Harper, 1946.

————. *The Philosophy of Symbolic Forms,* 3 vols. New Haven: Yale University Press, 1947.

————. "Structuralism in Modern Linguistics." *Word,* I, 1945, pp. 99–120.

Catford, J. C. *A Linguistic Theory of Translation: An Essay in Applied Linguistics.* London: Oxford University Press, 1965.

Cavell, Stanley. *Must We Mean What We Say?* New York: Scribners, 1969.

Ceccato, S., ed. *Linguistic Analysis and Programming for Mechanical Translation.* New York: Gordon and Breach, 1960.

Chafe, Wallace. "Meaning in Language." *American Anth. (Formal Semantic Analysis),* 67, No. 5, Part 2, October 1965, pp. 23–36.

————. "Phonetics, Semantics, and Language." *Language,* 38, 1962, pp. 335–344.

————. "Some Indeterminacies in Language," in *Monograph Ser. Lang. and Ling.* No. 16, R. J. di Pietro (ed.). Washington, D.C.: Georgetown University Press, 1963.

Chappell, Vere, ed. *Ordinary Language.* Englewood Cliffs, N.J.: Prentice-Hall, 1964.

Charbonnier, Georges. *Entretiens avec C. Lévi-Strauss.* Paris: Plon-Julliard, 1961.

Cherry, Colin. *On Human Communication.* New York: Wiley, 1961.

Cherry, E. C., M. Halle, and R. Jakobson. "Toward a Logical Description of Languages in their Phonemic Aspects." *Language,* 29, No. 1, Jan.-Mar., 1953, pp. 34–46.

Chomsky, Noam. *Aspects of the Theory of Syntax.* Cambridge: M.I.T. Press, 1965.

————. *Cartesian Linguistics.* New York: Harper, 1966.

————. *Current Issues in Linguistic Theory.* The Hague: Mouton, 1964.

————. "Current Issues in Linguistic Theory," in *The Structure of Language,* J. A. Fodor and J. J. Katz, eds. Englewood Cliffs, N.J.: Prentice-Hall, 1964, pp. 50–118.

————. "Deep Structure, Surface Structure, and Semantic Interpretation," in *Semantics*, D. D. Steinberg and L. A. Jakobovits, eds. London: Cambridge University Press, 1969.

————. "Explanatory Models in Linguistics," in *Proceedings of the International Conference on Logic, Methodology, and Philosophy of Science*. Stanford, Calif.: Stanford University Press, 1962.

————. "Formal Properties of Grammars," in *Handbook of Mathematical Psychology*, Vol. 2, ed. R. D. Luce, R. R. Bush, and E. Galanter. New York: Wiley, 1963, pp. 323–418.

————. *Language and Mind*. New York: Harcourt, 1968.

————. "Logical Syntax and Semantics, Their Linguistic Relevance." *Language*, XXXI, 1955, pp. 36–45.

————. "On the Notion 'Rule of Grammar.'" *Proceedings of Symposia in Applied Mathematics*, 12. American Mathematical Society, 1961. Reprinted in Fodor & Katz, *The Structure of Language*, 1964.

————. "Review of B. F. Skinner, Verbal Behavior, (1957)." *Language*, 35, 1959, pp. 26–58. Reprinted in Fodor & Katz, *The Structure of Language*, 1964.

————. "Semantic Considerations in Grammar," in *Report of the Fifth Annual Round Table Meeting on Linguistics and Language Teaching*, ed. Hugo Mueller. Monogr. Ser. on Lang. & Ling. No. 7. Washington, D.C.: Georgetown University Press, 1955.

————. "Some Methodological Remarks on Generative Grammar." *Word*, 17, 1961, pp. 219–239.

————. *Syntactic Structures*. The Hague: Mouton, 1957.

————. "The Logical Basis of Linguistic Theory," in *Proceedings of the Ninth International Congress of Linguists*, H. G. Lunt, ed. The Hague: Mouton, 1964.

————, and G. A. Miller. "Introduction to the Formal Analysis of Natural Languages," in *Handbook of Mathematical Psychology*, Vol. 2, ed. R. D. Luce, R. R. Bush, and E. Galanter. New York: Wiley, 1963, pp. 269–321.

Church, Joseph. *Language and the Discovery of Reality*. New York: Random House, 1961.

Clifton, C. Jr., Ida Kurcz, and J. J. Jenkins. "Grammatical Relations as Determinants of Sentence Similarity." *Journal Verb. Learn. Verb. Behavior*, 4, 1965, pp. 112–117.

Cohen, Jean. "La comparaison poétique, essai de systématique." *Langages*, 12, 1968, pp. 43–51.

————. *Structure du langage poétique*. Paris: Flammarion, 1966.

————, Tzvetan Todorov, Gerard Genette, Roland Barthes, et. al. *Recherches rhétoriques, Communications*. Paris: Seuil, 1971.

Cohen, Jonathan. *The Diversity of Meaning*. New York: Herder & Herder, 1963.

Collingwood, R. G. *The Principles of Art*. Oxford: The Clarendon Press, 1938.

Croce, Benedetto. *Aesthetic,* tr. Douglas Ainslie. London: P. Owen, 1967.

DeCecco, John P. *The Psychology of Language, Thought and Instruction*. New York: Holt, Rinehart & Winston, 1967.

de Condillac, Étienne Bonnot. *Cours d'Etudes,* II Grammaire, Part I, chapters 1–8, and, *De l'Art de Penser,* Part I, chapter 10. Paris: Chez Monory, 1776.

————. *Essay on the Origin of Human Knowledge,* Part II, Section I, Chapter 1. Gainesville, Fla.: Scholars' Facsimiles and Reprints, 1971.

DeGuy, Michel. "Pour une théorie de la figure généralisée." *Critique,* 1969.

Deleuze, Gilles. *Différence et répétition*. Paris: P.U.F., 1968.

de Muralt, André. *The Idea of Phenomenology,* tr. Breckon. Evanston, Ill.: Northwestern University Press, 1974.

Derrida, Jacques. *De la grammatologie*. Paris: Minuit, 1967.

————. "La mythologie blanche." *Marges,* Paris, 1972.

————. *L'écriture et la différence*. Paris: Seuil, 1967.

————. *Speech and Phenomena and Other Essays,* ed. Allison. Evanston: Northwestern University Press, 1973 (*Voix et phénomène*. Paris: Gallimard, 1967).

de Saussure, Ferdinand. *Course in General Linguistics*. New York: The Philosophical Library, 1959.

Descartes, Réné. *The Philosophical Works,* tr. Haldane and Ross. New York: Dover, 1955, 2 vols.

Dinneen, Francis P. *An Introduction to General Linguistics*. New York: Holt, 1967.

Dixon, Robert M. W. *Linguistic Science and Logic*. The Hague: Mouton, 1963.

————. "Logical Statement of Grammatical Theory." *Language,* 39, 1963, pp. 654–668.

Dreyfus, Hubert L. "Husserl's Phenomenology of Perception: From Transcendental to Existential Phenomenology." Unpublished dissertation, Harvard University, 1963.

————. *What Computers Can't Do, A Critique of Artificial Reason*. New York: Harper and Row, 1972.

Dufrenne, Mikel. *Language and Philosophy*, tr. Henry Veatch. Bloomington: Indiana University Press, 1963.

———. *Pour L'Homme*. Paris: Editions de Seuil, 1968.

Dumarsais. *Tropes*. Geneva: Slatkine-Reprints, 1967. Orig. published 1730.

Eco, Umberto. *Apocalittici e integrati*. Milano: Bompiani, 1964.

———. *Il problema estetico in Tommaso d'Aquino* 2nd ed. Milano: Bompiani, 1970.

———. *La definizione dell'arte*. Milano: Mursia, 1968.

———. *La struttura assente*. Milano: Bompiani, 1968.

———. *Opera aperta*. Milano: Bompiani, 1962.

———. "The Analysis of Structure," in *The Critical Moment*. London: Faber, 1963.

Edwards, J. "Pound's Translations." *Poetry*, 83, 1954, pp. 233–238.

Ehrmann, Jacques, ed. "Structuralism." Special issue, *Yale French Studies*, 36–37, 1966.

Eifermann, Rivka. "Negation: A Linguistic Variable." *Acta Psychologica*, 18, 1961, pp. 258–273.

Eight Papers on Translation, International Journal of American Linguistics, 20, 1954, Reprint Series.

Embler, Weller. *Metaphor and Meaning*. Deland: Everett/Edwards, 1966.

Emmet, Dorothy. *The Nature of Metaphysical Thinking*. New York: Macmillan, 1945, chapters 1, 5, 9, 10.

Empson, W. "The Need for 'Translation' Theory in Linguistics." *Psyche*, 15, 1935, pp. 188–197.

Entwistle, W. J. *Aspects of Language*. London: Faber & Faber, 1953.

Erlich, Victor. *Russian Formalism*. The Hague: Mouton, 1954.

Evin, Susan M., and Wick R. Miller. "Language Development," in *Readings in the Sociology of Language*, ed., Joshua A. Fishman. The Hague: Mouton, 1968, pp. 68–98.

Faccani, Remo, and Umberto Eco, eds. *I sistemi di segni e lo strutturalismo sovietico*. Milano: Bompiani, 1969.

Fages, J.-B. *Comprendre le structuralisme*. Toulouse: Privat, 1967.

Fang, A. "Some Reflections on the Difficulty of Translation," in *Studies in Chinese Thought*, ed. A. F. Wright. MAAA 75, 1953, pp. 263–287.

Farber, Marvin. *The Foundation of Phenomenology*. New York: Paine-Whitman, 1962.

Ferguson, Charles A. "Diglossia." *Word*, 15, 1959, pp. 325–340. Reprinted in Dell Hymes, ed., *Language in Culture and Society*, New York: Harper and Row, 1964.

Ferre, Frederick. "Metaphors, Models and Religion." *Soundings*, Fall, 1968.

Firth, J. R. "Modes of Meaning," in *Essays and Studies*. London: English Assoc. 1951, pp. 118–149.

———. *Papers in Linguistics 1934–1951*. Oxford: Oxford University Press, 1957.

Fishman, Joshua A. *Readings in the Sociology of Language*. The Hague: Mouton, 1968.

Fodor, Jerry A. "Projection and Paraphrase in Semantic Analysis." *Analysis*, 21, 1961, pp. 73–77.

———, and Jerrold J. Katz. *The Structure of Language, Readings in the Philosophy of Language*. Englewood Cliffs, N.J.: Prentice-Hall, 1964.

Fonagy, Ivan. "L'information du style verbal." *Linguistics*, 4, 1964, pp. 19–47.

Fontanier, Pierre. *Les figures du discours*. Paris: Flammarion, 1968. Orig. published 1830.

Foss, Martin. *Symbol and Metaphor in Human Experience*. Princeton, N.J.: Princeton University Press, 1949.

Foucault, Michel. *Les mots et les choses*. Paris: Gallimard, 1966.

———. *The Archeology of Knowledge*. New York: Pantheon Books, 1972.

Franck, Robert. "Langue, discours et significations." *Revue Philosophique de Louvain*, Vol. 67, May 1969, pp. 306–321.

Frege, Gottlob. *Philosophical Writings*, ed. Max Black and Peter Geach. Oxford: Blackwell, 1952.

Freud, Sigmund. *A General Introduction to Psychoanalysis*, tr. Joan Riviere. New York: Liveright, 1935.

———. *The Interpretation of Dreams*, tr. A. A. Brill. London: Allen and Unwin, New York: Macmillan, 1937.

———. *Wit and its Relation to the Unconscious*, tr. A. A. Brill. New York: Moffatt, Yard and Co., 1917.

Fries, Charles Carpenter. "Meaning and Linguistic Analysis." *Language*, 30, 1954, pp. 57–68.

———. *The Structure of English: An Introduction to the Construction of English Sentences*. New York: Harcourt Brace, 1952.

Fromm, Erich. *The Forgotten Language*. New York: Holt, Rinehart and Winston, 1962.

Frye, Northrop. *Anatomy of Criticism*. Princeton, N.J.: Princeton University Press, 1957.

Gardiner, Alan H. *The Theory of Speech and Language*. Oxford: Clarendon Press, 1932.

Garver, Newton. "Analyticity and Grammar." *The Monist,* 51, July 1967, pp. 397–425.

———. "Subject and Predicate." *Encyclopedia of Philosophy,* Vol. VIII, ed. Paul Edwards. New York: Macmillan, 1967, pp. 33–36.

Genette, Gérard. *Figures*. Paris: Seuil, 1966.

Gianturco, Elio. "Words and Meanings in Vico." *Ethics,* LXI, ii, 1951, pp. 151–153.

Gilson, Etienne. *Linguistique et philosophie*. Paris: Vrin, 1969.

Gleason, H. A. *An Introduction to Descriptive Linguistics*. New York: Holt, Rinehart and Winston, 1955.

Godelier, Maurice. "Système, structure et contradiction dans 'Le Capital.'" *Les Temps Modernes,* 55, 1966, pp. 828–864.

Goldmann, Lucien. *Pour une sociologie du roman*. Paris: Gallimard, 1964.

Goldstein, Kurt. "The Problem of the Meaning of Words Based upon Observation of Aphasic Patients." *Journal of Psychology,* 1936, pp. 301–316.

Gombrich, Ernst H. *Art and Illusion*. New York: Pantheon Books, 1960.

Goodenough, W. "Componential Analysis and the Study of Language." *Language,* 32, 1956, pp. 195–216.

Goodglass, H., and Jean Berko. "Agrammatism and Inflectional Morphology in English." *Journal of Speech and Hearing Research,* 3, 1960, pp. 257–267.

Goodman, Nelson. *Languages of Art*. Indianapolis: Bobbs-Merrill, 1968.

———. "On Likeness of Meaning." *Analysis,* 10, 1949, pp. 1–7.

———. "The Problem of Counterfactual Conditions." *Journal of Philosophy,* XLIV, 1947, pp. 113–128.

Grabmann, Martin. *Mittelalterliches Geistesleben, Abhandlungen zur Geschichte der Scholastik und Mystik,* Band II. München: Max Hueber Verlag, 1936.

Greenberg, Joseph H. *Essays in Linguistics*. Chicago: University of Chicago Press, 1957.

———. "Historical Linguistics and Unwritten Language," in *Anthropology Today,* ed. A. L. Kroeber. Chicago: University of Chicago Press, 1953, pp. 265–286.

———, ed. *Universals of Language*. Cambridge: M.I.T. Press, 1963.

———, and J. J. Jenkins. "Studies in the Psychological Correlates of the Sound System of American English." *Word,* 20, 1964, pp. 157–177.

Greimas, Algirdas J. *Du sens.* Paris: Seuil, 1970.

———. *Sémantique structurale.* Paris: Larousse, 1966.

Grice, H. P. "Meaning." *The Philosophical Review,* LXVI, No. 3, 1957, pp. 377–388.

Guillaume, Gustave. *Langage et science du langage.* Paris: Nizet, 1964.

Guiraud, Pierre. *La sémantique.* Paris: P.U.F., 1955.

Gurwitsch, Aron. "Edmund Husserl's Conception of Phenomenological Psychology." *Review of Metaphysics,* XIX, No. 4, June 1966, pp. 689–727.

———. *The Field of Consciousness.* Pittsburgh: Duquesne University Press, 1964.

———. "Toward A Theory of Intentionality." *Philosophy and Phenomenological Research,* XXX, March 1970, pp. 354–367.

Gusdorf, Georges. *Speaking.* Evanston, Ill.: Northwestern University Press, 1965.

Hall, Edward T. *The Hidden Dimension.* New York: Doubleday, 1966.

———. *The Silent Language.* New York: Doubleday, 1959.

Hall, Robert A., Jr. *Linguistics and Your Language.* New York: Doubleday, 1960.

Halle, M., et. al. *For Roman Jakobson.* The Hague: Mouton, 1956.

Halliday, M. A. K. "Categories of the Theory of Grammar." *Word,* 17, 1961, pp. 241–292.

———, A. McIntosh and P. Strevens, eds. *The Linguistic Sciences and Language Teaching.* London: Longmans, 1964.

Hallowell, A. Irving. "Ojibwa Ontology, Behavior and World View," in *Culture in History: Essays in Honor of Paul Radin,* ed. S. Diamond. New York: Columbia University Press, 1960, pp. 19–52.

Hampshire, Stuart. *Thought and Action.* London: Chatto and Windus, 1960.

Hanfman, Eugenia. "Analysis of the Thinking Disorder in a Case of Schizophrenia." *Arch. Neurol. Psychology,* 1939.

Harman, Gilbert H. "Three Levels of Meaning." *The Journal of Philosophy,* LXV, October 3, 1968, pp. 590–602.

Harries, Karsten. "Review: Alfred Schutz, *The Phenomenology of the Social World,* In Search of Social Science." *Journal of Value Inquiry,* IV, Spring 1970, pp. 65–75.

Harris, Zellig. "Distributional Structure," in *Linguistics Today*. New York, 1954, pp. 26–42. Also in *Word*, 10, 1954, pp. 146–162.

——. "From Morpheme to Utterance." *Language*, 22, 1946, pp. 161–183.

——. *Methods in Structural Linguistics*. Chicago: University of Chicago Press, 1951.

Hartmann, Peter. *Zur Konstitution einer Allgemeinen Grammatik*. The Hague: Mouton, 1961, Chapter II.

Hattori, S. "The Analysis of Meaning," in *For Roman Jakobson*. The Hague: Mouton, 1956, pp. 201–212.

Head, Henry. *Aphasia and Kindred Disorders of Speech*. New York: Hafner, 1963.

Heger, Klaus. "Les bases méthodologiques de l'onomasiologie et du classement par concepts." *Travaux de Linguistique et de Litterature*, III, no. 1. Strasbourg-Paris: Klincksieck, 1965.

Heidegger, Martin. "Hölderlin and the Essence of Poetry," in *Existence and Being*. Chicago: Regnery, 1949.

——. *On The Way to Language*, tr. Hertz. New York: Harper, 1971.

Henle, Paul, ed. *Language, Thought and Culture*. Ann Arbor: University of Michigan Press, 1959.

Henry, Albert. *Métonymie et métaphore*. Klincksieck, 1971.

Herdan, Gustav. *The Calculus of Linguistic Observation*. The Hague: Mouton, 1962.

Hesschberger, R. "The Structure of Metaphor." *Kenyon Review*, 1943, pp. 433–443.

Hesse, Mary. "The Explanatory Function of Metaphor," in *Logic, Methodology, and Philosophy of Science*, Yehoshua Bar-Hillel, ed. Amsterdam: North Holland, 1965.

Hester, Marcus. *The Meaning of Poetic Metaphor*. The Hague: Mouton, 1967.

High, Dallas M. *Language, Persons, and Belief*. Oxford and New York: Oxford University Press, 1967.

Hildum, Donald C., ed. *Language and Thought*. Princeton, N.J.: D. Van Nostrand, 1967.

Hjelmslev, L. "Dans quelle mésure les significations des mots peuvent-elles être considérées comme formant une structure?" *Proceedings of the Eighth International Congress of Linguists*. Oslo, 1957, pp. 268–286.

Hjelmslev, Louis. *Essais linguistiques*. Travaux du Cercle Linguistique de Copenhague. Copenhagen: Nordisk Sprog-og Kulturforlag, 1959.

————. *Prolegomena to a Theory of Language.* Madison: University of Wisconsin, 1961.

————, and H. J. Uldall. *Outline of Glossematics: A Study in the Methodology of the Humanities with Special Reference to Linguistics.* Copenhagen: Nordisk Sprog-og Kulturforlag, 1957.

Hockett, Charles F. *A Course in Modern Linguistics.* New York: Macmillan, 1958.

————. "An Approach to the Quantification of Semantic Noise." *Philosophy of Science*, 19, 1952, pp. 257–260.

————. "Animal 'Languages' and Human Languages," in *The Evolution of Man's Capacity for Culture*, arr. J. N. Spuhler. Detroit: Wayne University Press, 1959, pp. 32–39.

————. *The State of the Art.* The Hague: Mouton, 1968.

Hoenigswald, Henry M. "The Principle Step in Comparative Grammar." *Language*, 26, 1950, pp. 357–364.

Holenstein, Elmar. "Jakobson and Husserl: A Contribution to the Genealogy of Structuralism." *The Human Context*, Volume VII, No. 1, Spring 1975, pp. 61–83.

————. "Jakobson und Husserl: Ein Beitrag sur Genealogie des Structuralismus." *Tijdschrift voor Filosofie*, XXXV, Number 3, September 1973, pp. 560–607.

————. "Roman Jakobson—un phénoménologue." *L'Arc*, June 1974.

Hollander, John. "Versions, Interpretations, Performances," from *On Translation*, ed., Reuben A. Brower. Cambridge, Mass.: Harvard University Press, 1959, pp. 205–231.

Hook, Sidney, ed. *Language and Philosophy.* New York: New York University Press, 1969.

Hospers, J. *Meaning and Truth in the Arts.* Chapel Hill: University of North Carolina Press, 1946.

Householder, Fred. W., and Sol Saporta, eds. *Problems in Lexicography.* Bloomington: Indiana University Press, 1962.

Hulme, T. E. *Speculations.* London: Routledge and Kegan Paul, New York: Humanities Press, 1965.

Husserl, Edmund. *Cartesian Meditations*, tr. Dorion Cairns. The Hague: Martinus Nijhoff, 1960, sections 49–54.

————. *Experience and Judgment*, tr. James Churchill and Karl Ameriks. Evanston, Ill.: Northwestern University Press, 1973.

————. *Formal and Transcendental Logic*, tr. Dorion Cairns. The Hague: Martinus Nijhoff, 1969.

————. *Ideas*, tr. W. R. B. Gibson. New York: Macmillan, 1931.

————. *Ideen II*, sections 44–47, 50–51. The Hague: Martinus Nijhoff, 1951.

————. *The Logical Investigations*, tr. J. N. Findlay. London: Routledge & Kegan Paul, 1970, 2 vols. *Logische Untersuchungen*, Tübingen: Niemeyer, 4th edition, 1968, 3 vols.

Hymes, Dell, ed. *Language in Culture and Society*. New York: Harper, 1964.

Irwin, John V., and Michael Marge, eds. *Childhood Language Disabilities*. New York: Appleton-Century-Crofts, 1972.

Isenberg, Arnold. "On Defining Metaphor." *Journal of Philosophy*, October 1963, pp. 609–622.

Jacobi, Jolande. *Complex, Archetype, Symbol in the Psychology of Jung*, tr. Ralph Manheim. New York: Pantheon Books, 1959.

Jacobs, Roderick, and Peter Rosenbaum, eds. *English Transformational Grammar*. Waltham, Mass.: Blaisdel, 1968.

Jakobson, Roman. *Deux aspects du langages et deux types d'aphasie*. The Hague: Mouton, 1956.

————. *Essais de linguistique générale*. Paris: Minuit, 1963.

————. "On Linguistic Aspects of Translation," in *On Translation*, ed. Reuben A. Brower. Cambridge, Mass.: Harvard University Press, 1959, pp. 232–239.

————. *Shifters, Categories, and the Russian Verb*. Cambridge, 1957.

————, and Morris Halle. *Fundamentals of Language*. The Hague: Mouton, 1956.

————, and C. Lévi-Strauss. "Les Chats de Charles Baudelaire." *L'Homme*, January 1962, pp. 5–21.

————, G. M. Fant, and M. Halle. *Preliminaries to Speech Analysis: The Distinctive Features and Their Correlates*. Cambridge: Acoustics Lab., M.I.T. Technical Report No. 13, 1952.

James, D. G. *Scepticism and Poetry*. London: Allen and Unwin, 1937.

James, William. *The Principles of Psychology*. New York: Holt, 1890.

Jesperson, Otto. *Analytic Syntax*. Copenhagen: Levin & Munksgaard, 1937.

————. *A Philosophy of Grammar*, London, Allen & Unwin, 1924.

————. *The Growth and Structure of the English Language*. New York: Doubleday, 1956.

————. *Language*. London: Allen and Unwin, 1956.

————. *Language, Its Nature, Development, and Origin*. New York: Henry Holt, 1921.

————. *Logic and Grammar*. Oxford: Clarendon Press, 1924.

————. *Progress in Language*. New York: Macmillan, 1909.

————. *Selected Writings*. London: Allen & Unwin, 1962.

————. *The System of Grammar*. London: Allen & Unwin, 1933.

Jung, Carl. *Modern Man in Search of a Soul,* tr. W. S. Dell and Cary F. Baynes. New York: Harcourt, Brace and World, 1966.

————. *Psychology of the Unconscious,* tr. Beatrice Hinkle. New York: Dodd, Mead, 1957.

Katchadourian, Haig. "Metaphor." *British Journal of Aesthetics,* vol. 8, July 1968, pp. 227–243.

Katz, Jerrold J. "Mentalism in Linguistics." *Language,* 40, 1964, pp. 124–137.

————. "Recent Issues in Semantic Theory." *Foundations of Language,* III, No. 2, 1967, pp. 124–194.

————. *The Philosophy of Language*. New York: Harper, 1966.

————, and J. Fodor. "The Structure of a Semantic Theory." *Language,* 39, 1963, pp. 170–210.

————, and P. M. Postal. *An Integrated Theory of Linguistic Descriptions*. Cambridge: M.I.T. Press, 1964.

Khaldun, Ibn. *Prolegomena*. Chapter IV, Sections 42–50, 56–57. Selections published as *An Arab Philosophy of History,* tr. Charles Issawi. London: Murray, 1950.

Klemke, E. D., ed. *Essays on Frege*. Champaign, Ill.: University of Illinois Press, 1968.

Knights, L. C., and Basil Cottle, eds. *Metaphor and Symbol*. London: Butterworth, 1960.

Kockelmans, Joseph J. *On Heidegger and Language*. Evanston, Ill.: Northwestern University Press, 1972.

Kofman, Sarah. *Nietzsche et la métaphore*. Paris: Seuil, 1972.

————. *Rhétorique et philosophie, Nietzsche et la métaphore, Poétique,* n. 5. Paris: éd. du Seuil, 1971.

Konrad, Hedwig. *Études sur la métaphore*. Paris: Vrin, 1939.

Koutsoudas, A., and K. Korfhage. "Mechanical Translation and the Problem of Multiple Meaning." *Mechanical Translation,* 3, 1956, pp. 46–51.

Kristeva, J., J. Rey-Debove, and D. J. Umikev, eds. *Essays in Semiotics–Essai de Sémiotique*. The Hague: Mouton, 1971.

Kuroda, S.-Y. "Edmund Husserl, *Grammaire Générale et*

Raisonnée, and Anton Marty." Foundations of Language, Vol. 10, 1973, pp. 169–195.

Lacan, Jacques. *Ecrits.* Paris: Seuil, 1966.

———. *The Function of Language in Psychoanalysis,* tr. Anthony Wilden. Baltimore: Johns Hopkins University Press, 1968.

Lacoue-Labarthe, Philippe. *Rhétorique et philosophie, Le détour, Poétique,* n. 5. Paris: éd. du Seuil, 1971.

Lado, R. *Linguistics Across Cultures.* Ann Arbor, 1957.

Lageux, Maurice. "Merleau-Ponty et la linguistique de Saussure." *Dialogue,* IV, 1965, pp. 351–364.

Lamb, S. "On Alteration, Transformation, Realization and Stratification," in *Linguistics and Language Study,* C. I. J. M. Stuart, ed. Monogr. Ser. Lang. and Ling. No. 17. Washington, D.C.,: Georgetown University Press, 1964.

———. "The Semantic Approach to Structural Semantics," in *Transcultural Studies in Cognition,* A. K. Romney and R. G. D'Andrade, eds. *Amer. Anth.* 66, No. 3, Part 2, 1964, pp. 57–78.

Lander, H. J. "A Note on Accepted and Rejected Arrangements of Navajo Words." *International Journal of American Ling.,* 26, 1960, pp. 351–354.

Langacker, Ronald W. *Language and its Structure.* New York: Harcourt, 1968.

Langer, Suzanne K. *Feeling and Form.* New York, 1953.

———. "Origins of Speech and Its Communicative Function." *Quarterly Journal of Speech,* April 1960, pp. 121–134.

———. *Philosophy in a New Key.* Cambridge, Mass.: Harvard University Press, 1942.

Lee, Dorothy. *Freedom and Culture.* Englewood Cliffs, N.J.: Prentice-Hall, 1959.

Lenneberg, Eric. *The Biological Foundations of Language.* New York: John Wiley, 1967.

———, ed. *New Directions in the Study of Language.* Cambridge, Mass.: M.I.T. Press, 1964.

Lepschy, Giulio C. *La linguistica strutturale.* Torino: Einaudi, 1966.

Levin, David Michael. "Induction and Husserl's Theory of Eidetic Variation." *Philosophy and Phenomenological Research,* XXIX, September 1968, pp. 1–15.

Lévi-Strauss, Claude. *Anthropologie structurale.* Paris: Plon, 1958.

———. *La pensée sauvage.* Paris: Plon, 1962.

————. *Le cru et le cuit.* Paris: Plon, 1964.

————. *Les structures élémentaires de la parenté.* Paris: P.U.F., 1947.

Levy-Bruhl, Lucien, *How Natives Think.* London: Allen and Unwin, 1926.

————. *Primitive Mentality.* London: Allen and Unwin, 1923.

Lewis, C. I. *An Analysis of Knowledge and Valuation.* LaSalle, Ill.: Open Court, 1946.

Linsky, Leonard. *Semantics and the Philosophy of Language.* Champaign: University of Illinois Press, 1952.

Lisker, L., F. S. Cooper, and A. M. Liberman. "The Uses of Experiment in Language Description." *Word,* 18, 1962, pp. 82–106.

Longacre, Robert E. "Items in Context: Their Bearing on Translation Theory." *Language,* 34, 1958, pp. 482–491.

Lotz, J. "Speech and Language." *Journal of the Acoustical Society of America,* 22, 1950, pp. 712ff.

Lounsbury, Floyd G. "Language," in *Biennial Review of Anthropology,* B. J. Siegle, ed. Stanford, Cal.: Stanford University Press, 1959, pp. 185ff.

————. "Language," in *Biennial Review of Anthropology,* B. J. Siegle, ed. Stanford, Cal.: Stanford University Press, 1961, pp. 279–322.

————. "Pausal, Juncture and Hesitation Phenomena," in *Psycholinguistics: A Survey of Theory and Research Problems,* C. E. Osgood and T. A. Sebeok, eds. Baltimore, 1954.

————. "The Structural Analysis of Kinship Semantics." *Proceedings of the 9th International Congress of Linguistics,* The Hague: Mouton, 1964.

————. "The Varieties of Meaning." *Monogr. Ser. on Lang. and Ling.,* No. 8. Washington, D.C.: Georgetown University Press, 1955, pp. 158–164.

Lyons, John. *Introduction to Theoretical Linguistics.* Cambridge: Cambridge University Press, 1968.

————. "Review of Paul Ziff's *Semantic Analysis.*" *IJAL,* 29, no. 1, 1963, pp. 82–87.

————. *Structural Semantics.* Oxford: Blackwell, 1963.

————, ed. *Psycholinguistics Papers.* Edinburgh: Edinburgh University Press, 1966.

MacKay, D. S. "The Analogy of Mind," from *The Nature of Mind.* University of California Publications in Philosophy, Vol. 19. Berkeley: University of California Press, 1936, pp. 63– .

Macksey, Richard, and Eugenio Donato, eds. *The Languages of Criticism and the Sciences of Man: The Structuralist Controversy.* Baltimore: Johns Hopkins University Press, 1968.

Malinowski, B. *Magic, Science, and Religion.* Garden City, N.Y.: Doubleday, 1954.

Malmberg, B. *Structural Linguistics and Human Communication.* New York: Academic Press, 1963.

Marckwardt, A. H., ed. *Studies in Languages and in Honor of Charles C. Fries.* Ann Arbor: English Language Institute, University of Michigan, 1964.

Margolis, Joseph. "Notes on the Logic of Simile, Metaphor and Analogy." *American Speech,* 32, October 1957, pp. 186–189.

———. *The Language of Art and Art Criticism.* Detroit: Wayne State University Press, 1965.

Martinet, André. *A Functional View of Language.* London: Oxford University Press, 1962.

———. *Elements of General Linguistics.* London: Faber and Faber, 1960.

———, and U. Weinreich. *Linguistics Today.* 1954.

Matthiessen, Francis O. *Translation, An Elizabethan Art.* Cambridge, Mass.: Harvard University Press, 1931.

McCall, Marsh H. *Ancient Rhetorical Theories of Simile and Comparison.* Cambridge, Mass.: Harvard University Press, 1969.

McIntosh, Angus. "Patterns and Ranges." *Language,* 37, 1961, pp. 325–337.

———, and M. A. K. Halliday. *Patterns of Language.* Bloomington: Indiana University Press, 1967.

McKeon, Richard. "Aristotle's Conception of Language and the Arts of Language." *Classical Philology,* XLI, No. 4, October 1946, pp. 193–206.

McNeil, David. *The Acquisition of Language.* New York: Harper and Row, 1970.

Meillet, Antoine. *Linguistique historique et linguistique générale,* 2 vols. Paris: E. Champion, 1935.

———, and Marcel Cohen, eds. *Les langues du monde.* Paris, 1952.

Menyuk, Paula. *The Acquisition and Development of Language.* Englewood Cliffs, N.J.: Prentice-Hall, 1971.

Merleau-Ponty, Maurice. *Consciousness and the Acquisition of Language,* tr. Silverman. Evanston, Ill.: Northwestern University Press, 1973.

———. "Linguistics," in *The Primacy of Perception.* Evanston, Ill.: Northwestern University Press, 1964, pp. 84–97.

―――. "Review, J.-P. Sartre, L'Imagination." *Journal de Psychologie,* xxxiii, 1936, pp. 756–761.

―――. "The Body As Expression and Speech," in *Phenomenology of Perception,* tr. Colin Smith. London: Routledge & Kegan Paul, 1962, pp. 174–199.

―――. *Themes from the Lectures,* tr. William O'Neill. Evanston, Ill.: Northwestern University Press, 1970.

―――. "The Phenomenology of Language," in *Signs,* tr. Richard McCleary. Evanston, Ill.: Northwestern University Press, 1964, pp. 84–97.

―――. *The Prose of the World,* tr. O'Neill. Evanston, Ill.: Northwestern University Press, 1973.

―――. *The Visible and the Invisible,* tr. Alphonso Lingis. Evanston, Ill.: Northwestern University Press, 1968.

Mill, John Stuart. *A System of Logic.* London: Longmans, 1906.

Miller, George A., and G. G. Beebe-Center. "Some Psychological Methods for Evaluating the Quality of Translations." *Mechanical Translation,* 3, 1956, pp. 73–80.

Minsky, Marvin, ed. *Semantic Information Processing.* Cambridge, Mass.: M.I.T. Press, 1968.

Mohanty, J. N. *Edmund Husserl's Theory of Meaning.* The Hague: Martinus Nijhoff, 1964.

―――. *Phenomenology and Ontology.* The Hague: Martinus Nijhoff, 1970.

―――. *The Concept of Intentionality.* St. Louis: Warren Green, 1972.

Mohrmann, C., A. Sommerfelt, and J. Whatmough, eds. *Trends in European and American Linguistics, 1930–1960.* Utrecht and Antwerp: Spectrum Publishers, 1961.

Morier, Henri. *Dictionnaire de Poétique et de Rhétorique.* Paris: P.U.F., 1961.

Morris, Charles. *Signs, Language and Behavior.* New York: Braziller, 1946.

Moulton, W. G. "What Standard for Diglossia? The Case of German Switzerland," in *Monogr. Ser. Lang. and Ling.,* No. 15, E. D. Woodworth and R. J. di Pietro, eds. Washington, D.C.: Georgetown University Press, 1962.

Nabokov, Vladimir. "Problems of Translation: 'Onegin' in English." *Partisan Review,* 22, 1955, pp. 496–512.

Natanson, Maurice. "Phenomenology and the Natural Attitude." *Literature, Philosophy and the Social Sciences.* The Hague: Nijhoff, 1962, pp. 34–43.

Oettinger, A. G. "A New Theory of Translation and Its Application." *Proceedings of the National Symposium on Machine Translation*, H. P. Edmundson, ed. Englewood Cliffs, N.J.: Prentice-Hall, 1961, pp. 363–366.

———. *Automatic Language Translation*. Cambridge: Harvard University Press, 1960.

Ogden and Richards. *The Meaning of Meaning*. New York: Harcourt, 1930.

Ohman, Suzanne. "Theories of the 'Linguistic Field.'" *Word*, 9, 1953, pp. 225–240 (also listed as pp. 123–134).

Oliver, G. Benjamin. "'Depth Grammar' as a Methodological Concept in Philosophy." *International Philosophical Quarterly*, XII, March 1972, pp. 111–130.

———. "The Ontological Structure of Linguistic Theory." *The Monist*, LIII, April 1969, pp. 262–279.

Olmsted, D. L., and O. K. Moore. "Language Psychology and Linguistics." *Psychological Review*, 59, 1952, pp. 414–420.

Olshewsky, Thomas, ed. *Problems in the Philosophy of Language*. New York: Holt, 1969.

Ortega y Gasset, José. *The Dehumanization of Art*, tr. Willard Trask. Garden City, N.Y.: Doubleday, 1956.

Osgood, Charles, G. J. Suci, and P. H. Tannenbaum. *The Measurement of Meaning*. Urbana: University of Illinois Press, 1957.

Otto, Rudolf. *The Idea of the Holy*, tr. John Harvey. London and New York: Oxford University Press, 1968.

Panofsky, Erwin. *Meaning in the Visual Arts*. Garden City, N.Y.: Doubleday, 1955.

Pap, A. "Types and Meaninglessness." *Mind*, January 1960, pp. 41–54.

Pederson, Holger. *The Discovery of Language: Linguistic Science in the 19th Century*. Bloomington: Indiana University Press, 1931.

Peirce, Charles Sanders. *Collected Papers*. Cambridge, Mass.: Harvard University Press, 1931–1935.

———. "The Logic of Abduction," *Peirces' Essays in the Philosophy of Science*, ed. Vincent Tomas. New York, 1957, Chapter XIII, pp. 235–255.

Phillips, H. P. "Problems of Translation and Meaning in Fieldwork." *Human Organization*, 18, 1959, pp. 192–194.

Piaget, Jean. *Language and Thought of the Child*, tr. Marjorie and Ruth Gabain. London: Routledge & Kegan Paul, 1965.

———. *Le Structuralisme*. Paris: P.U.F., 1968.

Pitcher, George. *The Philosophy of Wittgenstein.* Englewood Cliffs, N.J.: Prentice-Hall, 1964.

———. *Wittgenstein.* New York: Doubleday, 1966.

Pos, H.-J. "Phénoménologie et linguistique." *Revue Internationale de Philosophie,* I, 1939, pp. 354–365.

Pottier, Bernard. "La définition sémantique dans les dictionnaires." *Travaux de Linguistique et de Littérature,* III, 1, 1965, pp. 33–39.

Pouillon, Jean. "Présentation: un essai de définition." *Les Temps Modernes,* November 1966, pp. 769–790.

Poulet, Georges, ed. *Les chemins actuels de la critique.* Paris: Plon, 1968.

Preston, W. D. "Problems of Attestation in Ethnography and Linguistics." *International Journal of American Ling.,* 12, 1946, pp. 173–177.

Price, H. H. *Perception.* London: Methuen. New York: Barnes and Noble, 1973.

Quine, W. V. O. *From a Logical Point of View.* Cambridge, Mass.: Harvard University Press, 1953.

———. *Word and Object.* New York: Wiley, 1960.

Quintilian. *De Institutione Oratoria,* VIII. English tr., *Institutes of Eloquence,* William Guthrie, tr. London: T. Waller, 1756.

Reed, David W. "A Statistical Approach to Quantitative Linguistic Analysis." *Word,* 5, 1949, pp. 235–237.

Reibel, David, and Sanford Schane, eds. *Modern Studies in English.* Englewood Cliffs, N.J.: Prentice-Hall, 1969.

Reichling, Anton. "Meaning and Introspection." *Lingua,* 11, 1962, pp. 333–339.

———. "Principles and Methods of Syntax: Cryptanalytical Formalism." *Lingua,* 10, 1961, pp. 1–17.

Rey, J. M. *L'enjeu des signes, Lecture de Nietzsche.* Paris: Seuil, 1971.

Richards, I. A. *Principles of Literary Criticism.* New York: Harcourt, Brace & World, 1925.

———. *The Philosophy of Rhetoric.* Oxford: Oxford University Press, 1936, 1950.

———. "Towards a Theory of Translating," in *Studies in Chinese Thought,* A. F. Wright, ed. American Anthropological Association Memoir 75, 1953, pp. 247–262.

———, and R. G. Ogden. *The Meaning of Meaning.* London: Routledge and Kegan Paul, 1924.

Ricoeur, Paul. *Le conflit des interpretations*. Paris: Seuil, 1969.

———. *De l'interpretation*. Paris: Seuil, 1965.

———. "La structure, le mot, l'événement." *Man and World*, I, 1968, pp. 10–30.

———. "New Developments in Phenomenology in France: The Phenomenology of Language." *Social Research*, 34, 1967, pp. 1–30.

———. "The Symbol Gives Rise to Thought," in *The Symbolism of Evil*, tr. Emerson Buchanan. Boston: Beacon Press, 1972, pp. 347–357.

Rieser, Max. "Analysis of Poetic Simile." *The Journal of Philosophy*, 37, 1940.

Robins, R. H. *Ancient and Medieval Grammatical Theory in Europe*. London: Bell, 1951.

———. *A Short History of Linguistics*. London: Longmans, 1964.

———. *General Linguistics, An Introductory Survey*. London: Longmans, 1964.

Rorty, Richard. *The Linguistic Turn*. Chicago: The University of Chicago Press, 1968.

Russell, Bertrand. *Analysis of Mind*. London: Allen & Unwin, 1921.

———. "Philosophy of Logical Atomism," in *Logic and Knowledge*, ed. R. C. Marsh. London: Allen & Unwin, 1956.

Ryle, Gilbert. "Categories," in *Logic and Language*, Vol. II, Antony Flew, ed. Oxford: Blackwell, 1963.

———. *Dilemmas*. Cambridge: Cambridge University Press, 1954.

———. "Letters and Syllables in Plato." *Philosophical Review*, LXIX, 1960, pp. 431–451.

———. *The Concept of Mind*. New York: Barnes and Noble, 1965.

Salzmann, Zdenek. "A Method for Analyzing Numerical Systems." *Word*, 6, 1950, pp. 78–83.

Sapir, Edward. "Communication," in *Encyclopedia of the Social Sciences*, 4, 1931, pp. 78–81.

———. "Grading: A Study in Semantics." *Philosophy of Science*, II, 1944, pp. 93–116.

———. *Language*. New York: Harcourt, 1921.

———. "Language," in *Selected Writings of Edward Sapir*, ed. David G. Mandelbaum. Berkeley and Los Angeles: University of California Press, 1949, 1958, pp. 73–82.

———. "The Concept of Phonetic Law as Tested in Primitive

Languages by Leonard Bloomfield," in *Methods in Social Science: A Case Book,* ed. Stuart A. Rice. Chicago: University of Chicago Press, 1931, pp. 297–306.

Saporta, Sol. "A Note on the Relation between Meaning and Distribution." *Libera,* 4, 1957, pp. 22–26.

————, ed. *Psycholinguistics, A Book of Readings.* New York: Holt, Rinehart & Winston, 1961.

Sartre, Jean-Paul. *Being and Nothingness,* tr. Hazel Barnes. New York: The Philosophical Library, 1956.

————. *Psychology of the Imagination.* New York: Citadel, 1961.

————. *Jean-Paul Sartre répond,* in *L'Arc.* Paris, 1966.

————. *What is Literature?* New York: Harper, 1959.

Schaff, Adam. *Introduction to Semantics.* London: Pergamon Press, 1962.

Schilpp, Paul, ed. *The Philosophy of Rudolf Carnap.* LaSalle, Ill.: Open Court, 1963.

Schneider, David. *American Kinship: A Cultural Account.* New York: Prentice-Hall, 1968.

Searle, John R. *Speech Acts.* Cambridge: Cambridge University Press, 1969.

Sebag, Lucien. *Marxisme et structuralisme.* Paris: Payot, 1964.

Sebeok, T. A. "Coding in the Evolution of Signalling Behavior." *Behavioral Science,* 7, 1962, pp. 430–442.

————, *Current Trends in Linguistics,* Vol. 1, *Soviet and East European Linguistics.* The Hague: Mouton, 1963.

————, *Style in Language.* Cambridge; M.I.T. Press, 1960.

————, et. al., eds. *Current Trends in Linguistics,* Vol. III. *Theoretical Foundations.* The Hague: Mouton, 1966.

————, A. S. Hayes and M. C. Bateson, eds. *Approaches to Semiotics.* The Hague: Mouton, 1964.

Serrus, Charles. "Categories grammaticales et categories logiques." *Les Études Philosophiques,* 1929, pp. 20–30.

————. "Le conflit du logicisme et du psychologisme." *Les Études Philosophiques,* 1928, pp. 9–18.

Sève, Lucien. "Méthode structurale et méthode dialectique." *La pensée,* I, 1967, pp. 63–93; "Réponse par Maurice Godelier," *La pensée,* 1970, pp. 3–28; "Réponse par Lucien Sève," *La pensée* 1970, pp. 29–50.

Shelley, Percy B. *Defense of Poetry.* Boston: Ginn, 1891.

Shibles, Warren A. *An Analysis of Metaphor.* The Hague: Mouton, 1971.

————. *Metaphor: An Annotated Bibliography.* Whitewater, Wisc.: The Language Press, 1971.

Smith, Alfred G., ed. *Communication and Culture*. New York: Holt, 1966.

Smith, F., and G. A. Miller, eds. *The Genesis of Language*. Cambridge, Mass.: M.I.T. Press, 1966.

Smith, H. L., Jr. "Syntax and Semology," in *Monogr. Ser. Lang. and Ling.*, No. 16, R. J. di Pietro, ed. Washington, D.C.: Georgetown University Press, 1963.

Snell, Bruno. *Der Aufbau der Sprache*. Hamburg: Claasen, 1952.

———. *Poetry and Society*. Bloomington: Indiana University Press, 1961.

———. *The Discovery of the Mind*. New York: Harper, 1960.

Sojcher, Jacques. "La métaphore généralisée." *Revue Internationale de Philosophie*, vol. 23, 1969, pp. 58–68.

Sokolowski, Robert. *The Development of Husserl's Notion of Constitution*. The Hague: Martinus Nijhoff, 1964.

———. "The Logic of Parts and Wholes in Husserl's *Investigations*." *Philosophy and Phenomenological Research*, XXVIII, June 1968, pp. 537–553.

———. "The Structure and Content of Husserl's *Logical Investigations*." *Inquiry*, 14, pp. 318–347.

Spiegelberg, Herbert. *The Phenomenological Movement*, 2 vols. The Hague: Martinus Nijhoff, 1960.

Sternberg, D. D., L. A. Jakobovits, eds. *Semantics*. London: Cambridge University Press, 1969.

Stevenson, Charles. *Ethics and Language*. New Haven: Yale University Press, 1953.

Straus, Erwin W. *Phenomenological Psychology*. New York: Basic Books, 1966.

———. *The Primary World of the Senses*. New York: Macmillan, 1963.

———. *Psychologie der menschlichen Welt*. Berlin: Springer, 1960.

Strawson, P. F. "On Referring." *Mind*, 1950, pp. 320–344.

Sturtevant, E. H. *An Introduction to Linguistic Science*. New Haven: Yale University Press, 1947.

Sweet, Henry. *Collected Papers*, arr. H. C. Wyld. Oxford: Clarendon Press, 1913.

Taylor, Daniel M. *Explanation and Meaning*. Cambridge: Cambridge University Press, 1970.

TeHennepe, Eugene. "Ordinary Language Philosophy: Historical Perspectives." Unpublished dissertation, Northwestern University, 1969.

Todorov, Tzvetan. *Littérature et signification*. Paris: Larousse, 1967.

——, ed. *Théorie de la littérature—Textes des formalistes russes*. Paris: Seuil, 1965.

Trager, George L., and Edward T. Hall, Jr. "Culture and Communication: A Model and an Analysis." *Explorations*, 3, 1954, pp. 157–249.

Turbayne, Colin Murray. *The Myth of Metaphor*. New Haven: Yale University Press, 1962.

Tytler, A. F. *Essay on the Principles of Translation*. Edinburgh: A. Constable, 1813.

Uldall, H. J. "On the Preparation of a Text." *Archivum Linguisticum*, Vol. 11, Fasc. 1, 1959, pp. 1–17.

——. *Outline of Glossematics: Part One, General Theory*. Copenhagen, 1957.

Ullmann, Stephen. "Descriptive Semantics and Linguistic Typology." *Word*, 9, 1953, pp. 225–240.

——. *Semantics, An Introduction to the Science of Meaning*. New York: Barnes & Noble, 1962.

——. *The Principles of Semantics*. Oxford: Basil Blackwell, 1951.

Urban, W. N. *Language and Reality*, chapters 9–10. London: Allen and Unwin, New York: Macmillan, 1961.

Ushenko, Andrew Paul. *The Field Theory of Meaning*. Ann Arbor: University of Michigan Press, 1958.

Verhaar, John W. M. "Method, Theory, and Phenomenology," in *Method and Theory in Linguistics*, Arel L. Garvin, ed. The Hague: Mouton, 1970.

Vico, Giambattista. *Autobiography*, tr. Fisch and Bergin. Ithaca, N.Y.: Cornell University Press, 1944.

——. *On The Study Methods of Our Time*, ed. Elio Gianturco. Indianapolis: Bobbs-Merrill, 1965.

——. *The New Science*, ed. Thomas G. Bergin and Max H. Fisch. Ithaca, N.Y.: Cornell University Press, 1968.

Voegelin, C. F. "Distinctive Features and Meaning Equivalence." *Language*, 24, 1948, pp. 132–135.

——. "Linguistically Marked Distinctions in Meaning," in *Selected Papers of the 29th International Congress of Americanists*, Sol Tax, ed. Chicago, 1952.

——. "Multiple Stage Translation." *International Journal of American Ling.*, 20, 1954, pp. 271–280.

Vygotsky, L. S. *Thought and Language,* ed. and tr. Eugenia Hanfmann and Gertrude Vakar. Cambridge, Mass.: M.I.T. Press, 1962.

Waldenfels, Bernhard. "Die Offenheit sprachlicher Strukturen bei Merleau-Ponty." Unpublished.

———. "Verstehen und Verständigung Zur Sozialphilosophie von A. Schütz." Unpublished.

Waterman, J. T. *Perspectives in Linguistics.* Chicago: University of Chicago Press, 1963.

Weinreich, U. "Explorations in Semantics," in *Current Trends in Linguistics,* VIII, T. A. Sebeok, ed. The Hague: Mouton 1966, pp. 395–477.

———. "Lexicographic Definition in Descriptive Semantics," in *Problems in Lexicography,* ed. Fred W. Householder and Sol Saporta. Bloomington, Ind., 1962, pp. 25–43.

———. "On the Semantic Structure of Language," in *Universals of Language,* J. H. Greenberg, ed. Cambridge, Mass.: M.I.T. Press, 1963, pp. 114–171.

———. "Travels through Semantic Space." *Word,* 14, 1958, pp. 346–366.

Weir, Ruth. *Language in the Crib.* The Hague: Mouton, 1962.

Wells, Rulon. "A Mathematical Approach to Meaning." *Cahiers Saussure,* 15, 1957, pp. 117–137.

———. "Meaning and Use." *Word,* 10, 1954, pp. 235–250. Also in *Linguistics Today,* 1954.

———. "Some Neglected Opportunities in Descriptive Linguistics." *Anthropological Linguistics,* 5, No. 1, 1963, pp. 38–49.

———. "To What Extent Can Meaning Be Said to Be Structured?" *Reports 8th International Congress of Linguists,* I, Oslo, 1957.

Werner, Heinz. *Comparative Psychology of Mental Development,* tr. E. B. Garside. New York: Harper, 1940.

Whatmough, J. *Language a Modern Synthesis.* London, 1956.

Wheelwright, Philip. *Metaphor and Reality.* Bloomington: Indiana University Press, 1962.

———. *The Burning Fountain.* Bloomington: Indiana University Press, 1959.

Whitehead, Alfred North. *Symbolism, Its Meaning and Effect.* New York, 1927.

Whorf, Benjamin Lee. *Language, Thought and Reality.* New York: Wiley, 1959.

Wild, John. "Introduction to the Phenomenology of Signs." *Philosophy and Phenomenological Research,* 1947.

———. "Is There A World of Ordinary Language?" *Philosophical Review* Vol. LXVII, No. 4, October 1958, pp. 460–476.

Wimsatt, W. K. "Symbol and Metaphor," and "The Chicago Critics," in *The Verbal Icon*. Lexington: University of Kentucky Press, 1967, pp. 41–68, 119–132.

———. *The Verbal Icon*. Lexington: University of Kentucky Press, 1954.

Wimsatt, W. K., Jr., and Cleanth Brooks. *Literary Criticism: A Short History*. New York: Knopf, 1957.

Wisdom, John. "The Logic of God," in *Paradox and Discovery*. Oxford: Basil Blackwell, 1965.

Wittgenstein, Ludwig. *Philosophical Investigations*. Oxford: Basil Blackwell, 1953.

———. *The Blue and Brown Books*. Oxford: Basil Blackwell, 1958.

———. *Tractatus Logico-Philosophicus*. London: Routledge & Kegan Paul, 1962.

Yoos, George E. "A Phenomenological Look at Metaphor." *Philosophy and Phenomenological Research*, 1971, pp. 77–88.

Ziff, Paul. "About Ungrammaticalness." *Mind*, 13, 1964, pp. 204–214.

———. *Semantic Analysis*. Ithaca, N.Y.: Cornell University Press, 1949.